The Sexual Circus

To my parents

The Sexual Circus

Wedekind's Theatre of Subversion

ELIZABETH BOA

Basil Blackwell

Copyright © Elizabeth Boa 1987

First published 1987

Basil Blackwell Ltd
108 Cowley Road, Oxford, OX4 1JF, UK

Basil Blackwell Inc.
432 Park Avenue South, Suite 1503
New York, NY 10016, USA

British Library Cataloguing in Publication Data

Boa, Elizabeth
   The sexual circus : Wedekind's theatre
   of subversion.
   1. Wedekind, Frank—Criticism and
   interpretation
   I. Title
   832'.8   PT2647.E26
   ISBN 0-631-14234-7

Library of Congress Cataloging in Publication Data

Boa, Elizabeth.
   The sexual circus.

   Bibliography: p.
   Includes index.
   1. Wedekind, Frank, 1864–1918—Criticism and
interpretation. 2. Sex in literature. 3. Sex role in
literature. I. Title.
PT2647.E26Z58 1987   832'.8   87–820
ISBN 0-631-14234-7

Typset in Plantin 11pt on 13pt
by Opus, Oxford
Printed in Great Britain by
T.J. Press Ltd, Padstow

Contents

Acknowledgements

I should like to express my thanks for permission to consult the Wedekind Archive in the Stadtbibliothek, Munich, to the late Frau Pamela Regnier-Wedekind and Frau Kadidja Wedekind-Biel, who was also most kind in answering my questions. I am also grateful to Herr Richard Lemp and Dr Georg Brenner for allowing access to the transcriptions of Wedekind's notebooks.

I wish to thank Robert Black, Steve Giles and Hinrich Siefken for all their suggestions and help.

Plates 1–8 are reproduced by kind permission of Frau Kadidja Wedekind-Biel and the Handschriften und Monacensia-Abteilung, Stadtbibliothek, Munich.

1
Introduction: Texts and Contexts

Productions in London and the provinces of *Spring Awakening* and the Lulu plays, *Earth Spirit* and *Pandora's Box*, have established Wedekind's reputation in Britain as an orginator of modern theatre whose work is interesting but not very familiar. He is known to cinema buffs through G. W. Pabst's *Pandora's Box* of 1928, and to opera-goers since the Paris premiere in 1979 of the completed version of Alban Berg's *Lulu*, which was followed by the Covent Garden production in 1981. *The Marquis of Keith* was broadcast as a radio play in 1972 and produced in 1974 by the Royal Shakespeare Company in a translation by Ronald Eyre and Alan Best. Along with *Spring Awakening* and the Lulu plays, *The Marquis of Keith* is among the most frequently performed of Wedekind's works in Germany. Productions of *Earth Spirit* or twin productions of both Lulu plays are common, and *Pandora's Box* is also occasionally produced on its own. These four most familiar works are the topic of this study.

Wedekind began writing in the late 1880s – *Spring Awakening* was published in 1891 – and the major works were all written by the turn of the century, though he continued to revise the Lulu plays for the next decade. Wedekind writes as a radical libertarian attacking threats to personal freedom. Yet increasingly his work also conveys the limitations of the individualist values which inform his critique of authority. His work is thus subversive in intention and doubly subversive in effect. It attacks head-on authoritarian practices and institutions in bourgeois society and, more ambiguously, calls into question the ideals and beliefs of the liberal middle class, exploring an outer world of material social relations and inner worlds of dreams and illusions. Central to Wedekind's plays are the generational and sexual relations linking parents and children, men and women, while the material and spiritual condition of the artist in the world of the market is a pervasive theme.

Plots and Themes

Least ambiguous in its libertarian thrust is the first major play *Spring Awakening*, subtitled *A Children's Tragedy*. This offers a child's-eye view of adult society, following the fates of three children exposed to the pressures of parental expectations, a competitive school-system and a punitive sexual morality. Two of them come to grief: Moritz Stiefel commits suicide on failing at school and Wendla Bergmann, kept in ignorance of sexual matters by her foolish mother, becomes pregnant and dies of a botched abortion, a sacrifice on the altar of respectability. The third child, Melchior Gabor, by whom Wendla became pregnant, escapes from the penitentiary to which his outraged parents have sent him; in a last surreal scene he is saved from the ravages of guilt and the cold, dead grasp of the now headless Moritz by a mysterious Masked Man who preaches a liberating doctrine of hedonistic vitalism. Moritz, in contrast to his friend Melchior, had earlier failed to seize the chance of life offered by Ilse, the Masked Man's female alter ego. Ilse, slightly older than the other children, had escaped from the provinces to the glitter and excitement of bohemian city life. She offered Moritz the pleasures of sex, but he chose instead the path of suicide.

In this play Wedekind attacks the education system, the middle-class family and the professions as the organs of an oppressive and repressive culture. Ilse and the Masked Man offer hope of escape from conservative provincial Germany into the new world of the city, but the shape of this new world remains unknown and the promise of freedom abstract. Until the last surreal scene the plot in outline sounds like a grim Naturalist tragedy, but a vein of mocking humour undermines the pathos and many decorative and lyrical motifs draw this work, of all Wedekind's plays, closest to the *Jugendstil* manner, the German version of the international aesthetic movement, which flourished in the arts in the 1890s.

Lulu, the central figure in *Earth Spirit* (1895) and *Pandora's Box* (1904), is Ilse's successor. She is the embodiment of liberated eros. In the Lulu plays we move from childhood into the adult world and from the provinces to the city and thence to the metropolis, first Paris and then London. The plays follow the disastrous career of a woman from the lower depths untrammelled by moral inhibition, who was taken up from the gutter at the age of twelve by the wealthy newspaper proprietor, Schön. Schön marries off his youthful mistress as child bride to the elderly roué, Goll. But Goll dies of a heart attack on discovering Lulu in the embrace of the young painter, Schwarz, from whom he has commissioned a portrait of her. Schwarz marries Lulu, now a wealthy widow, but dies in turn, by his own hand, when he discovers her scandalous provenance. After an interlude as a theatre dancer under the direction of Schön's son, Alwa, Lulu finally marries Schön. But Schön is torn by jealousy of his beautiful young wife and her disreputable friends and admirers: her original protector Schigolch, the lesbian Countess Geschwitz, the acrobat Rodrigo, the schoolboy Hugenberg and Alwa, his own son. Schön tries to force Lulu to shoot herself but in their struggle she shoots him; thus the first play closes with the death of Lulu's third victim.

In the second play, *Pandora's Box*, Geschwitz and Lulu's other friends help her to escape from prison. She flees to Paris with Alwa (as his wife in name only) and becomes mistress to the dubious Marquis Casti-Piani, a white-slave trader. In Paris, the great financial centre, money overshadows all other values. Casti-Piani, interested in the price on Lulu's head rather than in her body, offers her the choice of returning to prison or living in a Cairo brothel. Rodrigo and the journalist Heilmann also threaten to betray her to the police. Lulu seeks the aid of Schigolch who murders Rodrigo (the fourth victim), and she, Alwa and Schigolch escape to London where they are joined by the faithful Geschwitz. Lulu returns to the streets from which she once escaped and Schigolch, the protector, now leaves her to her fate. One of her clients murders Alwa, and Lulu and Geschwitz finally fall victim to Jack the Ripper. The play closes with Schwarz's portrait of Lulu looking down on a scene of blood-drenched horror.

The Lulu plays assert the value of sexual liberation against bourgeois marriage in which men own women as possessions, but show that freedom is impossible in the world of the free market and in the face of murderous male possessiveness. The prophets of freedom in *Spring Awakening*, the Masked Man and Ilse, are here respectively transmogrified into destructively and self-destructively rapacious men, and their object of desire, the woman. The Lulu plays are Wedekind's richest and most ambiguous statement on the forms sexuality assumes in bourgeois society.

In *The Marquis of Keith* (1901) relations between the sexes still loom large, but the play centres on the situation of the would-be enterprising and creative individual in the market economy. The central character, Keith, is a businessman. The slogan of free enterprise – 'business is business' – takes on the aura of an elevated assertion of spiritual freedom when the business is art. Keith is an impresario who plans to found a palace of the arts and seeks commercial backers in Munich for a project designed to free avant-garde artists from material cares so that they can pursue art for its own sake: 'business is business' becomes *l'art pour l'art*. The only limiting factor is the need to attract backers and a paying public. On this rock the project founders: Keith's scheme is taken over by Casimir, the most powerful businessman in Munich, and the avant-garde will have to bow to the demands of the market and the vulgar taste of beer-brewers and tradesmen.

In the name of his high purpose Keith claims total freedom from the restraints of conservative morality. The argument on freedom is pursued through an elegant *pas de quatre* played out between Keith, Ernst Scholz (a wealthy, earnestly moralizing childhood friend), and two women: domestic Molly (Keith's long-term mistress and house-keeper), and the glamorous Anna (his new lover). Fearful of losing Keith, Molly commits suicide, Anna deserts him for Casimir, and moral Ernst refuses financial support and retreats to a lunatic asylum, leaving Keith alone to pursue an elusive freedom in the world of Casimir.

This play, written a decade after *Spring Awakening*, explores the freedom of urban life which the Masked Man once promised Melchior Gabor. It subtly intertwines the themes of sexual and artistic freedom in capitalist society. Less drastic than the Lulu plays in its treatment of the sexual theme, it is Wedekind's most elaborate and intellectually challenging exploration of individualist values. Technically, too, in its intricate dismantling of individual character to lay bare the workings of social relations, it is, like *Spring Awakening* and the Lulu plays, a strikingly innovative work.

In my study of these four texts I shall be concerned with Wedekind's attack on authoritarianism and conservative morality, with his treatment of the themes of social mobility and individual freedom, with his response to the impact of the market on the arts, and above all with the theme of sexual relations. After chapters on each of the four main plays and Berg's opera *Lulu* I have included a chapter on the turn-of-the-century debate on 'the woman question', which looks at one or two of Wedekind's less well-known works in which the sexual theme is particularly salient. Two final chapters are devoted to the critical debates provoked by Wedekind's work and to the theatrical techniques which make Wedekind a key figure in the history of modern theatre.

Throughout, I shall argue that technique crucially determines the sense of the plays so that their impact is heavily dependent upon choices of production. The study follows a composite approach, asking what the plays convey as texts now, and as documents of their time with the benefit of a century's hindsight. This is not to argue that material history can simply be read off from works of literature, but to emphasize that a conception of history is one of the values which necessarily inform our reading. In the rest of this opening chapter I shall first set the historical context, then outline the main themes of shifting relations between the generations and the sexes in a world of rapid social and economic change. It is these themes, and the explosive theatricality of their treatment, that give Wedekind's work its resonance today.

Wilhelmine Germany

During the nineteenth century the trebling of the population and the migration from the countryside led to an explosive growth of Germany's cities, the realm of promise for Melchior Gabor in *Spring Awakening*. Between 1848 and 1914 Berlin grew tenfold, to become a city with a population of four million. Other towns grew in proportion: by the early 1890s Munich had a population of 390,000. (This rapid growth generated, among other phenomena, vast numbers of urban prostitutes, the real Ilses and Lulus.) By the 1870s, Germany had overtaken France in industrial production and by 1910 it had surpassed Britain, to become the second largest industrial power in the world after the USA. But the growth was uneven. The effects of the foundation of the Reich in 1871, along with victory over France, indemnity payments and the acquisition of the rich provinces of Alsace and Lorraine led to a speculative boom in the early 1870s, the *Gründerjahre*, when over 800 companies were founded. Increased banking activity promoted industrial development which in turn fuelled the financial sector. But for many speculators the bubble burst in the crash of 1873, giving rise to an upsurge of anti-semitic feeling directed against Jewish businessmen and bankers. Further crises followed in the mid 1880s, the early 1890s and at the turn of the century (Born, 1985: 111–12).

The 1873 crash set off wide-ranging commercial and political change. Free trade gave way to protectionism, a growing alliance between conservative agrarian interests and industry, and a consequent split between right-wing liberals and the left-liberal proponents of libertarian ideals. A more active social policy, fuelled by paternalist reformism, was administered by the predominantly Prussian civil service, which grew from 700,000 in the early 1880s to two million in 1910 (Green, 1974: 7). This accompanied an upsurge of nationalist rhetoric and an aggressive armaments policy. Imperial power-politics found symbolic expression in the cult of the Kaiser, who as father of the nation embodied that authoritarian ideology of law, order and conservative morality which is Wedekind's prime target.

This history is reflected in Wedekind's plays in many motifs. In *Spring Awakening* the city offers an escape from narrow provincialism but, as the Lulu plays suggest, at enormous cost. The ups and downs of capitalist enterprise are a central theme in both *The Marquis of Keith* and *Pandora's Box* which also features the anti-semitic reaction to the financial crash, and the international and colonial aspects of capitalism. The reformist civil service is shown through the figure of the well-meaning Ernst Scholz in *The Marquis of Keith* to be absurdly incompetent when faced with the disorderly operations of capitalism. The contradictions between the liberal rhetoric of free enterprise and the conservative ideology of order are a constant theme, and one of continuing relevance in our neo-liberal times.

The German education system laid the foundation of Germany's industrial power, in developing the scientific research which fuelled the great chemical industries. The technical schools trained an educated work force and the *Gymnasien* nurtured a professional and bureaucratic elite. In the *Gymnasien*, Latin and Greek still prevailed, but in conjunction with mathematics. This combination is present in the literary and mathematical motifs in *Spring Awakening*, which shows a school system designed to produce a proportion of failures, to encourage competition, to classify children for their future economic role and to inculcate respect for authority and conventional morality. Schooling was compulsory, giving teachers considerable power over their charges. There was a marked increase of suicide among schoolchildren, whose sufferings became a recurrent literary motif, as in Emil Strauss's *Freund Hein* of 1902 or Hesse's *Unterm Rad* of 1906 (Rutschky, 1983). Moritz Stiefel in *Spring Awakening* is an early exemplar; here and in *Earth Spirit* Wedekind aligns schools with penitentiaries and the police force as the state organs of an oppressive order based on the patriarchal family. The education system made it exceedingly difficult for proletarian children to rise socially – at the turn of the century, less than one per cent of students were of working-class origin – and impossible for women to compete with men in the middle-class professions (Fläschen, 1981: 134; Kassner and Lorenz, 1977). In *Spring Awakening* the girls and boys show characteristic differences in ambition and self-esteem. Despite some feminist successes, a long anti-feminist tradition remained effective through to the *Kinder, Küche und Kirche* ideology of the Third Reich. Wilhelmine Germany lagged behind Scandinavia, Britain, the United States and Switzerland in admitting women to higher education and by the turn of the century 'the woman question', a central theme in Wedekind's work, had become a topic of widespread debate. I examine this theme in detail in chapter 7.

The fragmentation of the liberal parties sealed the failure to reconcile economic progress with libertarian political ideals. National Liberal representation in the Reichstag fell from 152 in 1874 to 45 in 1881. Opposition to authoritarian forces was overwhelmingly borne by the German socialist party, the SPD, itself divided between reformist and revolutionary tendencies. A significant section of the middle class saw its interest threatened by the growing strength of proletarian politics and fell prey to what Gordon Craig (1978: 100) calls 'feudalization': a subservient alliance with a conservative aristocracy and an aping of aristocratic style. Casti-Piani, the dubious Marquis in *Pandora's Box*, is an ambiguous exemplar of a man of commerce turned aristocrat or an aristocrat turned man of commerce, and Keith tries to dazzle the Munich businessmen with an assumed title. The failure of liberalism and the changing economics of the art world led to a sense of marginalization among middle-class intellectuals. Even in the socialist camp, whose theorists and publicists were largely middle-class, there was distrust, often expressed by the intellectuals themselves; at the 1903 SPD congress August Bebel advised rigorous scrutiny of intellectuals and academics claiming to be socialists.

As a result of this political and cultural disarray, a sense of crisis pervades the literature of the end of the century. This is evident in the worship of art as an end in itself elevated above the market and the masses (where Keith would place it); in the obverse image of the artist as decadent outsider (represented by the inadequate Alwa of *Pandora's Box*) and in the self-reflection of art works questioning their own function and validity. Wedekind's plays are particularly interesting in that they portray art not as a cult but as a business like any other. Liberal freedom of expression comes into conflict with the market, as artists try to sell a commodity which attacks the class of potential buyers. Thus the artist's dilemma can become a measuring rod for the state of the body politic. This is a central argument in *The Marquis of Keith*.

Munich in the 1890s

In 1884, Wedekind went to Munich, ostensibly to study law, but spent most of his time immersed in his own artistic and personal concerns. In 1886 he returned to Switzerland, where he had been brought up, and worked for a short while with the soup-cube manufacturer, Maggi, before attending University in Zurich. He did not finally settle in Munich until 1908, and as a man of the theatre was constantly on the move between different cities. He spent much of his time in Berlin, but Munich, as a centre of the arts – visual and musical as well as theatrical – is the more significant of the two for Wedekind's work. Berlin only came to rival and then surpass Munich as a cultural centre in the 1890s with the advent of theatrical Naturalism and Otto Brahm's new *Freie Bühne*. From the start, Wedekind rejected Naturalism. His work abounds with features to which the art-historical term *Jugendstil* can be applied. In the mid-nineteenth century, Munich had been the most important art market in Germany, and after Paris the most important in Europe. As Robin Lenman (1982) notes, a number of factors came together in Munich, which from the 1860s became the intersection point of the new railway axes running from Paris to the East and from Scandanavia and Ostend south to Italy. The Munich Art Academy rose to prominence, drawing many artists away from Düsseldorf, among them the American colony. Along with Lenbach, Makart and Leibl, American realists such as Chase, Duvenek or Rosenthal worked in Munich. The city was not an industrial centre – the only big employers were the breweries – and this is no doubt one reason for the absence of factory workers from Wedekind's plays. Along with this freedom from industrial development, it had a wealth of attractions for the tourism stimulated by the railways, notably its art collections and the magnificent hinterland. In 1854 the *Glaspalast*, the first glass and steel construction on the continent in the style of London's Crystal Palace, was built as a centre for art exhibitions, a project reminiscent of Keith's Magic Palace. Though the patronage of the Wittelsbachs, Bavaria's royal house, declined from a high point under Ludwig I, Ludwig II's support of Wagner was a further attraction (the combination of beer and opera remains to this day a Munich speciality). Patronage also extended to the theatre. Ibsen lived for a while in Munich and there was a series of Ibsen premieres in the 1870s, before the threatrical centre of gravity moved to Berlin (Jelavich 1985: 25). Ludwig's castles in the Bavarian mountains provided employment for innumerable craftsmen, and on his death became an instant tourist attraction. By the late 1880s, Berlin was becoming more of a true capital and the newly wealthy Rhineland cities were coming into their own. In the face of this competition, the Bavarian authorities continued to encourage tourism and the arts, and the reputation of Munich bohemian life still drew artists and writers from all over Germany and Europe, especially Eastern Europe; Kandinsky was only the most famous of a whole generation of Poles, Hungarians and Russians who for political reasons felt more at home in Munich than in Vienna or Berlin. In 1898 the Munich *Secession* (a breakaway group of progressive artists founded in 1892) put on an exhibition organized by Diaghilev, with works by painters such as Jawlensky, Kardovsky, Werefkin and Sacharoff, some of whom were either already in Munich or stayed for a while (Zweite, 1982: 8). Wedekind's Keith is a would-be Diaghilev.

By the 1890s, however, provincial Munich with its inflated numbers of artists and craftsmen was struggling to sustain prominence in an increasingly national and international art market. The American depression in the early 1890s affected art sales, and there was insufficient local patronage to compensate for this. Furthermore, reliance on the tourist trade and local patrons heightened the pressure to pander to conservative tastes or to produce decorative kitsch, a major theme in *The Marquis of Keith*. The Munich *Secession* movement of 1892, the first in Central Europe, was a response to these difficulties, as artists banded together to publicize their work and to try to determine the market themselves, rather than be determined by it. There were also calls for state patronage: the Munich *Secession* received the token patronage of the Prince Regent Luitpold. While the *Secession* embraced several styles, pre-eminent among them was the *Jugendstil*, a manifestation of the international aesthetic movement which flourished in Parisian *art nouveau*, in the Glasgow of Charles Rennie Macintosh, in Vienna and in New York. William Morris, the Arts and Crafts movement and the Pre-Raphaelites were important English influences. The style was already well established before the term was coined from the journal *Die Jugend (Youth)*, founded in 1896 by Georg Hirth, the same year as the publisher Albert Langen founded the satirical journal *Simplicissimus*, to which Wedekind was a major contributor in the early years. Peter Jelavich (1982: 19) suggests that although the *Jugendstil* had no official political affiliation it can be seen as a revival of the left-liberal spirit. Though in retrospect the *Jugendstil* appears predominant, it was not to all tastes in provincial Munich, and the Munich *Secession* failed to live up to its radical programme. In 1906, for example, it rejected all nine paintings submitted by Kandinsky. Such preference for Mammon rather than the avant-garde is prophesied in the *The Marquis of Keith*.

Like the *Secession*, the journals had an economic aim to provide work for graphic artists, poets and writers and the liberal spirit survived better in a medium more independent of patronage. Hirth aimed to propagate more liberal religious and sexual attitudes and to emancipate the middle class from subservience to the Prussian elite and from its fears of social democracy, while Langen's *Simplicissimus* quickly became the leading radical journal in Germany. In Bavaria cases against the press on grounds of blasphemy, obscenity and so forth had to go to trial by jury, and juries are reluctant to convict. This allowed the radical journals some freedom of expression, but when Wedekind was imprisoned in 1899 for *lèse majesté* over a satirical poem published in *Simplicissimus*, the case was brought not in Munich where the journal was edited but in Leipzig where it was printed. After this, production was moved to Stuttgart where trial was also by jury (Lenman, 1978).

The connections between Wedekind's work and the Munich art scene are legion. As a verbal art, theatre can scarcely attain the abstraction of the visual arts. But there are affinities between the two modes. *Jugendstil* decoration came increasingly to overlie representation, opening the way to Kandinsky's breakthrough to abstract expressionism. Wedekind's technique of patterned episodes and characters fragmenting into elements recurring kaleidoscopically in different combinations is a comparable tendency of the decorative towards abstraction. *Jugendstil* blending of the sensual with the visionary recalls Wedekind's mythicized eroticism in the imagery of nymphs and dryads in *Spring Awakening*, or the aura of mystery surrounding Lulu. Analysis of the plays will show direct assimilation of *Jugendstil* motifs. In the visual arts the *Jugendstil* was not directly critical, unlike the contemporary Naturalist tendency, and certainly not funny, unless inadvertently in some of its steamier pictures of *femmes fatales*. But the precise line-drawing of the caricatures in *Simplicissimus* is comparable to Wedekind's etched mockery of stock representatives of authority. The shallowness of the liberal spirit comes out in the vein of anti-feminism in *Simplicissimus*, which has its counterpart in Wedekind's scorn of the women's movement, though he has nothing of the anti-semitism which crept into *Die Jugend* after the turn of the century.

Munich's bohemian café life gave birth to the cabaret in imitation of Paris. Like the *Secession* and the journals, cabaret was an aesthetic development strongly influenced by economic factors, though the Munich cabarets were less commercial than their Berlin counterparts, the *Überbrettl* (founded in 1900 by Ernst von Wolzogen) and Reinhardt's *Schall and Rauch* (founded a year later). The two Munich cabarets were *Die elf Scharfrichter* (*The Eleven Executioners*) and *Simplicissimus*, named after the journal, and featuring literary figures such as the anarchist Erich Mühsam and Hans Bötticher (later Ringelnatz). Like the journals, the cabarets brought together writers and artists creating lines of connection between the arts. *Die elf Scharfrichter* opened in 1901, the same year as the *Phalanx*, yet another breakaway group, was established by artists dissatisfied with the *Secession*. A poster by Kandinsky anounced the first exhibition, which contained works by members of *Die elf Scharfrichter* such as Hüsgen, who was the mask-maker for the cabaret. Wedekind's mask was shown in the second *Phalanx* exhibition (Weis, 1982: 40). Theodor Heine, the main caricaturist for *Simplicissimus*, made a famous poster of Marya Delvard, a founder of the *Die elf Scharfrichter*; a portrait of her by Albert Bloch was also included in the *Blaue Reiter* exhibition of 1911. Some joint members of *Die elf Scharfrichter* and the *Phalanx* were also active as theatrical set designers. Wedekind was a leading performer in *Die elf Scharfrichter*, singing songs to lute accompaniment and reciting extracts from his plays. One of his pantomimes, entitled *The Empress of Newfoundland*, was a further item. He regarded his journalistic and cabaret activities as hack-work performed out of economic necessity. Yet the cabaret combined several aesthetic tendencies of great significance for the twentieth-century theatre: the intimate contact with the audience; the use of masks, puppets, improvisation and mime; the emphasis on lyric poetry embracing popular themes from street ballads, dramatized to give it immediacy for a café public. The cabaret was conceived in analogy to the *Jugendstil* applied arts. The poems performed were *angewandte Lyrik* (applied lyrics), a term coined by Otto Julius Bierbaum, a poet and journalist who early on identified cabaret with the *Jugendstil*. *Angewandte Lyrik* is not the expression of a self-absorbed poetic subject, but is audience-directed and serves a rhetorical purpose. It is an ancestor of Hindemith's *Gebrauchsmusik* and of applied lyrics and music in Brechtian theatre. Common to all these forms was the combination of critical satire with an aestheticization of life. Beauty was to be a weapon against reactionary philistinism, whether in politics, sexual and social relations or the arts. The cabaret and the *Jugendstil* artists generally were not as hostile to the modern world as other groups in Munich (such as Stefan George's circle and its journal *Blätter für die Kunst*); they retained an element of optimistic faith in new energies and new techniques. This kind of mixture of the critical with the aesthetic is characteristic of Wede-kind's plays. So too is the ambiguous relationship to the market, which was to be attacked for its philistinism, yet wooed and exploited with enterprising vigour.

Memories and Memoirs

Wedekind's left-liberal father emigrated to America after the failure of the 1848 revolution. He established a medical practice in San Fransisco, married in 1862 and returned to Germany in 1864, the year of Wedekind's birth. Disappointed with the shape of the new Reich, in 1872 he moved with his family to Switzerland, where Wedekind attended the canton school in Aarau. Even as a schoolboy, Wedekind began to write poems and sketches, transforming elements of his own experience into theatre. Artur Kutscher (1970) records exhaustively how this process of transformation continued throughout his work.

Sol Gittleman (1969), and Hugh Rank, in his edition of *Spring Awakening*, offer surveys in English of some striking autobiographical features in Wedekind's plays, such as the suicide of two school friends, Franz Oberlin and Moritz Dürr, echoed in the death of Moritz in *Spring Awakening*. Frau Gabor is in part a portrait of Wedekind's mother, who never liked the play. The last scene of *Earth Spirit* conceals painful memories of quarrels between his parents; according to his daughter Kadidja, Wedekind drew on memories of exchanges between his parents in composing the dialogue leading up to the death of Schön. Wedekind's father was much older than his mother and in his later years became increasingly embittered, eccentric and reclusive. Quarrels over finance and Wedekind's failings as a law student culminated in 1886, when in the course of an argument Wedekind struck his father; there was however, a reconciliation some months later just a year before his father died in 1888. As his letters show, Wedekind was deeply attached to both of his parents and – apart from the dark shadow of their disturbed relations – seems to have spent a happy childhood in idyllic surroundings in the little castle, Schloss Lenzburg, where the family lived. The very strength of his feeling for his parents must have made the family problems all the more painful. The diary of 1889 tells of constant dreams about his father, and of his deep grief (Hay 1986: 57; 99–100). In the plays, childhood is a lost paradise filled with pain while adult love results in the mutual torture of the sexes.

Wedekind may also have drawn material for his work from his mother's memories of her early life, which are set down in her memoirs. Emilie Kammerer came from a middle-class Zurich family who for political reasons had moved to Switzerland from Ludwigsburg near Stuttgart. Her father owned a match factory and the family was fairly prosperous, though they did experience the ups and downs of competition in manufacturing. Like Wedekind's father, his maternal grandfather was a convinced democrat and in 1848–9 the household was often filled with political refugees. After the death of her mother, however, Emilie's life became much less happy. Her brother and her father both wanted to marry the housekeeper, Hanne, who chose the elder man amid scenes of threatened murder and mayhem. The brother moved to Ludwigsburg and married, but the marriage was not happy and he became an alcoholic. The marriage between the housekeeper and the father did not prosper either. Emilie's father eventually became insane and lived out his final years in an asylum. As he fell ill, his speech was impaired so that he talked in fragmented phrases, and he plagued his much younger wife with jealous scenes which culminated in a murderous attack on her.

His parents' marriage and his mother's memories suggest that, from an early date, Wedekind had good reason to see that it is not the *femme fatale* who produces insane and murderous jealousy, but the jealousy which invents the *femme fatale*. This situation in which a father and son are in love with the same woman, like Schön and Alwa in *Earth Spirit*, is foreshadowed in Emilie's recollections as are Schön's murderous impulses and the detail of his disturbed speech at the height of his madness. Emilie's memoirs strikingly illuminate the melodramas of family life which Wedekind transformed into theatre. They tell a story which sets a sexual conflict between a father and son firmly in the context of the social conditions of family life at the time.

Wedekind inherited his love of theatre and opera from his mother. Virtually an orphan after the decline of her father into insanity, Emilie came increasingly under the protection of her elder sister Sophie, who was a singer. Sophie trained in Zurich, Vienna and Milan and was successful in her debut at La Scala. When, in her early teens, Emilie joined Sophie in Vienna, then Milan, she was fascinated by the social life in her sister's little salon. Sophie's many admirers included a monocled marquis, a figure reminiscent of the ridiculous Escerny, Lulu's aristocratic admirer in the theatre episode in *Earth Spirit*. Sophie had no wish to marry and give up her career, but she found it virtually impossible to live and dress in the manner required of a leading singer without having a wealthy protector. She was unwilling to turn to such means of support, despite her brother's urgings, and she escaped into marriage, emigrating with her husband to South America. In 1856, at the age of fourteen, Emilie made the hazardous journey alone to Valparaiso. She discovered her sister in a parlous state: the planned photography business had failed, and the husband was a compulsive gambler. The two sisters set about a career singing in concerts to earn a living, travelling all over South America, earning money which Sophie's husband gambled away.

Eventually, en route for San Fancisco, Sophie, debilitated and exhausted, died of yellow fever on Christmas Eve 1858 and was buried at sea. Helped by the local German community, Emilie continued her singing in San Francisco and eventually married an elderly German who kept a bar. For a while she sang in a *Tingeltangel*, a café-bar of dubious repute, which led to her temporary exclusion from the German community, even though she was treated with perfect respect in the nightclub. When it emerged that her husband had heavy debts which her earnings as a singer could not have paid off in decades, she decided to avoid her sister's tragic destiny and divorced him. Ill with stress and anxiety, she consulted Doctor Wedekind who confessed that he had been in love with her for over a year. He offered her a choice: financial support for singing lessons to repair her voice, damaged by too much singing at too early an age, or marriage, in which case she must give up all thoughts of singing. Emilie chose marriage. At the end of her memoirs she comments sadly that her one dearest wish was to make the father of her children happy and to prove her gratitude through total devotion. In this, however, she failed, and she turned her feelings and thoughts increasingly to her children, through whom her own inner education was completed, as she puts it.

Fragments of this adventurous history, particularly the exotic setting, appear disguised in the prose fragment *Mine-Haha* which I shall discuss in chapter 7. Wedekind's sister Erika, more fortunate than her aunt and her mother, managed to combine marriage and a career. She became a celebrated soprano, achieving success long before her brother, whose career she tried to further. Like childhood, opera and theatre are a mixed motif in Wedekind's work; they represent at once a utopia of freedom set against marriage and the family, and a market where artists starve or prostitute themselves. The memoirs of Emilie, a child of the Zurich bourgeoisie, suggest how narrow was the gap between respectable society, the *demi-monde*, and the abyss of poverty and social exclusion. Sophie's early experiences in Milan graphically illustrate the difficulty faced by women in retaining financial independence or social respectability as artists, a theme in both *Earth Spirit* and *The Marquis of Keith*. Emilie's temporary loss of reputation when she worked in the *Tingeltangel* shows how suddenly a woman might shift in the eyes of others from an innocent, pathetic creature to a whore, irrespective of her actual experience. This ambiguity afflicts Lulu and her low-life companions in *Earth Spirit*. The motif of women working to keep feckless men, prominent in *Pandora's Box*, may well look back to the experiences of Wedekind's mother and of his beautiful and gifted Aunt Sophie, dead of yellow fever by the age of twenty-four, long before he was born.

Anti-Naturalism, Aestheticism and Melodrama

Wedekind's first major play, *Spring Awakening*, was written in 1890, at the height of the Naturalist movement. In the 1880s, the novel had been the leading Naturalist medium, but by 1890 the theories propagated in journals, essays and manifestos had spread to the theatre, which became the principal vehicle for Naturalist experiment. Naturalism in its extreme form was short-lived, and by the mid 1890s it was already waning. From the start, Wedekind rejected the Naturalists' aim of exact representation and their fatalistic theories of determinism by heredity and environment. His hostility was heightened by a quarrel with Gerhard Hauptmann, a leading Naturalist writer. Wedekind met Hauptmann in 1888 in Zurich, where there was a colony of German intellectuals in exile following the passage of Bismarck's anti-socialist law of 1878. Hauptmann and his circle called themselves *Das junge Deutschland* (*Young Germany*), the term used of the liberal agitation in the 1830s and 1840s which culminated in 1848, the year of revolutions. Hauptmann had written a play drawing on personal details about Wedekind's family, and Wedekind responded with an anti-Naturalist comedy he later entitled *Die junge Welt* (*The Young World*). It was written in 1889, the year in which Hauptmann's *Vor Sonnenaufgang* (*Before Dawn*) heralded the arrival of Naturalism on the Berlin stage. Wedekind attacked Naturalism on the grounds similar to those of Melchior's attack on charity in *Spring Awakening*: he exposed what he saw as the condescending pity of Naturalism which battened on suffering.

Unlike the Symbolist theatre of Maeterlinck or the verse drama of the young Hofmannsthal, Wedekind's work is not non-Naturalist: it is anti-Naturalist. It calls for acting against the Naturalist grain, and mixes details of contemporary life and social themes with myth and symbol, subversive humour and melodrama. The playwright's experiences in Paris reinforced this tendency. From 1888 Wedekind's share of his father's bequest left him financially free until the money ran out in 1905. In December 1891 he went to Paris and with short interruptions stayed till early in 1895. In 1894 he spent a few months in London which he found drab and dull, though there is a vivid description in his London diary of an evening at the Middlesex Music Hall (Hay: 314–16). The acts mixed sentimentality and imperialistic patriotism with thinly disguised pornographic appeal: a four-year-old girl dancer in a revealing dress; a white-clad English virgin, her hands tied behind her back, saved just in time from a mob of blacked-up savages. The yelling, whistling audience is clearly a prototype for the audience in the Prologue to *Earth Spirit*. As the Paris diaries show (Hay: 167–310), it was the life of the streets, the brothels and the bohemian underworld which fascinated Wedekind; not high art but variety theatre, circus and music hall. The true protagonists of the diaries are the many prostitutes. Wedekind admired their spirit, their erotic skills and the magnificence of their dancing. He played masochistic games and returned their love-bites despite problems with his false teeth. The diaries reveal a disjunction between free-ranging desire and recognition of exploitation as the aesthete-sensualist first enjoyed then rejected the girls he picked up at the *Moulin Rouge* or the *Café de la Paix*, like sweet Henriette who only a few months later was dead of syphilis. One, a lesbian, was called Lulu, another Kadudja. The latter name, turned into Kadidja, appears in the cast-list of *Pandora's Box* and is the name of Wedekind's second daughter.

Towards the end of his time in Paris, Wedekind wrote less in his diary about prostitutes and regularly visited Emma Herwegh, the elderly widow of the radical poet Georg Herwegh, one of those older, intelligent women whom he admired in the way he admired his own mother or his mother's friend Olga Plümacher, who introduced him to the pessimistic philosophy of Eduard von Hartmann. (The narrator of *Mine-Haha* is a similar figure.) Emma introduced him to her circle of friends, which included several women writers and painters. Two of the women helped him to revise the French in the original version of the Lulu plays; alas, he met no such helpers in London and the English remains bizarre. In the summer of 1894 he also met August Strindberg and his second wife Frida, who had a child by Wedekind in 1897. The nightmarish final phase of Strindberg's first marriage, when he became convinced that his wife Siri had many lovers, including their short-haired emancipated friend, Marie David, may have contributed, along with Wedekind's memories of his parent's troubles and his mother's recollections, to the closing act of *Earth Spirit* where the lesbian Geschwitz appears as the very devil to Schön's fevered imagination.

These experiences are contemporary with the first five-act version of the Lulu plays, *Pandora's Box*, subtitled *Eine Monstretragödie*, which Wedekind began towards the end of 1892 and completed in 1895. The gruesome and bloodthirsty in Wedekind's work has multiple sources in life and literature. *Spring Awakening*, written before Wedekind's experiences in Paris, looks back to Büchner's *Woyzeck*, a major influence also on the Naturalists, who were drawn by the theme of the sufferings of the poor; Wedekind follows the loose structure, the mix of grotesque caricature with visionary expression of Woyzeck's inner life, and the element of horror in Marie's end. The melodramatic vein in Wedekind's plays recalls Romantic melodrama, like some of Ibsen's early work and the sublimated melodrama and farce in Chekov. Wedekind drew material from real experiences within his own family and in the Paris *demi-monde* and from reports of the London murders in the late 1880s, as well as being influenced by street ballad and boulevard farce. Wedekind and Alfred Jarry, whose *Ubu Roi* dates from 1896, stand as joint ancestors of black theatre, which exploits the perverse, the grotesque and the horrific. The tradition of black Romanticism continues in the decadent features of aestheticism. Lulu, as a doll-like creation of the male imagination, has forebears in the work of E. T. A. Hoffmann, and can be compared with her contemporary Trilby, the eponymous heroine of George du Maurier's novel of 1894. The presentation of the monster Jack at the heart of respectable society has affinities with Stevenson's *Dr Jekyll and Mr Hyde* (1886) and Wilde's *The Picture of Dorian Gray* (1891). The *femme fatale* is a leading motif in the *Jugendstil*, notable examples being Judith and Salome as in the paintings of Franz von Stuck. The heroine of Oscar Wilde's *Salome* (1893) is an exact contemporary of Wedekind's Lulu. Violent death in turn-of-the-century art is some-times beautiful – Stuck's head of John the Baptist on a golden platter or some of Stefan George's early poems, for example – and sometimes horrifying, as in Stuck's *Murder* or the more abstract horror of Munch's *The Scream*. The beauty and the horror are later combined in the morbid and monstrous motifs of Expressionism. Wedekind's work shows the affinities between Parisian melodrama, German *Jugendstil* and the English literature of decadence.

In 1895, after his return to Germany, Wedekind submitted the manuscript of the *Monstretragödie* to his publisher Albert Langen, but it remains unpublished to this day. In the same year Langen published a revised version of the first three acts under the title *Der Erdgeist. Eine Tragödie* (*The Earth Spirit. A Tragedy*) with an inserted third act set in the theatre. The second edition of 1903 included the Prologue Wedekind had added for the tenth performance of the play in 1898. This version, with minor corrections, was the basis of Reinhardt's successful Berlin production of 1902 and, without the definite article in the title, of the standard text in the *Gesammelte Werke (Collected Works)*, published in 1913. The last two acts of the *Monstretragödie* appeared first in the journal *Die Insel* in 1902, with considerable revisions and an added first act. In 1904 this came out in Berlin in book form under the title *Die Büchse der Pandora. Tragödie in drei Aufzügen (Pandora's Box. A Tragedy in three Acts)* published by Bruno Cassirer. This edition was seized by the public prosecutor, and Wedekind and Cassirer stood trial in 1905 on a charge of disseminating obscene material. They were eventually acquitted in January 1906 but the book was destroyed. In the same year a third revised edition was published, and in 1911 a fourth edition appeared, in which considerable passages in French and English in Acts II and III were revised and translated into German. It is scarcely possible to disentangle the effects of censorship and self-censorship from changes of basic conceptions; and many of the changes were prompted by the particular requirements of stage production. This study follows the texts of the Lulu plays in the *Gesammelte Werke* as the versions through which Wedekind has become known to the public, while taking account of major departures from the *Monstretragödie*.

The Actor-Playwright

The Nuremberg premiere of *Earth Spirit* in 1898 was the first stage production of a work by Wedekind. During the decade following the Paris years, Wedekind barely earned a living. He wrote for *Simplicissimus* and gave readings from his work, but was still helped financially by his sister Erika. From 1898 onwards, some of his plays were performed, but with only moderate success, partly because they demanded an acting style not yet discovered. In 1898, Wedekind was engaged briefly in Nuremberg and then in the Munich *Schauspielhaus*, as *Dramaturg (dramatic producer)* and actor. The 1898 Munich production of *Earth Spirit* was not a success. On the eve of the first performance Wedekind was warned that he was about to be arrested for his satirical poem on the Kaiser's visit to Palestine, and on the following day he fled to Zurich. Under the impact of this experience, he began work on *The Marquis of Keith*, initially called *Der Genußmensch (The Hedonist)*. At the end of the year, on the advice of his publisher Albert Langen, he moved to Paris, where he met up again with his friend Willy Grétor, a painter, art dealer, forger and confidence trickster whom he had first met in 1894. Grétor is the immediate model for the reworked version of *The Marquis of Keith*, which was completed in the spring of 1900 during Wedekind's imprisonment after his return to Germany. The play was at first a flop, though it went on to become one of the most performed works in the 1920s, and has continued to be popular ever since. Although Wedekind's major works were all written by the turn of the century, he only slowly became widely known. The two significant break-throughs both took place in Berlin: Reinhardt's 1902 production of *Earth Spirit* and the highly successful 1906 production of *Spring Awakening*, which was greatly enhanced by the revolving stage, first used the previous year. In 1906, Wedekind married Tilly Newes, who had played Lulu in Karl Kraus's 1905 production of *Pandora's Box*. The couple went on to appear together in productions of his work all over Germany. Judging from Tilly's autobiography (1969), Wedekind showed many of the symptoms of jealous anxiety of an older man married to a younger, talented actress which he had so acutely diagnosed in his plays even before meeting Tilly or contemplating marriage. His work enjoyed increasing success, though censorship remained a problem. *Pandora's Box* was premiered in 1904 in Nuremberg, but after that it was scarcely played during his lifetime apart from occasional private productions. *Spring Awakening* was played only with major cuts. In celebration of Wedekind's fiftieth birthday in 1914 (just before the outbreak of war), fellow writers and academics organized a banquet, and a six-volume edition of his work was published along with a volume of tributes, *Das Wedekindbuch*, edited by Joachim Friedenthal. Then, for a year or so, the number of performances of his plays dropped, but before his death in 1918 his work was coming into vogue again. With the abolition of theatrical censorship after the war, Wedekind became one of the most frequently performed playwrights in Germany.

Much of the literature on Wedekind touches on other contexts in the German intellectual tradition, in particular the pessimistic philosophy of Schopenhauer and Edward von Hartmann, and Nietzschean vitalism. By the turn of the century social Darwinism mixed with Nietzschean power-worship had become a pervasive influence. Wedekind's characters are marked by self-awareness and self-division; they play roles consciously and unconsciously. No single model of the psyche emerges; sometimes the self appears as a field of impersonal biological and social forces, sometimes as a construct of the imagination. But it remains unclear whether the writer-imagination who creates the self is an essence, a transcendental ego, or a mirror reflecting myriad images from the surrounding culture. This exploratory quality offers points of comparison with a variety of different theories, from Hegelian and Marxian alienation or Freudian psychology of the unconscious through to Barthesian codes or the post-structuralist notion of language as the script in which the fictional self is written prior to individual utterance. The multiple readings Wedekind's plays can give rise to are part of their continuing vitality. My aim, however, is to argue that the plays are still very much alive *as theatre*. Whatever Wedekind may have absorbed from direct influence, or more indirectly from a climate of opinion, has been transformed into theatrical language which speaks immediately to a public.

Wedekind Today

Wedekind's plays have not become classics, and they can still elicit shock. Their unclassical rawness stems from the way in which both institutions and individuals are portrayed. Marriage and the nuclear family, the institutions at the heart of the bourgeois social order the plays explore, still stand as models against which the changing mores of today are measured and welcomed or condemned. The decorative surface of sets and costumes belongs to the past, but the emphasis on the collapse of familial and sexual relations presages anxieties of today. *Spring Awakening* attacks not just a particular morality, but the core generational relationships between parents and children, the circuit which transmits values through time. If the ordering of generation in the family is the very basis of culture, the Lulu plays strike at the heart of order. In his study *Adultery in the Novel* (1979), Tony Tanner offered a taxonomy of the bourgeois family under threat in a group of European novels. In the last act of *Earth Spirit* the kind of features Tanner identifies appear magnified to the point of travesty. The disruptive stranger bringing the threat of adultery has multiplied into lovers popping out of every nook and cranny. If the monstrosity at the heart of Goethe's *Elective Affinities* is the interchangeability of women underlying relations of individual love, at the heart of the Lulu plays is the much more shocking interchangeability of men, a blow at the very roots of patriarchy. Adulterous pollution runs riot: where is the order if a woman may murder the mother (as Lulu claims to have murdered Alwa's mother), marry the father, steal the offspring, murder the father and become potenial mother to the offspring of the offspring? The father's murderess in union with the son is a complicated abomination linking the house of Atreus with the Oedipal family. No good can come of it, and by the end of *Pandora's Box* no potential couple is left, however disorderly, as Jack the Ripper departs taking Lulu's genitals with him, unwomaning her in a novel twist to the classical practice of unmanning. If the family orders generation, then *Earth Spirit* subverts the order and *Pandora's Box* does away with the generation. The end of *The Marquis of Keith*, less horrific but no less drastic, leaves an unresolved question: should one retreat backwards into patriarchal order, as Anna does, or follow the hero past a drowned female victim down a slide to a no-man's-land of exclusion from society? Such visions are not prophetic. The family continues through its sea-changes, and propagation thrives. But Wedekind's plays constitute an unsettling vision of the fragility of the core social institutions, rendered all the more unsettling through the Polonius-like comical-lyrical-satirical-tragical-farcical-melodramatic mixing of the modes. The threat to the foundations of society comes from two related sources, one psychological, the other socio-economic. Wedekind's characters tend towards two extremes: the fluidly underdefined and the grotesquely overdefined. In today's pluralistic society, multiple images penetrate every household. The media unremittingly propagate ideology reflecting dominant interests, yet also purvey an eclectic variety of competing images, fashions and alternative models to emulate. The two sides of Wedekind's coin – the personality narrowing into a dominant convention or exploding into fragments – still provide a disturbing vision. The characters play roles transmitted through family, school, the community and a host of religious, literary and cultural sources. The metaphor of role-playing does not necessarily deny individual autonomy; it conveys a sense of social beings whose personality is culturally shaped and modified in interaction with others. Such fluidity may offer an exhilarating freedom to change and grow; but sometimes the pressure of convention destroys all autonomy in figures reduced to the mechanical mouthpieces of impersonal cliché. The person hardens into a single, heteronomous role concealing impersonal drives towards power and sexual gratification.

At the opposite extreme, the fluidity can become so great that the self fragments into a myriad of masks and appearances. The adults in *Spring Awakening* exemplify the extinction of individuality under the weight of convention. The Lulu plays explore the potential freedom of multiple roles first suggested in the children of *Spring Awakening*. But already here the central theme of *The Marquis of Keith* emerges: the double threat of narrowing into a conventional mould or exploding into fragments. The existence of these two extremes reflects rejection of established order yet fear of social disintegration and a growing scepticism of individualist utopias, whether outside society or hidden within it.

The plays present fashions and styles of the past, but the costumes and sets are also a language of signs with meaning beyond their mimetic function. They convey how any culture is generated and expressed through artefacts and furnishings, clothes, ways of moving and looking. Like the characters, these visual signs tend towards two extremes. The conventional is set against a fantastic flouting or eclectic mix of styles collapsing into absurdity. The dialogue too breaks up into competing manners originating not in the mind of the speaker but in the surrounding culture, so that the characters appear less as individuals than as vessels of cultural tensions originating outside themselves. The fractured dialogue in part conveys an authorial commentary, as Jörg Jesch (1959) suggests, but it also comes from Wedekind's own involvement in contemporary styles and manners. Now, in a later time, the fascination of Wedekind's work lies in the blending of critically self-reflective language with what we can now perceive as period style. Language appears as a given system into which we are born, determining the terms in which we see ourselves and so making us what we are; but it is also presented as constantly changing in ways we cannot see, and as changing us too.

The game with convention extends to mode. Karl S. Guthke (1961: 327) classifies the plays as tragicomedies in which the characters play comic roles superimposed on a fundamentally tragic existence. But they resist such classification; the mixing of modes in *Spring Awakening* and the Lulu plays subverts, rather than confirms, metaphysical fatalism. Conversely, in *The Marquis of Keith*, a well-made conversation-piece in the comic mode, every element of the genre – sharply defined characters, elegant act divisions, strong plot, happy ending – is travestied to sceptical, rather than tragic effect. Volker Klotz (1972) sees open dramtic form as distinctively modern. *The Marquis of Keith* apes closed form so that the open ending is all the more shocking. The metaphysical and formal uncertainty informing Wedekind's plays is still disturbing and enlivening; it leaves scope for producers and audience to construct their own reading.

The fragmenting figures, the artefacts surrounding them, the codes they speak and the mixed modes all create the sense of a culture in flux as the core institutions of marriage and the family threaten to fall apart. This instability is still both exhilarating and frightening, for Wedekind writes as a radical critic of tradition, but without a blueprint for the future. Twice in *Earth Spirit*, amidst threatened suicides and murders, declarations of love and horrid revelations, first Alwa then Schön bursts in with the news that Revolution has broken out in Paris. The incongruity between amatory and revolutionary upheavals is farcical, but the juxtaposition raises a serious issue. Emancipation may be psychological or it may be political, and the perennial question of priorities still applies today: can political revolution free human beings, or is political change impossible until individuals free themselves from the inner slavery of psychological conditioning by the social institutions underlying the political order? In a sonnet on Lenz's bourgeois tragedy, *Der Hofmeister (The Private Tutor)*, Brecht writes of Figaro on the German side of the Rhine (1967, vol. 9: 610). Whereas Beaumarchais' Figaro outwits his rapacious master, Lenz's lackey castrates himself, a symbol of the self-castration of Germany's bourgeois intellectuals. *Earth Spirit* gives the impression that while Paris is always exploding, the Germans continue to implode, destroying themselves rather than the structures which enslave them. But in their farcical context, these intimations from abroad are sceptical in effect; the French political games are no more substantial than the German individual posturings. *Pandora's Box* leaves no hope of emancipation in Paris, where unleashed private enterprise brings short-lived fortunes to some and enslaves others. The plays constantly explore paths to individual freedom which lead only to dead-ends blocked by social and economic barriers. Whether the failings of the individuals are caused by the barriers, or the barriers by the failings, remains unclear.

In obvious ways, Wedekind's plays are partial and dated as a picture of the body politic. They show gradations within the middle class: the provincial petit-bourgeoisie, the ambitious professional caste of teachers, doctors and lawyers, the beer-brewers, newspaper proprietors and civil servants in the city or Munich, the bankers and shareholders in Paris. The aristocracy features fleetingly in grotesque caricature; the lumpenproletariat looms large; but the industrial working class is entirely absent. The young people come to town as servants to the middle-classes. They never work in factories, at most in shops or restaurants, the men hoping to rise by artistic and the women by sexual talent. Political activity appears as administration in the civil service or the police. Revolutionary and reformist politics are equally farcical; and socialism rears its ugly head only to be rejected in favour of champagne. Wedekind portrays the social mobility of early industrial capitalism as a matter of individuals either rising from rural obscurity or the urban underworld, or else falling back into the abyss. The mobile individual and the economic environment which makes such changing fates possible both appear in an ambiguous light. They exemplify a freedom impossible in the rigidly stratified order of pre-industrial society; but the mobility has to be fought for and the freedom bought. The battle is so brutal and the cost so high that in the end, little is left of individual freedom.

Rather than the primacy of the psychological over the political, the plays inadvertently demonstrate the indivisibility of personal and political emancipation. The plots demonstrate this indivisibility in negative form, as the characters come to grief. But the last scene of *Spring Awakening* and the anti-fatalistic manner of all the plays open the way to more activist readings, though the kind of action is not specified. The demonstration is most powerful in sexual, rather than class politics. The pursuit of sexual emancipation is a thread which, once pulled, threatens the whole fabric of society, since the way in which relations between the sexes are perceived and enacted is intimately connected with the socio-economic structure as a whole. In spite of his evident hostility to the feminist movement, Wedekind follows the feminist thread a long way, inwards into the desires underlying the respectable moral surface and outwards towards economic forces which intrude into the imagination with drastic effects on sexuality. I shall therefore argue that while he remained trapped in some of the more virulent sexist ideas of his time (as some of his less well known works clearly show), the theatrical effect of the major plays, depending on production, undermines that very ideology. His contempt for feminist and socialist ideas sounds alongside, without obscuring, an exploration of sexual psychology which subverts still potent sexual stereotypes. That theatrical subversion is the main topic of this study.

2
Spring Awakening

Spring Awakening offers an individualistic response to problems it diagnoses as social. Critical analysis of a sexually oppressive culture is combined with vivid evocation of the sexual fantasies bred by that culture. The play marries dramatic form and theatrical effects with the social, psychological and moral argument. As self-reflective theatre, the play in production becomes a metaphor for human nature as self-reflective. Self-consciously theatrical and anti-illusionist, it is a seminal work in the history of modern theatre.

Nature and Human Nature

The title *Spring Awakening*, evocative of love in life's springtime, is contradicted by the subtitle, *A Children's Tragedy*, with its message of young lives blighted. The subtitle, in turn, is denied in the closing phantasmagoric vision of a new beginning for Melchior in the world of the Masked Man and his female alter ego, the bohemian Ilse. This unseen world is conjured up in Ilse's stories of city life, fantastic fictions when measured against the small-town environment pictured in the play. Equally fantastic is the Gothick vision in the final act, of Moritz as a comic voice issuing from the head he carries under his arm. A fractured character from the now completed children's tragedy, he has become the disembodied voice of an aesthetic attitude, as detached from biographical definition as the Masked Man.

Like the dismantled Moritz, the play as a whole can be taken apart into pieces which do not fit together neatly to form a mimetic representation of a closed world, whether a lyric realm of nature and young love or a fatally determining social environment. The last scene breaks the action, its location, the dialogue and the characters into a kaleidoscope of fragments from which the play was constructed, and undermines the authority of its plotting in an inevitable catastrophe. The fragmentation begins with the title and subtitle. The words *Frühlings Erwachen* (*Spring Awakening*) recall a vast poetic tradition, most immediately the Romantic lyric introduced in Germany with the young Goethe's Sesenheim poems of the early 1770s, such as *Mailed* or *Erwache Frederike*, with its repeated motif of awakening. By the time Wedekind was writing, his title contained echoes of a hundred clichés: 'Schöner Frühling, komm doch wieder,/Lieber Frühling komm doch bald!' (Fairest springtime, come please quickly,/Dearest springtime come now soon!) wrote Hoffmann von Fallersleben in the same metre as his 'Deutschland, Deutschland über alles . . .'. Joseph Völk's cry, 'Jetzt ist Frühling geworden in Deutschland!' (Spring is now come in Germany), at the Zollparlament of 1868, was a tag of the time. Spring is come in the play, but only in the imagination, not in narrow provincial Germany. The first scene, with pubescent Wendla, a slim virgin in her child's dress, dreaming of elfin draperies, recalls a late outgrowth of Romanticism, the decorative and sinuous *Jugendstil*. *Jugendstil* characteristically portrays children or androgynous adolescents, often with an underlying homosexual appeal, as in Aubrey Beardsley's work. The cult of sterility, of sex without procreation, mocked a decade later by Thomas Mann in his story *Tristan* and commented on by Walter Benjamin (1974: 672), was a reaction against authoritarian family conditioning. In this context, the title with its subtitle sounds a note of lyrical pathos. The irony is bitter-sweet: the awakening leads to death.

But the play immediately moves beyond *Jugendstil*. The first scene introduces non-decorative nature as biology, in the form of dryads who might get pregnant or catch diptheria. Later, the boys discuss wet dreams and pass round anatomical drawings, while one scene is set in a lavatory, a hyper-Naturalist flourish in this anti-Naturalist play, looking back to Büchner's *Woyzeck* whose hero urinates, and beyond that to the *Sturm-und-Drang* realism of Goethe's *Götz von Berlichingen* in which natural functions figure fleetingly. The age of *Jugendstil* was also the age of positivist science. *Spring Awakening* connotes not just meadow flowers, but involuntary erections. In this context at least, two voices sound in the title and the subtitle. There is the grim voice, denied in the last scene, of scientific determinism, plotting the inevitable effects of biology and environment; and there is the polemical voice of sarcastic protest at a culture pervaded by Romantic cliché, which keeps its children in ignorance, condemning them to death by abortion or to the living death of the penitentiary.

In yet another context, the title evokes Dionysian nature, not Sinding's *Rustle* but Stravinsky's violent *Rite*. The cult of natural vitality, the *Lebensphilosophie*, had twin roots in science and metaphysics, in social Darwinism and derivatives of Schopenhauer's philosophy of will. The play evokes life as a struggle for mastery over chaotic natural forces. Moritz speaks of being born into a whirlpool (I, 2). Just before he shoots himself, he speaks of the river heavy as lead, transferring to an external force the inner weight which drags him down – sex, he says, must be a sensation like passing over rapids (II, 7). Whereas Moritz drowns in the river of his feelings, Melchior survives, an outcome anticipated when Thea tells how Melchior almost drowned during a raft party, but survived because he could swim (I, 3). Ilse conjures up the synthetic excitements of *la vie bohème* and a game of Russian roulette with a lover, but the instinct for survival limits such dangerous sexual experiments (II, 7). Sex, the fertile source of life and pleasure, is also potentially deadly: like the river, it threatens to overwhelm and extinguish the individual. Only those strong enough to swim, to explore their sexuality and survive, enjoy a truly full life. Moritz goes under, while the adults avoid the challenge by escaping into hypocrisy and repression, satisfying unadmitted instincts in devious ways, usually to the detriment of others. In this context, the tragedy announced in the subtitle is first affirmed, then denied in the last scene as Melchior breaks out of a living death to be reborn into the world of the Masked Man. The cataclysmic eruption of sexual energy, deadly in its outcome for Wendla and Moritz, can burst the moral conventions asunder and promise new life.

The title, subtitle and structure produce competing senses of nature and human nature and a variety of voices or tones. Nature as *Jugendstil* mourning for youthful love, nature as the science of biology and nature as the vitalist cult of Life correspond roughly to three kinds of play Wedekind might have written: a neo-Romantic Symbolist verse drama; a tragedy in basic German enriched with coughs, grunts and Naturalist noises; or an early Expressionist, ecstatic if humourless, vision of rebirth. The last, vitalist reading might seem pre-eminent if the Masked Man is seen to be the mouthpiece of the author. But if there is an author behind the mask, he has taken care to hide his face; his voice does not drown out the other voices in the play. There is no single image of human nature, no definitive answer to the question: what is a human being? The various images mutually undermine one another to an effect which may be comic or melancholy, bitter or polemical in turn, but which is always sceptical. The play is less the reflection *of* a view of human nature than an experimental reflection *on* a variety of views with only one clear conclusion: that human beings are never natural in the sense of being purely instinctive or spontaneous like animals or Nietzschean blond beasts. The children are reflective and self-conscious: they constantly watch themselves and make images of themselves, just as the play as a whole experiments with different ways of looking at human nature. The metaphors pervading the dialogue are often images of nature, but nature mediated through cultural traditions in which the shifting concept is a coin in the ideological currency. The Masked Man who points the way to Life is a highly unnatural figure in a mask and elegant evening dress. He offers a mode of sensibility at the opposite extreme from natural vitality – one that demands self-awareness and the complicated blend of indulgence, restraint and deception symbolized in the mask. It is a recipe for survival through acceptance of alienation, of self-division and cool distance from others, an aesthetic rather than a natural mode of being.

Self-awareness and Role-playing

Human beings are shown in *Spring Awakening* to be self-reflective. Their self-image is deeply affected, if not wholly determined, by the culture and social relations they inhabit. Self-reflection goes along with role-playing as the characters produce themselves, acting out roles they create or assume in accordance with the rules of the social game. The adult world is pervaded by hypocritical moral posturing and sentimental self-deception. The roles of the two mothers, for example, should be alienated in proto-Brechtian fashion to show that the characters are mouthing received ideas, playing the appropriate part, that part in turn projected for our inspection: Frau Gabor the would-be liberal who consigns her son to the penitentiary; Frau Bergmann, the sentimentalist who prattles of storks and babies and delivers her daughter into the hands of an abortionist. Rentier Stiefel, the man of property, twice rhetorically denies paternity at his son's graveside (III, 2). The fact that the father of Wedekind's suicide schoolfriend did likewise, only goes to show that life often imitates bad art. There follows Rektor Sonnenstich's incantation:

> Der Selbstmord als der denkbar bedenklichste Verstoß gegen die sittliche Weltordnung ist der denkbar bedenklichste Beweis *für* die sittliche Weltordnung, indem der Selbstmörder der sittlichen Weltordnung den Urteilsspruch zu sprechen erspart und ihr Bestehen bestätigt.

> *As the greatest conceivable offence against the universal moral order suicide is at the same time the greatest possible proof of the universal moral order, in as much as the suicide saves the universal moral order the trouble of pronouncing its verdict and so confirms its existence.*

The babble of assonances, alliterations and repetitions in Sonnenstich's speech is reminiscent of the Captain's disquisitions on morality in Büchner's *Woyzeck*: 'Moral, das ist wenn man moralisch ist, Woyzeck . . .' (Morality, that's when one is moral, Woyzeck . . .). The definitions are circular. The words fail to refer; they are an end in themselves, the self-display of a pendant assuming the mantle and style of Kant. The argument fits Freud's category of the logical error in his study of jokes. The joke (which I shall not try to explain) shines through the rubbish and anticipates later attacks on cliché in Ionesco and the Theatre of the Absurd. The adults mouth received ideas transmitted through the institutions of family, school, church, and the law, the bastions of the social order. Frau Bergmann has acted by Wendla as her mother did by her: 'Ich habe nicht anders getan als meine liebe gute Mutter an mir getan hat.' (I acted no differently by you than my dear good mother did by me: III, 5.) Mothers are always dear and good. The abortionist is by title another mother, Mutter Schmidtin, a name at once cosy and sinister, affording a glimpse of the witch's face behind the mask of the dear, good mother.

Whereas the adult mask of convention has become indistinguishable from the face, the children still play with different ways of seeing themselves. Wendla imagines herself as an elfin queen (I, 1) and Melchior as a dryad (I, 2), for a moment shifting from his male identity, just as Moritz later imagines the greater sexual pleasure girls must feel, or identifies with the headless queen in his grandmother's fairy-tale (II, 1). When Ernst and Hänschen kiss among the vines, they move not just in imagination beyond sexual stereotypes (III, 6). But the real moment is also an image in the mind: the two boys imagine themselves looking back in the future to this moment in the past, so transforming it, even as it happens, into an image. Ernst, more earnest than Hänschen with his playfully diminutive name, imagines a future as the happy father of children. But the *Biedermeier* genre painting of philoprogenitive bliss in the sentimental manner of the first half of the century is swept aside in favour of the sterile *Jugendstil* charm of androgynous youths in the spring of their life among autumnal vines, the manner of the *fin de siècle*. The picture of two boys kissing could be seen in many ways, provoking various responses. Ernst and Hänschen choose to see their action framed, translated into a beautiful observable image. The kiss becomes a theatrical pose in a tableau the boys enact and observe simultaneously, a tableau within the tableau we the audience watch on the stage.

The metaphor of role-playing reaches a climax with the Masked Man, heralded by his female counterpart Ilse (II, 7). Ilse models for painters and photographers. She wears a myriad of costumes and strikes endless poses. Even asleep, she is a reflected image in the ceiling mirror: in her lover's words, beautiful enough to murder. She tells of other girls dressed as Andalusians or beer-nymphs – an urban variety of the ubiquitous dryads – and recalls children's games in which she played a brave with a tomahawk. Isle imagining herself as Ganymede only underlines her femininity, but the tomahawk for a moment breaks through the female image. On stage we see an actress in a ragged dress, bright scarf and ball shoes, playing the role of Ilse in a play: theatre as metaphor for Ilse inside the play is a myriad of roles. Unlike Ilse, the adult characters play parts unwittingly: the mask has coalesced with the face. But the mask worn by the gentleman in evening clothes can be changed at will. His mask suggests not self-deception, but deception of others, a mocking game of conceal-ment and survival. It allows a double freedom: to present himself to others in a guise of his choosing and to look as he likes behind the mask. By extension, he can see the beautiful or ludicrous mask on the face of others, or see behind it to the pitiable or despicable face underneath. He can choose his own perspective on the world.

The children's fluidity suggests that the vicious circle of condition-ing can be broken. The human capacity for self-reflection offers the potential for freedom. The imagination constantly interprets basic sense perceptions, feelings and experience, and influences action. The path to freedom from social pressure lies through a shift of attitude or perspective: we may unconsciously play the roles society imposes upon us, or we may consciously choose our own roles and live our own fictions. The play points to desirable education reform, but primarily to individual self-transformation as the means to emancipation. Conscious choice of role within society is combined with a perspectivistic, x-ray vision which sees through the masks presented by others. The play itself offers a variety of perspectives on one set of events. It starts off a Children's Tragedy apparently in the Naturalist mode, showing the inevitable effects of the moral environment and biology. The opening is reminiscent of Hebbel's *Maria Magdalene* of 1844, a crucial work in the history of realist forms in the German theatre. There too, a mother and daughter talk of clothes, a sense of foreboding is created by talk of death, and the pregnant heroine is doomed to fall victim to a destructive social morality. This is Wendla's fate in *Spring Awakening*. But in the final scene, her counterpart Moritz is transformed from a helpless victim of tragedy into a spokesman of decadent pleasure, and he and Melchior appear to be less two individuals than two modes of sensibility coexisting in one imagination. From the opening onwards, incongruous shifts in tone and register give rise to multiple possible readings. Wendla's premonition of death is over-theatrical, a nudge and wink to the audience to expect the worst; but the tragic inevitability of the worst is finally denied. Moritz's transformation into a decadent aesthete is anticipated when the horror of a child blowing out his brains is turned by Ilse into a grotesque and beautiful image of red blood on yellow Aaron's rod, and of brains hanging on the willow tree (III, 2). The notion that the same events and experiences can change in meaning depending on perspective is thus embodied in the structure and manner of the play as a whole.

The next two sections will consider two sets of roles and perspectives: first the imaginative world of the children, then the sterotyped roles the adults play and which they seek to impose upon their offspring.

Fairy-tales, Legends and Children

The children's speech constantly fluctuates between the colloquial and the lyrical, between naive simplicity and sophisticated irony. The different manners prevent the emergence of fixed types, and suggest contrasting ways of seeing and feeling. In the opening scene, for example, Wendla speaks variously as a typical young girl concerned with clothes, as the heroine of a tragedy, as a sophisticated ironist gently mocking her silly mother and as a lyrical visionary. These different manners – the child-like, the tragic, the ironically mocking and the lyrical – function throughout the play as perspectives through which the characters are at once constructed, and presented to one another and to the audience. The final disruption of the tragedy with Wendla as victim turns her initial premonition into a theatrical joke, a piece of mock dramatic irony. The children appear as real children, but also as mythical beings: comic, grotesque or beautiful elves and dryads. The child's-eye view, filtered through legendary and fairy-tale motifs, is particualry salient. Wedekind draws on eerie folk tales, children's stories and Romantic fairy-tales, a tradition embracing the brothers Grimm, E. T. A. Hoffman and Wilhelm Busch. The fascination with the child's imagination, also marked in Victorian England, reflects the strains felt by members of a prudish and authoritarian society.

The scene where Wendla and Melchior meet in the wood is full of fairy-tale echoes (I, 5). Melchior greets Wendla as a dryad. But beautiful spirits of nature may arouse forbidden desires and become threatening, like Keats's *belle dame sans merci*. Wendla, gathering herbs as wise women do, turns from dryad into witch, the pagan spirit of nature transformed by Christian teaching into the seat of evil, as Melchior tries to beat Satan out of her. Initially, the two children recall Hansel and Gretel; but the threat that lies in wait comes from inside themselves. Wendla, lost in the woods, meets Melchior, a knight errant who will rescue her. But young girls in woods should beware of a harmless exterior and invitations to lie down under the trees. If Melchior turns Wendla into a witch, he himself turns into a demon, the demon he would beat out of her. At the same time, the meeting is between two ordinary children: 'No, no, I am Wendla Bergmann', says Wendla on being greeted as a dryad, a childishly naive – or is it a delicately ironic? – deflation of Melchior's poetic vision. Either way, the comic effect does not dispel the magical atmosphere. A different echo sounds in Wendla's dream of the poor beggar girl wandering among hard-hearted people, beaten at night by her cruel father. Such sentimental fiction, of the type of Dickens's *A Christmas Carol*, is a genre intermediate between realism and the fairy-tale. Wendla falls victim not to a hard-hearted public but to a

soft-hearted mother and her alter ego, the abortionist who serves a
public of sentimental hypocrites. Wendla's dream becomes more grim
as a premonition of her death; but at the same time the dream
undermines pathos, for we recognize in it the sentimentality of
children's tragedies purveyed for a sobbing adult public full of people
like Frau Bergmann. The sentimentality of the genre is undermined
by the ugly motif of abortion and is finally destroyed at the end of the
play.

The scene in the woods shows that childhood is not innocent. The
child's-eye view is inflitrated by conventional morality which turns
dreams about dryads into nightmares about witches. But two further
examples of the child's-eye view – the presentation of the schoolmasters and Moritz's fairy-tale – suggest how the imagination can combat
conditioning. The grotesque schoolmasters are monstrous enemies
seen through the eyes of a child. Wedekind has given them as real
names the perennial mocking nicknames pupils apply to their
teachers. Naming is a potent way of deflecting evil and of demystify-
ing authority through ridicule. The ludicrous teachers, more concerned with draughts than suicide, are seen from the viewpoint of
childish mockery rather than of adult satire. The mockery is one of the
most hopeful elements in the play; it evokes a mentality not yet cowed
into submission. The children are generally presented from their own,
albeit shifting, point of view; when they kiss, Ernst and Hänschen
impose their own angle of vision which, for the moment, becomes the
focus of the play. The teachers, by contrast, are seen externally
through the child's eye which destroys their authority: who, after
seeing or reading such a play, could be driven to suicide by a
Sonnenstich or an Affenschmalz (Sunstroke and Monkeygrease)? The
attack is not on education as a whole, only on educators and a
competitive examination system. The children draw on literary images
and the Masked Man speaks the language of mathematics: there is no
crude setting of nature against culture.

The most striking fairy-tale motif, introduced by a character and
subsumed into the structure, is Moritz's tale of the headless queen
told him by his grandmother (II, 1). (Grandmothers are better tellers
of stories and of truth than mothers, as witness the grandmother's
grim story in Büchners's *Woyzeck*.) The headless queen cannot eat,
drink, see, laugh or kiss. Although she is all body, she feels no
pleasure and is at war with everyone. She is finally won by a king with
two heads which keep quarelling. The court magician transfers the

smaller head to the queen, and bodies and heads, king and queen, live happily ever after, exchanging kisses. The story implies that girls must acquire brains from boys, though smaller ones, while boys have to escape the domination of the mind and acquire sensuality from girls: many fairy-tales have such sexist undertones. But it is the boy Moritz who imagines himself as the headless queen, and who appears in the last scene, having blown his brains out at the end of Act II. A tendency towards headlessness, then, is less a matter of sex than of temperament, though Moritz does have characteristically feminine attitudes. Besides sketching gender types, the story implies that all human beings, male or female, are happier and more able to love when senses and intellect interact. To remain a prey to unreflected instinct is to be less than fully human; it is better to have a head with eyes to see yourself and others, to be conscious and to know. In depositing his brains over a willow tree, Moritz reverses the order of events in the grandmother's story and regresses to an inhuman condition. His appearance with his head under his arm suggests that he might put it on again sometime, and sustains the hope of the fairy-tale against the hopelessness of the children's tragedy.

Finally, the child's-eye view – which is not childish – embraces the most celebrated classic of German literature, Goethe's *Faust*. Frau Gabor regards *Faust* as adult reading, a view her son Melchior rejects: it is the adults who reduce everything to 'p . . . And v . . .' (penis and vagina: III, 1). The technical terms for the sexual organs are comically incongruous with the language of the Gretchen tragedy, and uncover the hidden prurience of adults who impose their pornographic vision on a work they purport to admire. The closing scene, however, rejects the Gretchen tragedy as a masked Mephistopheles briskly disposes of Wendla's fate. Melchior departs as a Faust with his mentor. He is also a Don Juan who, unlike his predecessor, refuses Moritz's cold dead hand that would draw him down to hell.

Adults and Morality

Whereas the children experiment with roles and attitudes, the adults are rigidly hypocritical or self-deceived. The mask of moral authority conceals hidden desires for power, status and sexual gratification. In the name of morality, but in reality to satisfy personal desires, they abuse the children or attempt to impose on them their own ideal self-image. Melchior's view of morality is amply illustrated in his argument with Wendla about her charitable activities (I, 5). All human behaviour, Melchior argues, arises from desires; we do what we do because we want to. We present our behaviour as moral, but this is either hypocrisy or self-deception, role-playing with ourselves or others as audience. Wendla gives to the poor because she enjoys it; the dirtier and iller the women and children and the more the men hate her for her prosperity, the greater her pleasure! How can the miser help it that he does not enjoy giving? We cannot choose our desires or decide what to take pleasure in. Hence the absurdity, later, of Herr Gabor's claim that Melchior will learn to desire the good in the penitentiary, irrespective of the education methods of that establishment (III, 3). Melchior does not quite argue with Nietzsche that pleasure in giving derives from pleasure in humiliating. But the young Lady Bountiful enjoying her own goodness unmasks charity as a palliative which brings more pleasure the greater the inequality between giver and receiver. The point is psychological rather than political: Wendla's fascination with power emerges in her imagined role-reversal when she dreams of herself as a poor beggar girl. As benefactress she enjoys the power of giving, as beggar girl the masochistic pleasure of submission.

No rigorous moral position emerges from this play; one could abstract hedonist, egoist or utilitarian conclusions. The strongest note is an anti-Kantian moral scepticism which lends the play some intellectual bite. The most immediate influence was probably Schopenhauer, though with the values reversed, for Wedekind takes a less gloomy view of the scourge of desire than the great pessimist. In one possible reading of Schopenhauer, morality is necessarily yet another manifestation of will, but will which wills its own denial. Wedekind endorses the first claim, but rejects as death-directed a morality which could deny desire. If morality can be reduced to desire for the death of desire, it is to be rejected as illusion or self-contradiction. This is arguably a more logical conclusion than Schopenhauer's. The attack is not simply on particular conventions, but on all moral discourse as at best an obstacle to self-knowledge, at worst harmful and potentially deadly. It induces guilt in the children who fail to conform to some ideal, at first externally imposed and then internalized, which conflicts with other desires and temperamental propensities. It allows adults to vent their frustration under the guise of moral correction. In this sense, morality is real enough in its effects.

As the Masked Man says, it is the real product of two imaginary numbers, should and would: 'das reele Produkt zweier imaginärer Größen: Sollen und Wollen' (III, 7). This gnomic statement has been much puzzled over. One critic suggests that it is just a piece of impressive-sounding nonsense, a view that has much to be said for it (Best, 1975: 80). Two interpretations suggest themselves, however. 'Sollen' – ought – is imaginary in that there are no objective moral truths to be discovered in the external world. Moral imperatives are inventions of the imagination (White, 1973) or internalized social conventions (Shaw, 1970: 61; Burns, 1975). They become imaginary in the sense of delusory if held to have objective reality or absolute binding power. 'Wollen' – wanting or desire – also issues from the subject and is not normally regarded as existing outside the individual (unless by metaphysicians like Schopenhauer or Sartre). Since 'want' is the more authentic expression of the self, to lend 'ought' more binding status is especially foolish. Thus the interaction of subjective desire with moral principles, equally subjective but generally heteronomous rather then autonomous, produces actions which have real consequences for ourselves and others, and which always represent desire disguised as moral imperative. This is in keeping with Melchior's view of Wendla's good deeds and with many other passages in the play. J. L. Hibberd (1977) reaches a broadly similar conclusion in a reading which takes account of the strictly mathematical sense of 'imaginary'. Another interpretation follows if 'Wollen' means the faculty of will which Kant took to be a bridge between causality and freedom in moral matters: our actions are caused by the will, but we can will according to the moral imperative; that is, we can choose to act morally, which in Kant means *not* in accordance with desire. The Masked Man's formula would then take on an anti-Kantian sense: we imagine that we will what we ought, but such free will is imaginary. We cannot choose what to want. On either reading the conclusion remains the same: we will in accordance with our desires and call it morality. Peter Jelavich (1985: 93) takes the Masked Man to be Wedekind's spokesman preaching the necessity of compromise between the contradictory dictates of obligation and volition. But the mask suggests the necessity of deception rather than compromise.

Desires can, of course, be altruistic – the children show traces of solidarity – but this is not true of the adult desires in *Spring Awakening*. The action constantly strips away the moral posture. The adults want three main things: power; extension of the ego in their children; and sexual pleasure. This analysis places the play within a complex of ideas stretching from Schopenhauer, social Darwinism, and Nietzsche's philosophy of power through to Freud or Adler. Besides applying to Christian charity, the critique extends to parental and filial duty and sexual morality. The appeal of children in an authoritarian society is ambiguous. They can be moulded into the ideal shape their parents have failed to achieve, or they can be punished for failing or arousing forbidden fantasies in their frustrated elders and betters.

The men, as main agents of discipline in the patriarchal family, come under cruder satirical attack than the women. As well as fathers, middle-class professionals are singled out – the gargoyle school-teachers, the doctor who connives at Wendla's fate, Melchior's lawyer father, the sanctimonious Pastor Kahlbauch, and the man of property Rentier Stiefel whose downmarket name suggests that his riches may be *nouveaux*. All are figures who traditionally present a facade: the bedside manner, the *ex cathedra* prounouncement, the pulpit tone or the self-made man's pursuit of refinement. They suggest too how the professionals, especially lawyers, sustain an oppressive social order they call justice, though Wedekind's analysis of this hypocrisy is psychological rather than political. When Moritz fails to reproduce his father's self-image of competent success, Rentier Stiefel denies paternity. Herr Gabor's horror seems to be provoked less by Melchior's seduction of Wendla than by his promise to stand by her, a crime against social status, a betrayal of masculine double morality and a threat to the paternal right to dispose of a child as a valuable possession. The stock authoritarian types allow actors to demonstrate palpably that morality is play-acting, a point reinforced by the very fact that these figures recall butts of comedy which have been traditional since the seventeenth century.

The men are caricatured more heavily than the women, but by the end of the play it is difficult to say which is more unpleasant, overt male lust for power or the raging self-pity of the lapsed liberal and the sickly sentiment of a mother who hands over to the abortionist the daughter whose trouble she sees as an offence against herself – 'Oh, warum hast du mir das getan?' (O, why have you done this to me: III, 5). At first sight, Frau Bergmann and the dominant Frau Gabor, who seems to challenge patriarchy, are contrasting figures. But Frau Gabor's liberal reform programme is demolished from a more radical standpoint. Frau Gabor is liberal in theory but not in practice:

children may know but not do; discipline must be internalized; the children must police themselves (II, 1). If they do not, then all the external sanctions are brought back. When she learns that Wendla is actually pregnant by her son Frau Gabor relapses into subservience to her husband and collaborates vigorously in consigning Melchior to the penitentiary. Frau Bergmann balks at theoretical knowledge, while Frau Gabor joins her in balking at practical experience.

Nevertheless, Frau Gabor's sudden retreat from liberalism is somewhat undermotivated. Her programme seems to be at least a step towards moderating repression while still protecting girls from premature or unwanted pregnancy in an age before the Pill, an issue the play raises and signally fails to deal with. The disposal of the liberal Aunt Sally is rather cavalier, as if her reasoned argument posed a threat to sexual pleasure and so, like Wendla's fate later on, has to be brushed aside. The attack is on Frau Gabor as a self-deceived person, rather than on her arguments. She does not truly desire the autonomous growth of her child; underneath, she is no different from the teachers or the silly Frau Bergmann. Her underlying desire to force her son into a mould of her making comes out in bathos as she contemplates the way in which the penitentiary will ruin her masterpiece:

> Und sehe ich ihn wieder – Gott, Gott, dieses frühlingsfrohe Herz – sein helles Lachen – alles, alles – seine kindliche Entschlossenheit, mutig zu kämpfen für Gut und Recht – O dieser Morgenhimmel, wie *ich* ihn licht und rein in *seiner* Seele gehegt als *mein* höchstes Gut . . .

> *And when I see him again – God, God, that heart full of springtime joy – his bright laughter – all, all – his young determination to fight for goodness and justice – O that morning sky, bright and fresh, which I tended in his soul as my highest good* . . . (III, 3)

The emphases are mine. 'Gut' may mean good, treasure or possession. Frau Gabor sees herself as a warrior for justice and wants her child-possession to reproduce her own ideal image. When he fails, the broken idol is swept into the dustbin of the penitentiary. Her angry reaction on hearing of Wendla's pregnancy recalls the vengeful rage of a betrayed lover, a jealousy close to sexual feeling. The love affair with her son over, Frau Gabor returns to conjugal consolations in the strong arms of her husband, as the Masked Man tells us.

The differences between the two mothers are not great. Frau

Gabor's 'my highest good' and Frau Bergmann's 'mein einziges Herzblatt' (my heart's precious: I, 1; III, 5) convey possessive and oppressive love, and a regressive infantilism as the adult women identify with their dream children. Frau Bergmann's delight in her daughter's slim pretty body, prettier than the other girls, reveals the ageing mother's dream of sexy yet innocent femininity, which makes her as reluctant as her daughter is to hide the young body. In a prudish society rife with sexual frustration, children have the appeal of presexual innocence, but it is the arousing innocence of the virgin. The girls have not yet become either of the stereotypes, boring good wives or exciting fallen women. Unlike the wives they are desirable; unlike the fallen women they are innocent. On the one hand, they allow for sexual dreams without sex, the dream Frau Bergmann dreams; on the other hand they arouse the perverse desire for the rape of innocence and the concomitant desire to punish the innocent object for arousing such desires. In adult eyes, the children are either angelic – Wendla in her princess dress or Melchior described by his mother as 'this morning sky' – or limbs of Satan – Melchior later, a Lucifer fallen from his morning sky into the hell of the penitentiary, or Martha whose father makes her wear sackcloth. In Martha's father the desires aroused by his child lie close to the surface and emerge as sadism (I, 3). Parental duty is a moral role concealing infantile wish-fulfilment, lust or the desire for power. Wedekind's critique is not of role-playing as such, but of harmful roles. Repression does not lead to good behaviour, but creates perverse desires which threaten the survival of the actor and his protagonist. The morality of guilt and punishment is particularly damaging to the 'sinful' children punished to assuage secret adult guilts and fantasies.

Les Fleurs du mal

Given human self-awareness, sexuality is never simply natural or instinctive; sex is always in the head as well as in the loins. Even during sleep, dreams accompany physical manifestations. Moritz dreams of legs in sky-blue tights climbing over a desk, and Georg Leeschnitz dreams of his mother, a pre-Freudian detail which complements sexual feeling in parents (I, 2). The age at which puberty begins is variable. Lämmermeier, older than Melchior, still only dreams of cake and apricot jam. Moritz, on the other hand, recalls his own experience of infantile sexuality: his uncomprehending arousal at the age of five, by the *décolleté* of the queen of hearts on a playing card. The predominant morality demands abstinence outside marriage, and therefore throughout adolescence, just when the sexual drive is at its most urgent. Religious and moral teaching associates sex with guilt and punishment. Since pregnancy is the only consequence of intercourse visible to the public, a double morality operates to ensure that unseen male guilt is offloaded onto the visibly guilty: women are guiltier than men. In competitive bourgeois society men have greater freedom of action and higher social status than women: men are superior to women.

These moral and social differences are linked to characteristic differences in sexual attitudes. The girls feel inferior to boys (I, 3): Martha would rather be a boy; Wendla who wants only boy children, is glad to be a girl, but only because it is more satisfying to be loved by a man than by a girl (the typical conjunction man-girl is used, probably unconsciously by Wedekind as well as by his creation). A man, she goes on, can be proud of his professional achievements, like the forester Pfülle whose Melitta receives from him ten thousand times more than she is in herself, the thousands of trees a ludicrous proliferation of phallic symbols. Boys are expected to be active, to choose a partner and to be admired for social and physical achievement. Girls are expected to be passive, to be chosen and to attract by beauty and dress. Yet because sex is taboo, both sexes are induced to feel guilt or shame. Moritz cannot look at a girl without thinking disgusting thoughts, though he does not yet know exactly what he is thinking or why it is disgusting: a case not of guilty knowledge, but of guilt before knowledge (I, 2). The boys project their guilt on the object which arouses sexual desire – Melchior beating Satan out of Wendla – while the girls helplessly accept their own guilt as grounds for punishment. Masculinity is also oppressive. Moritz, a 'feminine' type weighed down by his father's demands, likes to imagine the greater pleasure girls must feel in their passivity during sexual intercourse as they are forced to submit to what is wrong (II, 1) and finally punishes himself in a grim coalescence of masculine sadism and feminine masochism. This complex of biological, social and moral factors produces a sado-masochistic pattern of behaviour transmitted to the children by the adults: Wendla is fascinated by the beatings Martha's father inflicts on her, and twice asks Martha what he hits her with (I, 3). Pleasure is associated with pain, sexual arousal with dominance and servility, guilt and punishment. Sado-masochism may take several forms. It may remain an unconscious pattern of behaviour, as with Martha and her father; or it may become semi-conscious role-playing which finally becomes painful as with Wendla and Melchior; or it may turn into a fully conscious game, pleasurable if dangerous, as in Ilse's adventures. Finally, it may be simply comical, a grotesque game of the imagination, as in Bluebeard-Hänschen's execution of his painted and too chaste nudes who rouse wicked desires which they will not satisfy (II, 3).

In Moritz, sado-masochistic impulses turn against the self (II, 7). His suicide is ostensibly prompted by an excess of filial piety, guilt at disappointing his father. Yet he demolishes filial duty himself, arguing that children do not choose to be born nor to be who and what they are. As he comically puts it, had he not been born an infant he might have been clever enough to choose to be someone else. Then again, his existence arose from the sexual act, hardly grounds for gratitude, since his parents did not have him in mind at the time. Honouring his father and his mother has had the opposite effect from the Biblical promise: his days have not been long upon the earth (III, 7). But there are deeper grounds for scepticism. Moritz's piety has something of the self-deception Melchior sees in all supposedly moral actions. Moritz kills himself not out of duty but because he wants to die; life is a matter of taste, he says, a taste he does not have. He enjoys the 'little death' of masturbation before the greater masochistic consummation of self-destruction, in which his gun is a symbol of the phallus. The hidden desire to submit is fully overt in the closing words of the play as he lies supine (the female position), warms himself with dissolution and smiles in a grotesque and decadent transformation of his earlier image of girls dissolving in pleasure after initial violent violation. The battle of Life and Death is part of the vitalist argument, but Moritz also reveals the way in which sexuality may be affected by social morality. Death is here a metaphor for a mode of feeling in Moritz, who turns away from the pleasure Ilse offers, inwards into narcissism.

Besides Melchior's sadism, Wendla's masochism and Moritz's narcissistic masochism, the play touches on adolescent homosexuality, masturbation stimulated by mental images, desperation or erotic paintings, group-masturbation, and auto-voyeurism in ceiling mirrors. All of these sexual activities are accompanied by imaginings and dreams, except in the penitentiary, where masturbation becomes an athletic competition which could as well be replaced by boxing. The boys here represent the brutish and competitive male in his lowest form. Of all the children's behaviour, this is the most drearily sordid because the least sexual, dissociated as it is from the power of the imagination to transform and give meaning to physical activity. The female counterpart of the competitive male is the passive female object of male eyes. Rather than themselves desiring, the girls are excited by the thoughts of the desire they imagine they arouse in the boys. In the sexual act itself, Wendla cries out 'No – – no' before succumbing to Melchior's desire, just as Moritz had imagined it must be (II, 4). All this reflects a society where girls are encouraged to be attractive yet innocent of sex and where boys are supposed to be the initiators. By the same token, for a boy to be soft, yielding and sweet is unmanly, as the girls dimly feel when they laugh at Moritz for offering Thea chocolates which are soft and warm from his trouser pocket (I, 3).

On the other hand, the children are half aware of these sexual differences and do not simply take them as a fact of nature. They reflect upon, question and sometimes move beyond the stereotypes, as when the girls enjoy Melchior's handsomeness (I, 3), or Ilse takes the initiative with Moritz before rejecting him as still too childish (II, 7). To be sure, the girls are drawn to the conventionally masculine Melchior and reject the unmanly Moritz, but they undermine the purely passive female image. When Ernst turns away from his patriarchal vision, he plays the feminine role to Hänschen, the initiator, in a scene which suggests that the gender roles do not neatly match biological sex (III, 6). When Moritz and Melchior exchange ideas for a natural upbringing, Moritz proposes a unisex upbringing in the hope that this would do away with tensions and guilt (I, 2). Melchior, closer in his views to Wedekind than the naively idealistic Moritz, remains convinced that sex as difference would assert itself and with it the problem of pregnancy. Boys with their 'männliche Regungen' (male urges; I, 2) would still take the initiative. But he does think that girls would be curious too, and even toys with the notion that girls have 'Regungen' of a sort, a remarkable feat of imagination (I, 2). What remains unimaginable is a childhood without cultural imprinting. Even Moritz's unisex education is in typical neo-classical style, with emphasis on physical discipline and hardness, the very qualities he himself lacks. These still recognizable stereotypes are shown to originate in social conditioning. The children, not yet fixed in the adult mould, explore their feelings and try out roles. The games they play are shot through with cultural influences from literature, from popular traditions and stories, from their school reading and – disastrously – from an adult morality of shame, guilt and punishment which turns the fairy-tales into nightmares. Nothing in the gamut of sexual activities is purely natural, other than the physical reflexes; all else is culturally mediated and shaped by the imagination.

The authorial attitude to all this remains ambiguous. Adult sex is either boring or abominable: Wendla's married sister Ina is a dull, desexed mother; Frau Gabor seeking consolation in her husband's arms as their son rots in the penitentiary is abhorrent. The sexual activities of the children or of Ilse's bohemians all deviate in one way or another from conventional norms. Moritz's brief flirtation with a unisex assimiliation of the sexes is brushed aside in favour of the much more fascinating differences, however perverse or artificial. An aesthetic stance is more easily discerned than a moral one. Some of the scenes are simply funny, like Hänschen quoting Othello in the lavatory, some sordid, like the masturbation competition, some lyrical, like the homosexual kiss. Martha's story of her beatings conveys Wedekind's humane protest at paternal brutality, but the audience can still feel the thrill of masochistic curiosity which grips Wendla. The audience watches a slightly older actress knowingly playing an innocent girl child who uncomprehendingly plays in her imagination with the idea of being beaten. The audience does not directly see poor Martha's suffering but, along with Wendla, imagines a picture of a girl kneeling, her nightdress dragged off, being beaten, an intricate suite of images within images in which critique of cruelty and erotic appeal are inextricably entwined. Depending on production, the scene in which Melchior beats Wendla may be presented as the climax to this ambiguity. The audience watches two children who do not understand their own feelings, and who suffer when their fantasies become all too painful reality. But the audience is also watching two no doubt attractive young people on a stage, consciously acting out for an audience a sado-masochistic scene which will not turn into reality but may be enjoyed as an erotic image. A clever production can turn such ambiguity into a statement on sexuality more powerful than a straightforward moralistic condemnation of perversion. The play as theatre enacts its own thesis of the transforming power of the erotic imagination.

Individualist Amoralism and Social Ills

The example of sado-masochism highlights a basic unclarity in the idea of individual amoralism as a path to emancipation. The play implies that the distinction between inclination and duty is at best misleading, at worst harmful. The moral posture is a role superimposed on real motivations. Realization of this truth brings freedom to act on desires immediately, rather than deviously as in most so-called moral behaviour. 'Immediately' does not mean instinctively and without reflection, however. Once freed from morality, the imagination may seek other ways of interpreting and expressing the sexual drive. Our desires are thus complex: basic drives but clothed in specific form. We may be free to reject an imposed morality, but our desires are not subject to choice, and remain influenced by conditioning. The sado-masochistic pattern of feeling persists in Ilse's bohemia, where it becomes a conscious game. Individualistic amoralism does not do away with the desires rooted in a punitive morality and an authoritarian social structure. At most, it offers a way of enjoying them and making them less harmful by way of a complicated psychological balancing trick. This balance is not always easily maintained, however. The fantasies of power and subjection go along with objective power and weakness, whether socio-economic inequality or the physical differences which make women more liable than men to suffer when the balancing trick goes wrong (themes developed in the Lulu playes). The way to inner freedom of the imagination is limited by the persisting power of social models and conditioning, even when an individual rejects the predominant moral ideology. In order to change desires, profound social change would be needed, altering relations between the sexes and the social construction of gender. The very ambiguity of the sexual theme, however, makes the play a challenge to latter-day feminist debate, for it testifies to the strength and persistence of the sexual patterns of feeling it critically illumines.

The social limits to freedom which operate inwardly through the psyche also operate externally. Consider the difference between the two emanations of the Life Force, Ilse and the Masked Man. The chances of survival are considerably higher for a man in expensive evening dress than for a woman in rags, however exotic, and indeed it is Ilse, not her male counterpart, who has a premonition of early death (II, 7). Ilse enjoys some independence; she is not simply a prostitute or a rich man's bought wife; she enters sexual relations for pleasure, not for money. The commodity she sells is the female body as an object of observation. Feminine pleasure in being observed, and masculine pleasure in observing, are inculcated sexual tendencies: Melchior will go out into the world as the photographer, not as the photographer's model. Ilse's trade is dangerous and short-lived, and she has no other. Individual amoralism does not banish economic inequality or the stigma of motherhood outside marriage – what would happen to Ilse should she become pregnant? (The massive motherly body, intermittently a motif in twentieth-century art since Picasso, did not loom large in the *Jugendstil*.) Sexual inequality makes strong emotional attachment problematic. Only twice does a character claim to love rather than to desire: Wendla has only ever loved her mother, a bond separate from sex (III, 5); Ernst's declaration to Hänschen is love between equals for whom the problem of pregnancy cannot arise (though even here Ernst's feminine love meets Hänschen's masculine hedonism (III, 6). Love is a threat to pleasure. Responsibility for Wendla's death does indeed lie with a hypocritical morality, but the fact remains that Wendla alive and pregnant would not have been free and would have been a greater threat to Melchior than Wendla dead. Emotional attachment, shared responsibility for pregnancy or mere concern for another human being all threaten freedom. In sum, individualist amoralism is an inadequate response to essentially social problems in two crucial ways: first, desires are highly subject to cultural influence, and secondly personal freedom, especially for women, is constrained by economics. The focus in the play is masculine desire. Whatever Wedekind may have intended, *Spring Awakening* promises freedom of sorts for men but not for women.

Theatrical Language: Location, Time, Costume, Styles and Modes

On the face of it, the settings in *Spring Awakening* lend themselves perfectly to naturalistic production conveying aspects of a particular milieu, a provinical town. We see interiors, the urban out-of-doors (gardens, the school lawn, streets and the graveyard), and scenes in nature such as the river bank, the vineyard and the hayloft (an interior, but one which is essentially bucolic). The interiors range from the petit-bourgeois household of aproned Frau Bergmann and the book-filled rooms in the house of lawyer Gabor and his intellectual wife, to impersonal institutions such as the school and the penitentiary, while the scenes in nature have appropriate trappings of flowers and trees. They might all seem fairly naturalistic, but in the burial scene the pathetic fallacy is taken to ludicrous extremes, as pouring rain and umbrellas suddenly and theatrically give way to clearing skies and showers of anemones when the children begin to pay their tributes to Moritz; nature is a theatrical prop. The interiors become comically hyper-Naturalist, as in the lavatory scene with its grotesque juxtaposition of lavatory bowl and masterpieces of painting. Hänschen looks at pictures with a comic reductive realism, as if the painted ladies were real women who could open their chastely closed knees. The scene explores adolescent sexuality and mocks the Naturalist claim that art should show a slice of life: the human imagination is not bounded by the lavatory or chained by milieu, and paintings do not offer a slice of life, or of female flesh. Of course, Naturalist sets are loaded with symbolism: a weaver's frame is not just a weaver's frame but a monument to the dignity of labour. Here, however, the interplay of dialogue and set opens realms of the imagination beyond the scope of Naturalism. Verbal images of nature penetrate indoors and artificial images intrude into nature. Windows are often the passage between indoors and out: the open window in Melchior's study suggests the liberal atmosphere encouraged by his mother, in contrast to the walled-up window of the stuffy school conference room which denies the spirit of Rousseau and Pestalozzi whose busts look down on the scene. The blocked-up window is a deliberately heavy-handed symbol introduced for comic effect. In the penitentiary, the window through which Melchior escapes is about to be covered by an iron grille (III, 4). The last interior, Wendla's bedroom, is filled with ambiguous imitations of the world outside. Her sister Ina, whose imagination is already atrophied by domesticity, comments gloomily on the autumn glory of the plane tress: 'eine kurze Pracht, kaum recht der Freude wert, wie man sie so kommen und gehen sieht' (a short glory that comes and goes, hardly worth taking pleasure in: III, 5). Wendla still dreams of picking *Himmelschlüssel* (primroses, literally keys of heaven) in the evening sunshine, a weepy bit of botanical symbolism calculated – or too calculated? – to jerk a few tears. But darkness grows before her eyes and instead of butterflies 'ein Untier', a monster, flies in through the open window and a moment later Mutter Schmidtin enters; the indoors scene is flooded with natural images and the local abortionist becomes at the same time a black emanation of nature, a witch.

Many of the scenes in *Spring Awakening* recall the visual arts: nature and milieu are mediated through an aesthetic perspective. The riverside scene of Moritz's suicide, with its winding path and river heavy as lead, its sparse details of willow tree, reeds, and tall Aaron's rod outlined in the setting sun, is a *Jugendstil* landscape (II, 7). Ilse's descriptions of artists' ateliers, models of the pyramids, snow-white funeral urns and ceiling mirrors, Moritz's fantasies of plunging necklines, black silk stockings and patent leather shoes all intrude into this picture of decorative nature. Franz von Stuck, the artist-prince of Munich, who designed the cover for the first edition of the play in 1891 following an idea of Wedekind's, deploys both manners: exotic eroticism and decorative landscapes (Rank, 1976; Wagener, 1980). Wendla floating above the flowery carpet of her garden is reminiscent of not quite earthbound young people in flowery *Jugendstil* meadows (II, 6). Ilse's images of red drops of blood on yellow Aaron's rod, and of brains hanging on the willow tree are typical *Jugendstil* transformations of horror into beauty. Hänschen and Ernst could have modelled for Stuck's painting, *The Kiss*, or for Peter Behrens's woodcut of the same title. The hayloft scene with the reluctant, finally yielding Wendla has Rococo echoes, a major point of reference in the sinuous *Jugendstil* (II, 4). And there is the Gothick chiaroscuro of the close. Rather than offering Naturalist representation of a given environment, the play invites more exciting contrasts between the drab, finally monstrous constriction of the small-town milieu and imaginary worlds: nature is seen through the eyes of an aesthete, interiors are transformed into metaphors through the interaction of set and dialogue.

The plot recedes behind evocation of atmosphere and a lyrical, rather than dramatic, sense of time. Time and place are intimately linked, the scene headings sometimes specifying a time, sometimes a place, often both. The time of day or year is represented by visual detail; the sense of place depends as much on the light appropriate to the hour or season as on physical objects. Like the calendars popular at the time depicting decorative personifications of the seasons the three acts are set in spring, summer and autumn through to November. The seasons move forwards within the acts. The time of day progresses within each scene as the sun sets, darkness falls, the rain clears, or a storm blows up. The act divisions are not strongly marked, and the casual movement from scene to scene is an orchestral suite of shifting moods rather than a classically structured symphony. The frequent scene changes affect the quality of time. Different times of day and night are juxtaposed: a lamplit lavatory; a shadowy hayloft in a gathering storm; Frau Gabor writing her cold letter in motherly friendship (a contradiction in terms in this world) with no light or time specified; Wendla in morning radiance; the setting sun by the river (II, 3 to 7). Shifts in time and mood obscure the straight line of action, while some of the most memorable scenes – Othello/Bluebeard in the lavatory, Wendla in the morning garden – have no function in the plot. The linear movement from early spring to November is cut across by contrasting tableaux: lives do not procede in straight lines. The combination of seasonal flow of time with vivid tableaux of moments has a double effect. Weather, flowers and plants – warm wind melting winter snow, the woodruff for a May-bowl, the Aaron's rod of high summer, the scurrying clouds across a November moon – evoke the flow of the seasons in a lyrical lament for Wendla and Moritz crushed in the Spring of their lives. But the sharp contrasts from scene to scene fragment the lyricism, often to comic effect. Take Hänschen Rillow: the Spring of his life appears in two very different lights as he flushes his painted lady love down the lavatory or conjures up a sun-drenched picture of playful delicacy:

> Und jetzt ist alles so schön! Die Berge glühen; die Trauben hängen uns in den Mund und der Abendwind streicht an den Felsen hin wie ein spielendes Schmeichelkätzchen . . .

> *But now everything is so beautiful. The mountains glow, the grapes hang down in our mouths, the evening wind caresses the hills like a playful kitten . . .* (III, 6).

The eroticised *Jugendstil* landscape also anticipates Franz Marc's pictures of animals merging into landscape in the *Blaue Reiter* exhibition of 1911, some twenty years on. The natural succession of seasons contrasts jarringly with the human stages of life as beautiful youth confronts ugly maturity, a note struck in the first scene between the nymphet Wendla and her dreary mother who is so much more childish than her daughter. To grow up into such a mother would be a fate worse than death, at least in the eyes of the aesthete author – better to be cut off in the bud. The melancholy vineyard scene shows that human life culminates in its spring, not in a fruitful autumn (III, 6). In the preceding scene human fertility is destroyed by the perverse society which aborts a baby and kills the young mother. The sterile but charming image of the two boys underlines, but also undermines, the pathos of Wendla's end, and her tragedy is finally brusquely disposed of by the Masked Man. Eros and beauty, not fertility and babies lie at the heart of the cult of Life. Times of day and night, the seasons and the stage of life create a complex metaphorical language; but what would be natural in human affairs remains unknown. The multiple qualities of time contribute to the perspectivistic multiple voices which sound in the play and break open closed tragedy. 'Unnatural' elements, such as Ilse's adventures or Hänschen's activities with painted ladies or his friend Ernst, are enjoyed for their comedy or their beauty while nature itself is shaped by the aesthetic eye.

The opening scene introduces the recurrent motif of clothes. With clothes too, imaginative dimensions are added through dialogue: we see Wendla in her princess dress and imagine her in her *Bußgewand*, her robe of atonement, but clothed underneath in dryad draperies. Clothes signal cultural influence on sexuality and the excitement of clothed artifice rather than naked nature. Adults dress their children to underline gender and to make them conform to some dream: the princess dress at once stresses and denies sexuality. At the opposite pole is Martha's sackcloth. Both carry adult fantasies and transmit sexual attitudes across the generations. Wendla's married sister talks of the clothes she is buying her son: Mucki is getting his first proper little boy's trousers. Apart from Mucki's *Höschen* and the unisex discussion, the emphasis is overwhelmingly on female clothes, an indication of the masculine bias of the play. (Only in *Pandora's Box* and *The Marquis of Keith* does male dress become important, marking a shift of interest from sex to other concerns as well.) In a tradition set by Wedekind himself, the Masked Man wears elegant evening dress in contrast to Ilse's exotic rags, but there are no explicit directions concerning the details of his dress. Besides costumes on stage, there is a vast number of references to clothes: Martha's nightdress laced with a blue ribbon; the various dreams of pink dress, pink shoes, but stockings black as night, legs in sky-blue tights, décolletés, dryad draperies and so forth. The costumes we see on stage help create the characters in a realistic manner, but all the references suggest imaginative self-projection and role-playing.

The scenes and costumes create a small-town milieu, while the Masked Man and Ilse evoke a wider environment of high-bourgeois urbanity and its bohemian fringe. Beyond that again the dialogue constantly conjures up images which break open the closed milieu, a process extended by deliberately melodramatic effects and completed in the surreal chiaroscuro of the last scene with the headless Moritz. This range of visual and verbal images goes along with constantly changing manners of speech and tonal effects. Cumulatively, the varieties of language draw us into different ways of seeing and feeling, creating a perspectivistic structure initiated by Wendla's shifting manner in the opening scene which I examined earlier: the manner typical of a child of her milieu; the ironically witty (a manner beyond the realist compass of the character); the visionary; and finally the dramatic (as heroine of a tragedy – a metatheatrical intrusion). A passage from the following scene shows in detail the myriad effects in even a short extract. It opens with schoolboys talking about homework; they then go home, leaving Melchior and Moritz in the gathering dusk. Until then, the dialogue has been colloquial and naturalistic, but the tone begins to change, as the two boys start to walk:

MORITZ: Siehst du die schwarze Katze dort mit dem emporgestreckten Schweif?

MELCHIOR: Glaubst du an Vorbedeutungen?

MORITZ: Ich weiß nicht recht. – Sie kam von drüben her. Es hat nichts zu sagen.

MELCHIOR: Ich glaube, das ist eine Charybis, in die jeder stürzt, der sich aus der Skylla religiösen Irrwahns emporgerungen. – Laß uns hier unter der Buche Platz nehmen. Der Tauwind fegt über die Berge. Jetzt möchte ich droben im Wald eine junge Dryade sein, die sich die ganze lange Nacht in den höchsten Wipfeln wiegen und schaukeln läßt . . .

MORITZ: Knöpf dir die Weste auf, Melchior!

MELCHIOR: Ha – wie das einem die Kleider bläht!

MORITZ: Es wird weiß Gott so stockfinster, daß man die Hand nicht vor den Augen sieht. Wo bist du eigentlich? – Glaubst du nicht auch, Melchior, daß das Schamgefühl im Menschen nur ein Produkt seiner Erziehung ist?

MELCHIOR: Darüber habe ich erst vorgestern noch nachgedacht. Es scheint mir immerhin tief eingewurzelt in der menschlichen Natur . . .

MORITZ: *Look at the black cat with its tail up!*

MELCHIOR: *Do you believe in omens?*

MORITZ: *I'm not sure. – It came from over there. It doesn't mean anything.*

MELCHIOR: *In my view that's the Charbydis everyone falls into once they've struggled free of the Scylla of religious superstition. – Let's sit here under the beech. The spring wind is sweeping across the mountains. I'd like to be a young dryad up there in the woods, rocked and swayed in the tree-tops the whole night through . . .*

MORITZ: *Undo your jacket, Melchior.*

MELCHIOR: *O, how the wind blows through our clothes!*

MORITZ: *God, it's getting pitch dark, you can't see your hand in front of your eyes. Where are you actually? – Melchior, don't you also think that the sense of shame in human beings is just a product of education?*

MELCHIOR: *I was thinking only the day before yesterday about that. It seems to me at least to be deeply rooted in human nature . . .* (I, 2).

The first three exchanges are colloquial enough and suggest an indefinite emotion aroused by the cat, a twinge of fear in the eerie half-light calling up an intellectual response in Melchior. His syntactically elaborate attack on superstition is in a pedantic manner beyond his years, an adult voice from a child's mouth didactically warding off childish fears. This could still be the borrowed manner of the classically educated schoolboy; but after a pause, as the night mood reasserts itself, comes a lyrical outburst far beyond realism in its rhythmic structure and alliterations. The next short section shifts from the visionary to the sensual. Moritz's reference to jackets, with its simple syntax and its feel for the wind, is comically down-to-earth after Melchior's dryad in the treetops. The comic incongruity works both ways. The immediacy of Moritz's remark punctures Melchior's more high-flown vision, just as the vision had punctured the preceding pedantic voice, setting off imagination against dull reason. The dryad of the imagination is sandwiched between intellect and sensation. Finally, under cover of darkness, and in a carefully detached tone, the boys venture to begin an intellectual discussion of sex and shame. The register is not inappropriate to educated adolescents hiding embarrassment, and is less pompous than the Scylla and Charbydis passage. Once more, a touch of subterranean humour shines through, in the self-consciously abstract terminology and in Melchior's precise dating of 'only the day before yesterday'. His casual tone belies itself – we only remember the occasion of our thoughts so exactly when they are not as cool as Melchior implies.

The pauses, together with varied syntax of question, exclamation and more complex structures, create a subtle rhythm associatively linking sensation, emotion and thought. The two dashes in Moritz's final speech evoke the sensuous feel of the wind and the releasing darkness. Up to a point, the dialogue is fairly realistic, creating the figures through manners appropriate to each and to the situation: an intelligent schoolboy with his less intellectual friend, feeling, sensing, imagining and thinking on a spring night – an Impressionist rather than a Naturalist blend. The pauses, reminiscent of Wedekind's contemporary Maeterlinck, are especially suggestive of fleeting and fluid feeling and sensation too subtle to define. But the mixture of heightened lyricism, exaggerated pedantry and underlying comic incongruity undermines realism, even of the Impressionist variety. The manners separate into voices half emancipated from the figures, which build up the mixed modes of the play as a whole. The lyricism tends towards pathos and tragedy; the grotesque exaggerations, as in the treatment of the adults, towards satire. But lyrical pathos is counteracted by a pervasive humour which refuses tragedy, while mixed attitudes rob the satire of clear direction, as in the ambiguous treatment of sexual behaviour. The undermotivated leap from uniformly negative adult characters to the abstract and ambiguous figure of the Masked Man functions in a similar way: the Masked Man symbolizes mockery of bourgeois society, yet also accommodation by way of cynical exploitation. The play does not fall into any clear mode. If any mood predominates it is the humorous. But this is not the reconciliatory humour of integrative comedy. Nor is it Moritz's Olympian humour which measures human affairs against the universal fate of mortality, nor yet the humour of the political satirist who sets a vision of change against a corrupt status quo. The humour is a fragile and defensive psychological stratagem for survival, expressive of a temperament at once critically engaged and painfully entangled in the problems the play analyses. The recourse to surrealism and the faceless Masked Man are, like the humour, symptoms of an inability to see beyond the limits of bourgeois society or Ilse's fringe bohemia. Yet they are also a refusal of fatalism. The humour does not express a unified vision, but is a fluid medium carrying the many voices in the play.

3
Earth Spirit

In *Earth Spirit* late nineteenth-century bourgeois society becomes a laboratory for an experiment in amoral sexuality as a path to liberation. The experiment fails because of inner contradictions in the male characters. As in *Spring Awakening*, human behaviour appears as role-playing informed by conventional values and cultural models, with a bias towards presenting women as actresses performing to male spectators. The roles are linked to the social inequality of the sexes and the market economy, themes which loom even larger in *Pandora's Box*. The complex of subjective psychological and objective economic forces which shapes sexuality also affects the arts, in a society where sex and art alike are commodities on the market. The play itself, as an example of erotic art, derives its theatrical power from an ambiguous exploitation of the very sexual fantasies it shows to be exploitative of women and destructive to men and women alike.

The Three Faces of Lulu

The title of this play, the animal imagery of the Prologue and Lulu's mysterious provenance all suggest that she is an allegorical spirit of nature who enters human society. She also embodies and externalizes dreams and fantasies in a non-realist manner comparable to Expressionist theatre. Finally, she is a mimetic character in the round from a low-life milieu who is finally destroyed by bourgeois society. These three aspects of Lulu go some way towards explaining the different perceptions of critics and audiences; the reading proposed here attempts a partial assimiliation of these different responses. Lulu as a spirit of nature can be seen as one of the fantasies prevalent in a culture where the idea of nature as a source of redemption or corruption has traditionally held great importance. In other words, what we see is not a conflict between a natural force and a corrupt society, but the form sex assumes in a society where the concept of nature is part of the ideological currency. What sex would be like as a natural phenomenon remains unknown and unknowable. Furthermore, the view of Lulu as a shifting image in male eyes – fantasies become flesh – can be partially assimilated to the third way of seeing her, as a character from low-life milieu, a woman who plays up to men as the prime path to security, self-esteem and pleasure in a male-dominated society. The men, whether petit-bourgeois, bourgeois or aristocratic, see Lulu both as a vulnerable or corrupt creature from the lower depths and as an innocent or demonic natural creature. The play shows that it is impossible for a spirit of nature, a dream woman or a real woman to satisfy men whose desires are an incompatible *mélange* of religious and moral ideals and erotic fantasies.

Spring Awakening explored the corroding effect of moral conditioning on sexuality. The heroine of *Earth Spirit* has not been corrupted by the family or a middle-class education. She enters bourgeois society at the age of twelve, already sexually experienced. She seems to be a figure without conditioning. The opening of Kafka's *The Castle* is rather similar: there too, a figure who has apparently not been subject to its conditioning enters a society and comes to grief. Lulu is an experiment, a dream woman free of the inhibitions normally inculcated in women which stand as obstacles to pleasure. She is a magical gift, a woman who will be whatever men want her to be. But she cannot be seen as a model for sex without social distortion, since, in order to become sexually active at all, she has to enter into relations in late nineteenth-century society where what men want is conditioned by cultural traditions and economics. The disastrous outcome of the experiment is largely caused by contradictory desires in the men. But the initial dream is also undermined. Just as Kafka's K is not the empty cypher he at first appears, but is shaped inwardly by tendencies corresponding to the outer social structures he enters, so Lulu is destroyed both by the outer forces of society and by the inner force of her own temperament. The woman who will be what men want is the ultimate destructive fantasy, the female counterpart to contradictory and reductive male desires. In moulding her identity in response to male desires, Lulu collaborates in her own emotional and psychological destruction, before Jack the Ripper finishes the job. This outcome is only clear in *Pandora's Box*. In *Earth Spirit* Lulu still has considerable autonomy and fluidity. The next section will first examine Lulu as an image in men's eyes, then consider whether there is any reality behind the image, an autonomous continuing self capable of independent action, rather than merely of automatic responses to the expectations of others.

Image and Reality

Towards the end of Act I, Lulu looks into Schwarz's eyes and describes what she sees there: a reflected image of herself as Pierrot (I, 7). The passage suggests that she is nothing but an image in male eyes; it also captures her egoism, which so disconcerts the men: in Schwarz's eyes, the windows of his soul, she sees nothing of him, only her own image. Wholly given over to fulfilling male desires, Lulu is perhaps nothing in herself. She becomes no more than an image, and conversely reduces men to nothing but a blank surface in which that image is mirrored. In the dialectic of master and slave in Hegel's *Phenomenology of Spirit*, the slave, an inferior being, cannot recognize and so confirm the master's humanity. Here, the woman, reduced to an image by imperious male desire, cannot recognize and bestow identity on the man; the male master too is enslaved to and by the image. The projected image comes between the human protagonists who seem doomed never to meet, and reduces the self to a wraith which threatens to disappear when no one else is there. Hence the horror which grips Lulu under Goll's dead eyes: they threaten her too with extinction (I, 7). Yet the way in which Lulu acts out men's desires does not necessarily signify lack of autonomy, for she consciously chooses to act and enjoys her own skill. Her status as an actress is raised several times: is she or is she not a born actress? Does she know that she acts? When Alwa wants to write a play for her she says the stage is not her *métier*, but he avers: 'Sie sind als Tänzerin auf die Welt gekommen' (You were born a dancer: III, 1). It is Lulu's nature to relate to others by acting to please them and herself. Unlike Schwarz, Schön knows that Lulu's sexual appeal lies in her gifts of projection. Like a good actress she knows how to please an audience better than the audience itself; she can charm, intrigue and surprise. In running away from Schwarz she intuitively appeals to his hidden fantasy of reluctant, finally yielding innocence (I, 4).

Ideally, the sexual games should be played out between equals who recognize each other's skill. The problems come when the private games collide with the public institution of marriage. Lulu is not just an automaton like E. T. A. Hoffmann's doll Olympia in *The Sandman*, the creation of a Doctor Coppelius. Her power to act is an expression of personality and a conscious creative activity. Acting is a potentially positive metaphor for sociability in human beings whose personality is not rigidly fixed but constantly modified in interaction with others.

But Lulu has to interact with others in a particular environment, the bourgeois society she entered barefoot and penniless at the age of twelve. Acting cannot remain pure self-expression; it is also a means of adaptation and survival, adopted out of clear-sighted appraisal of economic facts. Lulu has clearly learned much from Schigolch in an anti-education at the opposite extreme from the conventional moral conditioning of middle-class girls like Schön's child fiancée. As the cynical Goll remarks, it is a part of woman's profession to know how to please (I, 2). Middle-class girls are taught this skill, but its purpose remains decently hidden: they learn to be (amateur) wives rather than (professional) mistresses. Lulu, by contrast, is prepared to go about the business of pleasing in a professional way in return for security – a parodistic unmasking of the bourgeois marriage contract. Her readiness to play the roles is both fuelled and limited by her will to survive. Just as the instinct for survival puts a stop to Ilse's game of Russian roulette, so Lulu does not willingly succumb to Schön's murderous fantasies or, finally, to Jack the Ripper. The other limit to role-playing is her own pleasure. Her motives, pleasure and the will to survive, fly in the face of both conventional morality and the romantic ideal of love.

There are doubts about Lulu's moral nature as well as about her acting; the play challenges us to judge whether she is a kind of psychopath, without those capacities for sympathy, altruism or love which are central to most conceptions of what it is to be human. This ambiguity continues the moral argument in *Spring Awakening* and pursues further the question of love side-stepped there. Towards the end of Act I Schwarz, shocked by Lulu's self-regarding reaction to Goll's death, asks her a series of questions about belief, the soul and love, similar to the religious question Gretchen asked Faust. She answers only: 'Ich weiß es nicht' (I do not know: I, 7). She has not learned the abstract language of morality, and the one role she will not play is the moralizer. Why should she weep dutiful tears for a man who acquired her as a commodity? Commodities owe no gratitude. Putting into practice without hypocrisy the amoral doctrine of *Spring Awakening*, she acts only out of desire, never out of duty. Accordingly, she seems to the sentimental Schwarz 'verwildert' (uncivilized), a savage who has not acquired civilized moral discrimination (I, 7). Later, Schön claims she has a sense of duty and has changed for the better (II, 4); but his words, spoken in the hearty tones of a man of the church preaching a bracing sermon, cannot be taken at face value. As a would-be Nietzschean revaluer of values, he turns normal ideas on their head: what he praises is Lulu's dutifulness as a bought woman.

Yet Schön's claim has force beyond the immediate context. Throughout most of the play, Lulu shows more humanity than the other characters except perhaps young Hugenberg, who is also moved not by duty but by his first sexual passion. Lulu is touched by the final isolation of even such an old reprobate as Goll, with no one to perform the final service of closing his eyes (I, 6). It was not for services such as these that he acquired her; but she is struck by the common fate of death and can feel for him too, though she will not play the sorrowing widow for Schwarz's benefit. She may be concerned with survival, but she is not caught up in the fetishism of commodities. She likes her carpet to go barefoot on, not as a sign of wealth, and she receives old friends, ignoring the snobbish conventions of the middle class (II, 2; IV, 5). She speaks with affection to Alwa (II, 1), and tries to draw Schwarz into love-making when all he can think of is a rich commission (II, 1).

Lulu often behaves and feels in ways that might be judged good, but not because it is her duty; nor does she assume an outer moral show. It is the same with love. She tells Schwarz she does not know whether she has loved (I, 7), Alwa that she has loved 'keine Seele', (not a soul: IV, 8). But her final desperate claim that Schön is the only man she has ever loved rings true, given her refusal until now to fulfil sentimental expectations (IV, 8). She does not love Schön better than life itself; she does not love his soul. But with Schön she does not simply respond passively to an image in another's eye. She actively fights to remain his lover, to become his wife if needs be. Here is the worthy protagonist for the sexual game which should be played out between equals who recognize each other's skill. Schön originally took Lulu up from the gutter to surround her with his wealth, but she does not remain a possession. In the power struggle between them she turns the tables and causes him to act according to her will when she composes the words he must write to his fiancée (III, 10). Here Lulu becomes the writer of roles. Thomas Elsaesser (1983) notes an equivalent reversal of roles in Pabst's *Pandora's Box*. The film constantly plays on who has the right to look and who is reduced to an object of the devouring gaze. Lulu turns Schön of the imperious gaze (heightened by his glittering monocle) into an object for spectators when the dressing room door opens to reveal him caught in her embrace. Yet the sexual encounter between these worthy protagonists culminates in disaster because the private games collide with the public institution of marriage, and because Schön's sexual desires clash with his moral delusions.

The Prologue: the Sexual Circus

The fantasies Lulu arouses derive from a vast arsenal of sources reflecting perennially ambiguous attitudes towards sex conceived of as a force of nature for good and evil. Sometimes, as with the Pierrot and Mignon fantasies, they express a lost ideal of harmony between art and nature. To a German audience the title of the play is immediately recognizable as a reference to the Earth Spirit in Goethe's *Faust*, a demon so powerful that it threatens to annihilate although it is the source of all life. The title therefore sets up the pervasive association of Lulu with creative yet destructive forces of nature. The Prologue seems to continue the theme of natural forces and instincts. The main characters are introduced through emblematic beasts: Schön the tiger, Goll the bear, Schwarz the monkey and Lulu the snake. The 'unbeseelte Kreatur', the soulless beast in this circus, is not just the snake, as many critics seem to assume, but all the creatures who are ready to leap at the throat of their human master. They seem at first to move to order as the ringmaster fires his revolver and cracks his whip, but in the struggle between man and beast sometimes the animal rears up on its hindlegs, sometimes the man goes on all fours. The creatures belong in the ringmaster--author's circus, they are creatures of his imagination, they live in his marquee and in his soul. Finally, the ringmaster throws away whip and revolver, symbols of domination over the animal instincts of the psyche, and relies on his wit to confront the final bloodthirsty animal, the audience.

The Prologue is an ironic pointer to what is to come, only

comprehensible in the light of the play as a whole; and is indeed a later addition. The play will offer to its bloodthirsty audience a double attraction, of violent unleashed instincts and intellectual wit. The Prologue invites the spectators to recognize themselves in the bloody conflicts which follow, to learn wit to understand themselves and, like the ringmaster, to throw away revolvers and whips. They may then turn into human beings who can learn to know themselves rather than remain in the grip of unreflected instinct, a message comparable to Moritz's fairy-tale. The animal imagery is potentially misleading, for it suggests two kinds of battle: between the human and the animal and between the male tiger Schön and the female snake Lulu. The temptation to assimilate the two is clear: man with his intellect and soul confronts soulless, instinctual woman to dominate her by whip and revolver, following the old woman's advice in Nietzsche's *Zarathustra*. This is *not* the picture the Prologue presents. But most of the men in the play see things in this light, as they turn Lulu into an image of animal sexuality to be enjoyed or put down depending on whether the lustful or the soulful mood is on them. The plot, and in retrospect the Prologue too, make clear enough that the murderous impulses reside in the men and arise from domination of woman in the name of morality. The battle between the human and the animal should be transformed into a game between human protagonists, male and female alike endowed with wit and instinct. That said, Wedekind does not entirely escape the imagery of a battle between the sexes. He bestows wit and intellect unevenly. Like Frau Gabor, the intellectual Countess Geschwitz remains rather monstrous, while the dream of the purely sensual woman is obviously hard to relinquish: learning a little French or reading sentimental novels are the sensual Lulu's only intellectual pursuits.

Lulu's Legendary Roles

The men, including the author, impose many roles on the woman Lulu as their own instincts and fantasies, projected onto her, confront the whip and revolver of bourgeois morality. Goethe's Earth Spirit, the role given by the title, was a demon, the spirit of natural creation. In fairy tales – *Rumpelstilzchen* is the best known example – naming gives power over demons. Such name-magic recurs throughout the play. The earliest name, used by the first protector Schigolch, is Lulu, and it has the seal of authorial approval by appearing in the cast-list. Wedekind probably took the name from a circus pantomine opened in Paris in 1888 by Félicien Champseur, and it also features in his Paris diary as the name of a prostitute (Hay: 264). Lulu hears her name as 'vorsintflutlich' (II, 2) – from before the flood, probably not Jehovah's but the flood sent by Zeus after Pandora opened her box. Pandora was an earth spirit too, fashioned from clay by Hephaestus. Wedekind may also have had another female demon in mind, Adam's first wife Lilith, sometimes called Lilu. These figures were made by gods; in Wedekind's play Lulu's features are man-made, dreams and visions imposed on her by the male characters and evoked in the names they give her. Rather like the parents with their children in *Spring Awakening*, here the men try to realize their own dreams in Lulu, Pygmalions creating a Galatea; the myth of Pygmalion creating Galatea underlies the whole play. When the real woman fails to correspond to the dream, the men try to break her like a botched statue, but destroy themselves instead; they are broken by their own contradictions as they turn the revolver of morality or possessiveness against their own instincts and passions.

Like the angelic or evil children in *Spring Awakening*, Lulu appears in a double light. Schwarz is first roused by her sexual appeal as she rolls up the leg of her Pierrot costume in a delicate game of striptease. Standing as still as a statue on her modelling dais, she heaves a sigh, Galatea coming to life with heaving bosom. Schwarz idiotically tells her to stop breathing like that, a premonition of his inability to accept her vital sexuality. During the chase through the studio, the exciting game of flight and pursuit gives birth to the dream of Lulu as a fearfully reluctant, chaste and chased nymph. Schwarz, a detumescent satyr turned sentimental petit-bourgeois, deceives himself into believing her *virgo intacta* despite her married state, forgetting the sexy images of Parisian underwear which first aroused him. The role of innocent virginal bride he imposes is boring, and Lulu is duly bored.

In this first appearance, Lulu is transformed from a wife wearing the fashionable clothes of the time into Pierrot holding a shepherd's crook, a role combining the twin themes of art and nature. Pierrot recalls the *commedia dell'arte* and the shepherd's crook evokes Arcadia, a utopia where art and nature are one. Pierrot's childlike floppy costume continues the preoccupation with childhood in *Spring Awakening*; worn by Lulu, it creates a *Jugendstil* image of epicene youth, an appropriate dream for the old aesthete Goll. Pierrot, a

French development from the original Italian Predrelino, a minor figure in the *commedia dell'arte*, is a clown, often a melancholy clown with a dream-like air: his world is not reality. In Watteau's magnificent *Giles*, the travelling players stand together in an Arcadian landscape, yet each is alone, their gaze never meeting. In the centre the sad real face of Giles looks out from his fantasy costume. Giles is a predecessor of Picasso's sad acrobats who reappear in Rilke's *Duineser Elegien*. The figure appears in another masterpiece of early Modernism, Schönberg's *Pierrot Lunaire*; where the text provided by Albert Giraud, whose poems Wedekind knew, presents Pierrot as an exile from a world that never was. Musil later associated the androgynous quality of the costume with the Platonic myth of a unity preceding the division of the sexes: in *The Man without Qualities* Ulrich and Agathe first meet as adults in their Pierrot pyjamas in an androgynous mirror-image of each other. Klee's round-faced child Pierrot is a comic and charming evocation of presexual innocence. There is perhaps an affinity too with the childlike acrobat in Kafka's story *First Sorrow*, one of the most touching figures in Kafka's oeuvre; never earthbound, he travels by train in the luggage rack, but at the first sense of division his youth and beauty wither. The Pierrot picture which accompanies Lulu to the end recalls the dream of sex without division.

Mignon, the name Schön and Alwa use for Lulu, comes from Goethe's *Wilhem Meister*. Like Pierrot, she too is an exile from the magic South she conjures up in her song *Kennst du das Land*, a land where nature glows with colour and statues speak. Mignon, like Lulu, cannot dance to order as a professional, but dances her egg-dance as free self-expression. She too is androgynous and pre-pubertal. Schigolch is a parodistic version of the harpist, an ambiguous father quite unplagued by guilt. Mignon's mixed feelings towards Wilhelm are transferred to Alwa, who sees Lulu as child and sister, as surrogate mother (a point to be argued later), then as potential mistress. Such a blend is reminiscent of Baudelaire's *L'Invitation au voyage* which conjures up a Northern counterpart to Mignon's Italy. Baudelaire's addresse, 'mon enfant, ma soeur', is an ambiguous mixture of child, sister, voluptuous mistress and muse. She represents the transformation of nature into aesthetic beauty in painted Dutch landscapes and interiors. The motif of incest with a child, sister or mother is a dream of unity with an alter ego preceding all differentiation and individuation and transcending all taboos. Barbara Johnson (1980) has shown how Baudelaire breaks the closed utopian perfection of the poem in its twin *petit poème en prose* by introducing the prosaic themes of economics and class. Wedekind does likewise with his Mignon.

Nelli, Goll's name for Lulu, is a ridiculous diminutive of Helen. In German culture, Helen inevitably recalls the Classical world in Part II of *Faust*. The embodiment of perfect beauty, she is an appropriate dream for the aesthete, Goll. But she is a dangerous dream too, for she once betrayed a husband and unleashed a war. Schwarz calls Lulu Eve, a name evocative of the many masterpieces of German medieval and Renaissance painting. Naturally innocent in the Garden of Eden, she becomes the origin of all evil and recalls the endless complexity of the concept of nature as it appears in religious, philosophical and literary traditions. The large-eyed Lulu frequently seems innocent to the men in the play. Her apparent innocence and natural goodness recall a vast pastoral tradition in which the source of evil is not nature but the corruption and artificiality of society. Her childlike quality suggests the child's closeness to nature, a salient motif in Romantic literature. The view of Lulu as corrupt or destructive echoes the strong Christian tradition of fallen nature and of sex as a natural instinct of bestial origin, part of man's material being doomed to corruption, as distinct from his spiritual or moral essence. It was Eve the temptress who brought about the expulsion from paradise. Evil is sometimes held to be not so much deliberate badness as an inhuman ignorance of good and evil; knowledge is the cause of the Fall but also the path to redemption through Christ; only by passing through recognition of guilt do human beings become fully human in the knowledge of their spiritual essence and through the exercise of conscience. Thus Lulu is at once innocent yet evil in her inhuman ignorance. Her seven-times repeated 'Ich weiß es nicht' (I, 7) in response to Schwarz's enquiry into her spiritual condition is surely an echo of Wagner's *Parsifal*. (Wedekind was a great admirer of Wagner's operas.) The reference is even more marked in what Jack Stein (1974: 226) calls the 'Parzifal' (*sic*) dialogue in Berg's *Lulu*. Parsifal's goodness is the ignorance of the pure fool, an inhuman innocence like that of the beasts. Such innocence results in unknowing evil when he shoots the swan. Unredeemed nature also appears in Kundry's animal writhings and total enthralment to sexual instinct. Thus nature as pure ignorance and nature as engulfing instinct are both redeemed through knowledge, with its inevitable concomitant guilt.

Innocence as subhuman ignorance also has philosophical roots in the Cartesian distinction between the man who thinks and animals who are unthinking, soulless machines. Or there is Hegel's distinction, repeated by the young Marx, between man's self-reflective condition and the state of the animals who remain purely 'an sich', who are without self-awareness. An animal cannot be alienated, but neither can it come to realize its oneness with Spirit. Women are often held to be closer to nature than men because of the greater centrality of their reproductive function in shaping the pattern of their lives. Accordingly they are sometimes deemed to be more naturally good than men, less engaged in the corrupting struggle for power or status, a natural goodness like that of children who are not yet caught up in the conflicts of adult life. In prelapsarian Arcadia they are the bountiful providers of sexual pleasure for Gods, satyrs and shepherds. By the same token, however, being closer to nature they are the evil instigators of bestial desires and are marked by soulless animality. They know little of man's moral, spiritual and intellectual aspirations. The intellectual Countess Geschwitz is denatured. In as far as women think at all, they think intuitively, a mode of thought closer to instinct than to intellect, or else they show the negative counterpart of intuition, the cunning of the snake, Lulu's emblematic beast.

Several of these motifs from opposing traditions combine in a Romantic motif popular also in the *Jugendstil* and continued in neo-Romantic and Symbolist writing (Hermand, 1968). This is the idea of the naturally good but soulless spirit of nature who bridges the Christian and pastoral traditions. Such spirits, who are generally female, come to save men from the corruption of power through their feminine gentleness, but must themselves gain through men the human attributes of a soul and knowledge of good and evil. The tension between eros and nature on the one hand and morality and society on the other sometimes finds a Utopian resolution, sometimes only a tragic end. Matthew Arnold's *The Foresaken Merman*, in an interesting reversal of each element, tells of a human woman who enters the natural realm of the sea, but is finally divided by Christianity from nature, motherhood and the merman father of her children with their 'cold, strange eyes'. The nymphs Melusine or Undine are the best-known examples in German Romantic literature, appearing in works by Tieck, Fouqué, Goethe, Grillparzer and in operas by Hoffmann and Lortzing. They have cousins too in Hauptmann's Symbolist plays or Hofmannsthal's *Die Frau ohne Schatten*

(*The Woman without a Shadow*). In Act II of *Earth Spirit* Melusine, who retreats every Saturday to her bath and resumes her fishy tail, is recalled twice: first when Lulu says she has come from the water (her bath and her natural fluid element), and secondly in Schigolch's sardonic remark that nymphs like the beautiful Melusine remain fascinating as long as they are young, but when they grow old they become animals for whom there is not even a place in the zoo (II, 1; II, 2). As this example suggests, the treatment of most of these motifs is parodistic. They illuminate the contradictory attitudes men have to female sexuality when it is neither sanitized in marriage nor rendered taboo in the family.

The aristocrat Escerny may serve as a final ludicrous example of a dreamer of an up-to-date fantasy appropriate to the age of German colonial ambitions. Escerny emerges from the unseen audience in Act III to pay court to Lulu. He offers her a situation as *grande cocotte*, the traditional culmination to a career as actress or chorus girl and no doubt what Schön has in mind when recommending tights rather than a mackintosh as Lulu's stage costume (III, 1). Sometimes even marriage could follow, the path Anna takes in *The Marquis of Keith*. The effete Escerny belongs to a class being displaced by a rising bourgeoisie, the men of the stock exchange like Schön, but he is still fit to go out and govern Africa. For him, Lulu is a creature from depths below or beyond money-grubbing bourgeois society. Whereas the petit-bourgeois Schwarz saw Lulu as 'verwildert' (I, 7) a pejorative term for uncivilized, the decadent aristocrat endows her with primitive nobility of body and spirit: she is a noble savage. Accordingly, he proposes to transport her to her true setting, the jungle – or at least to a villa in Africa with all mod cons. Escerny is a masochist of the kind to which Sacher-Masoch, whose best-known works date from the 1870s, gave his name. In reality, he rules despotically over his colonial subjects; in fantasy, he seeks submission to a symbolic revenge of the primitive in his vision of being governed by Lulu. The symbolic granting of power to a woman who is in fact a possession at the mercy of her male owner, associated here with colonial power politics, anticipates a similar motif in Heinrich Mann's study of Imperial Germany, *Der Untertan* (*Man of Straw*). There the hero, Diedrich Heßling, lords it over his factory workers by day while kneeling to be beaten by his wife at night. The myth of primitive nature is another piece of mystification surrounding relations shaped by class, economics and cultural conditioning in the family.

Family Relations

Lulu is strikingly lacking in biological relations. As far as we know she has never stood in anything but sexual relationships to men; a mother or sister remains unimaginable. The family, so central in *Spring Awakening*, here seems to have disappeared. The real blood relations of daughterhood, sisterhood and motherhood are transformed in *Earth Spirit* into metaphors. The estrangement uncovers hidden features in family relationships. In metaphorical terms, Lulu is daughter to Schigolch, Goll, even Schön. There is a whiff of fantasy-incest with Goll, who gives Lulu a name as a father would name his child (I, 2), and who dresses her in short skirts (II, 4). Even more dubious is dreadful old Schigolch who may or may not be her father. Probably not but he has certainly enjoyed her sexually at a time in her life when normal standards would have demanded fatherly feelings, though 'normal' standards were not normally observed in the cities of the nineteenth century. In his diaries Wedekind writes of being plagued by a sexual fantasy about an imagined daughter, long before he conceived of the Lulu plays or had a daughter (Hay: 108–13). The incest between brother and sister from which Goethe's Mignon sprang here becomes incest between father and daughter. Lulu was never pre-sexual but always 'das ewig Weibliche' (the eternal feminine); other qualities as daughter or sister are secondary, contingent, interchangeable. For Alwa, Lulu begins as a symbolic sister, her femininity taboo. But there are stranger features in their relationship. Lulu mysteriously claims to have murdered Alwa's mother (IV, 8), while her vicious attack on the portrait of Schön's fiancée suggests that she would not have been averse to a second murder (I, 4). It is unclear whether her claim that she murdered Frau Schön is to be taken literally or whether, like the destruction of the portrait, it was a symbolic murder. Schön's wife had been bedridden for two years before he took Lulu into his household (III, 1). The illness has symbolic undertones: marred by childbirth, ageing wives are banished to the sick-bed, to be replaced in the marriage-bed by a youthful concubine. Alwa is strangely indifferent to the monstous idea of his father's mistress murdering his mother, and it is never mentioned again. Whether Lulu's claim is to be taken seriously or not (probably not), the metaphorical sense of the murder is clear enough: Lulu replaces Schön's wife in Schön's bed and in Alwa's imagination as the ideal woman of his youth. Now, however, he has come consciously to desire the original forbidden ideal – whether mother or sister – suggesting repressed sexual feeling all along.

These symbolic father-daughter, brother-sister, and son-mother relations suggest that sexual feelings underlie the family taboos. In Pabst's film, the scene in which Lulu murders Schön is mirrored so that the spectator becomes uncertain of what is real, what is image. Elsaesser (1983) reads the scene as an Oedipal fantasy in Alwa's mind. The family taboos create an unreal ideal of purity in woman, beginning with the female family figures. The idealized pure mother, sister or daughter is as much a dream or legend as Eve, Mignon or Melusine. The myth of asexual purity calls forth its converse, an all-embracing sexuality which extinguishes all distinctions and taboos and threatens the basic ordering of generation.

None of the men who desire or marry Lulu ever contemplates having a child by her, though Alwa may once have dimly felt that he was her child. Nor does the thought ever seem to enter her head. It is part of the magical gift to men that she never gets pregnant and is not plagued by the mothering instinct, except perhaps fleetingly towards Alwa as he kneels, his face hidden childlike in her lap, confessing his love. Yet even as she runs her hands over his hair in a motherly fashion, she claims to have murdered his mother (IV, 8). It is clear that motherhood is not for her: to be a mother would desex her. (This is a departure from the original *Monstretragödie* in which Lulu is pregnant by Schwarz.) Lulu is just about marriageable to an elderly roué like Goll, for whom she can be child and bride simultaneously: another child would be superflous. Schwarz marries, as he believes, a rich young heiress of good family. He has not yet got round to considering fatherhood, though perhaps that might have come when he had collected enough rich commissions to think about an heir. In the meantime, Lulu is still his model for pictures that will produce money and fame. Motherhod would interefere with her beauty – she would become like Schön's first wife. Furthermore, her obscure origins present a problem reminsicent of Ernest's difficulties in Wilde's *The Importance of Being of Earnest*. Would a person with all these interchangeable personal names but no original family name be a fit mother of an heir? Bourgeois marriage, an institution for the handing on of property and the interlinking of peer groups in the social hierachy, is contracted in the name of love, unlike the arranged marriage or dynastic alliance. But desire and love cannot be felt by contract: 'Auf Kommando *lieben*, das kann ich nicht!' (I cannot *love* to order: II, 3). The disasters which befall Lulu's marriages arise from this fundamental contradiction.

Marriage for Love or Money

The idyllic mood of Lulu's friendship with Alwa (before he too dwindles into lover or husband) derives from the fact that brothers and sisters are peers in pre-economic childhood. To be a daughter or wife, however, involves more than biological or sexual relations in a society where women are either an economic burden, made lighter if they are attractive, or else valuable property if they stand to inherit or can be married well. The concern to see Lulu well settled shown by Schigolch and Schön is a grotesque parody of fathers placing their daughters to maximum benefit. Like Shaw's Alfred Doolittle, Schigolch is one of the undeserving poor, happy to benefit from protectors and husbands alike. Schön, a bourgeois roué, arranges matches for Lulu; first with Goll, an older version of himself, old and rich enough to be satisfied with flesh without money; then with Schwarz, for whom Lulu is an innocent, suitably rich childbride like Schön's own innocent child fiancée of good family. Goll is a stock figure of comedy: like the wrinkled Doctor Bartolo in *The Barber of Seville* he deserves to be betrayed. But he is more sophisticated than his predecessors, an aesthete unconcerned with technical virginity for whom Lulu, a clever actress, can play the virginal role over and over again, dancing to his whip and to his whims. Assumed virginity is much more fun than the real thing, had the foolish Schwarz had the wit to realize it. Schwarz is a hungry bohemian with a petit-bourgeois soul who hopes to rise socially and to sell pictures to bourgeois patrons. Lulu is to supply the status, the money and the inspiration, as well as being a virgin possession unsullied by previous owners. Escerny, on the other hand, follows aristocratic tradition, planning to install Lulu as mistress in a *Lustschloß* in Africa, well away from the ancestral home. After all these male arrangements Lulu finally arranges her own marriage to Schön, following the example of the lively heroines who have peopled emancipatory comedy and cast off the yoke of paternal authority. She has a German ancestress in Lessing's Minna von Barhelm who was unencumbered by a father (Boa: 1984). Like Lulu, Minna tries to persuade her lover that social status and physical constitution are irrelevant. In the earlier play, the woman stands higher in the hierarchy and the man is marred by a wounded arm. In Wedekind's play, the woman stands lower in the hierarchy and is marred, yet what does a missing hymen matter compared with the horror of a union without desire? But the model of emancipatory comedy breaks down. The lovers marry and do not live happily ever after: the question is why not?

Earth Spirit confronts directly the problem of love for the would-be free amoralist. The word 'love' is ambiguous: its meaning may be emotional or physical. Lulu once loved a student, but we do not know in what sense (I, 4). Faced with her initial resistance to his advances, Schwarz imagines she has never loved in any sense (I, 4). Later, she says that she does not know whether she has loved; she does not know the meaning of the word in its non-physical sense (I, 7). Schwarz neatly elides loving and making love in persuading himself that Lulu is a virgin. (There is less word-play in the *Monstretragödie* where Schwarz asks point blank if Lulu is a virgin, a habit Wedekind too apparently indulged in with female acquaintances.) The relationship between Schön and Lulu, however, explores love as an emotional, sexually fulfilling, freely chosen and persisting attachment between equal partners. It proves an inaccessible ideal in bourgeois society, if only because the partners cannot be equal. Women are property owned by men, bound to accept the role of mistress or wife if they are not to sink to the even more insecure status of prostitute. This is on the assumption that they are not, like the Countess Geschwitz, aristocratic heiresses in their own right, or workers who sell their labour rather than their bodies, a possiblity ignored here, where attention is focused on the middle class. The ideology of bourgeois marriage is fed by concern with property, traditional moral and religious teaching, and romantic idealism. In principle, both sexes are expected to conform to the ideal of purity and fidelity; in practice, pregnancy and childcare ensure that this ideal exerts greater pressure on women, as early analysts of bourgeois soicety such as Hume and Rousseau had already noted. Premarital purity is valued in aristocratic society as a guarantee of the mystic descent through blood. It is a luxury the bourgeois can afford since children do not represent labour-power as in peasant society, but are heirs to accumulated wealth.

Sexual innocence is a challenge to masculine prowess and the desire to dominate, but it is also boring. Goll squares the circle by taking an experienced girl who can feign innocence. But when innocence is the prelude to marital sex as the hallowed means of procreation, and to the asexual condition of motherhood demanding abstinence, fidelity and respect, it is unexciting. Thus, a pattern is established: dull licit sex and exciting illicit sex; dull good wives and desirable bad mistresses; ambiguous virgins either to be enjoyed, corrupted and punished for being bad or else to be married, betrayed and protected from knowledge. The contradiction reaches a climax in Lulu's taunting observation that Schön can hardly betray his boring wife with his exciting mistress since they are one and the same woman (IV, 8), an obeisance to Beaumarchais/Mozart's Almaviva who inadvertently achieves that feat. The one role Lulu cannot play is the asexual respectable wife: her boredom as the wife in an enclosed bourgeois household is unassuaged by reading novels or learning French. She pleads with Schwarz not to answer the bell and with Schön not to go off to the stock exchange, but both of them ignore her plea. And indeed one cannot make love all the time; that is the misfortune of the bourgeois wife who is not a mother and has nothing to do but be beautiful while her husband makes money. Despite a houseful of suitors, there is little sign that Lulu in fact betrays Schön with anybody. Her motley collection of admirers provides some diversion, illicit in being an intrusion into the sacred privacy of the household. In Pabst's film the clownish hangers-on penetrate the marital bedroom, heightening the sense that it is Lulu's sexuality Schön cannot bear in a wife. It scarcely matters whether Lulu yields to her lovers: their desire proves her corruption. Lulu is excitingly desirable, therefore she must be bad, therefore she must be unfaithful. Schön's imagination turns everyone into a lover. The farce of the last scene externalizes inner madness as Schön is torn apart by sexual fantasies and conventional morality – and by love, as his attitude to divorce shows: 'Läßt man sich scheiden, wenn die Menschen ineinander hineingewachsen und der halbe Mensch mitgeht?' (Do you get divorced when you have grown so together that half of yourself would go with your partner?) This is not a worn-out marriage, but a marriage of lovers, an impossible contradiction in terms.

All Lulu's theatrical skills fail to combat Schön's compulsive self-pity, as the role of *paterfamilias*, decent citizen and man of property is locked in mortal combat with the role of sensualist and aesthete amoralist:

SCHÖN (allein sich umsehend): Der reine Augiasstall. Das mein

Lebensabend. Man soll mir einen Winkel zeigen, der noch rein
ist. Die Pest im Haus. Der ärmste Tagelöhner hat sein
sauberes Nest. Dreißig Jahre Arbeit, und das mein Familien-
kreis, der Kreis der Meinen . . .

SCHÖN   (*alone looking round*): *A pure Augean stables. This, the evening
of my life. Show me a corner that's still clean. The plague is in the
house. The poorest labourer has his clean nest. Thirty years' work,
and this is my family circle, the circle of my nearest and dearest . . .*
(IV, 2)

The fragmented clichés are at once the heteronomous expression of a
conventional role invading Schön's mind, and the stereotyped cries of
the hero in a melodrama which destroys the play's comic happy
ending at the close of Act III. Schön's words can be read as an element
in a tragedy, the expression of an individual forced into a farcical role
by an unseen producer, Society, and at the same time as a comic game
with the mode of melodrama, which ridicules and thereby denies the
power of the unseen producer. Here and throughout the play, acting
in life, as self-creation or else as engulfment by an impersonal role, is
interwoven with acting in the theatre. This secondary artistic creation
of images is the topic of the next section.

Eros and Art

The ringmaster of the Prologue introduces the theatrical metaphor
which pervades the whole play. The animals issue from his soul, a
multiplicity of selves and modes of feeling to be explored in the course
of the circus act. The metaphor has a triple sense. First, it suggests the
fluidity of the human personality in interaction with others and the
threat conventional roles pose to the authentic personality. Secondly,
the play reflects on the creation and function of art. Finally, the
reception of art and the audience are both thematized within the play.
Various artistic activities are touched on: painting, dancing, singing,
and writing, producing and acting playes. The reception of art is
explored through the audience in the Prologue and in Act III, and in
the discussions in Act I between Schön, Schwarz and Goll about
painting, the theatre and actresses. Responses to Lulu's portrait are a
leitmotif in both plays. In the theatre, a real audience will watch a real
actress playing the role of an actress on stage who also acts in fictional

'real' life. The themes of art and sex are linked: there is a strong erotic element in aesthetic experience, while the play itself is liable to be erotically appealing yet aesthetically controlled. In the creators, executors and receivers of art, an ideal balance between eros and disinterested aesthetic distance tends to tip over into highly interested lust and possessiveness in the men and the desire to be possessed in Lulu. Gazing at herself in a mirror, a female Narcissus, she says she would like to be a man, so pleasing is the image she sees (IV, 7). She here projects her own image and its possession.

In Act I, Schwarz is at work on two pictures. His protrait of Schön's fiancée lacks the force of Lulu's portrait; the initial erotic impulse which fuels artistic creation is absent. But the erotic impulse must be restrained by aesthetic control: Schön advises, 'Malen Sie Schnee auf Eis' (Paint snow on ice: I, 4). If he is to write sucessfully, Alwa must not translate erotic feeling into flesh-and-blood contact. He must remain detached from the real woman whom he sees as raw material to be translated into a theatrical image: there is a cold curiosity in his interest. (Thomas Mann also explores in *Death in Venice* this artist's 'interest' which denies the distinterest Kant postulated.) Alwa wonders what will happen to Lulu next to provide him with material for the next act of his play: 'Über die ließe sich freilich ein interessanteres Stück schreiben'. (One could certainly write an interesting play about her: III, 2). His monologue goes on to echo the Prologue in evoking an audience lusting for blood, for whom the best climax would surely be the slaughter of Lulu, the climax Alwa's creator ultimately provides. Similarly, Schwarz for a moment tries to deny Lulu life when he tells her to stop breathing like that so that he may go on painting rather than loving (I, 4). Both as lovers and as artists, the men wish to possess and to exploit Lulu; the only difference is of temperature, between cold artistic feeling and the heat of lust. In both cases male 'interest' threatens to become deadly to the object of desire or contemplation.

Lulu, the performer who dances to Goll's command and plays the roles written by Alwa – herself alienated into an image on stage – has a double vision of the audience. It is a faceless darkness with which she can find no contact. The audience do not see her, they see only her surrogate image created by Alwa, and their excitement is not complemented by hers. She has to drink alcohol to warm herself, as she later drinks before going on the streets where she will meet Jack the Ripper; the parallel implies the impersonality common to acting and prostitution. Theatre is not the binding ritual Wagner dreamed of, but isolation and division. But then the audience begins to crystallize for Lulu into an as yet unknown stranger in whom lust displaces aesthetic contemplation (III, 1). The first stranger to emerge is Escerny, who wants to take her off to the jungle. He is a harbinger of Jack the Ripper, the beast who will emerge in the urban jungle to the delight of another bloodthirsty animal, the audience. Like Goll and Schön at the beginning of the play, the aesthetes who sit in the audience separated from the stage are filled with hidden lusts for which staged sex and violence are palliatives, a form of pornography. This is why Lulu refuses to dance in front of Schön and his fiancée. For her, acting is a personal erotic relationship with an individual, but to act in front of Schön's fiancée would turn her into a pornographic image for third parties. Lulu rejects the acting profession. In her view, art is a surrogate, hence her contempt for artists who are less than real men (I, 2) and for theatre which is so much duller than reality (III, 1). She prefers the primary fictions of real life to secondary acting on stage, which lacks flesh-and-blood consummation.

Artistic creativity and aesthetic experience are tainted by the evils which affect sexuality. The alienating image of the reflected Pierrot which came between Lulu and Schwarz (I, 7) points to the larger alienation of art as it divides the creative artist from the human raw material, just as the alienated image on stage divides the actress from herself and from the audience. The aesthetic order of art has affinities with social order; both control instincts, yet also shape them in a potentially destructive way. Lulu's costumes, white and childlike or red and animalesque (III, 7), hypostatize with all the symbolic power of art the contradictory image of woman which finally kills her. Art is an extension of socially rooted alienation and in bourgeois society is a commodity just as sex is. This theme is orchestrated more fully in *Pandora's Box*, where Casti-Piani proposes to use Lulu's image as a shop sign outside a brothel inside which Lulu herself will be on sale. At the beginning of Act II of *Earth Spirit*, Schwarz is clearly turning into a successful society painter whose work will lose the authentic erotic power of that early portrait of Lulu. As the producer of commodities, the artist, whether creative or executive, has to find buyers for the product and backers to invest in artistic talent. This theme, prominent in *The Marquis of Keith*, is touched on here in Schön's secret investment in his son's theatrical venture. Schön does not impose his vulgar desire to see Lulu in tights throughout her performance, and Alwa is allowed the more subtle effect of unveiling her *gradatim* (II, 7), but the risk of commercial vulgarization remains. Works of art in their rich frames, like beautiful women in their expensive elegance, are valuable possessions demonstrating the wealth of their owners: they are commodities become fetishes. That the aesthetic can slide into the purely erotic is a mixed blessing; that both turn into the commerical is merely depressing.

Of course, this view is altogether too gloomy: the tendency of the aesthetic to tip over into the erotic also appears in a comic and celebratory light. It deflates the high-priests who make a disembodied religion of art, like goatish old Goll talking of spirituality (I, 2). It is a mockery of Kantian theory reminiscent of Nietzche's. One is reminded of Renoir's remark that he painted with his penis. Schwarz in pursuit of Lulu round the studio is in the grip of the same power which enabled him to paint the portrait, the transforming erotic imagination, albeit the male erotic imagination working on the female object. The portrait testifies through its vicissitudes to the way in which art can create and transmit ways of seeing and of appearing, the loving and beautiful as well as the destructive and ugly. The Prologue celebrates theatre as a vivid spectacle and as an exploratory game of the imagination. It shows not the dull surface of everyday life but the extremes of passion and perversion, shaped by a controlling wit which uncovers the real perversion in ordinary social attitudes. In production, *Earth Spirit* itself should transcend the doubts about art. (In the next section I shall consider the extent to which it is successful in this.) In reality, the play is prophetic of the aesthetic and commerical problems of Wedekind's work encountered early on. It is perhaps also prophetic of a waning of erotic power and explosive rage after the turn of the century, when Wedekind enjoyed success and himself became a possessive husband.

Sexual Psychology and the Economic Position of Women

As in *Spring Awakening*, here too a powerful social argument is partially vitiated by an ambiguous attitude towards the sexual fantasies the play critically illumines. Attachment to an exclusively sexual image of women pervades the play. This vision was under threat at the time the play was written both by left-wing feminism and by the perennial necessities of childcare stressed by traditional moralists and liberal and conservative feminists alike. The hedonist value of sexual fulfilment predominates. Even on this central theme of sexual emancipation, the play is partial. Lulu may be a vivid dramatization of masculine sexual fantasies but she is an inadequate representation of female sexuality, to say nothing of women as full personalities. Sexual emancipation is indivisible from emancipation of the whole person. The men are scarcely full personalities either, but their interests and jobs contrast with the female status as mere sex object. The independent woman Wedekind chooses to develop is the Countess Geschwitz, a lesbian with inherited wealth. In *Earth Spirit* she is one of a gallery of farcical figures who parody motifs already explored elsewhere. In her attitude to Lulu, she is a mirror-image of the men seen in the distorting mirror of sexual role reversal. Like Lulu, she is defined entirely in sexual terms as a woman who rejects and repels men, a ludicrous monster created by a male author for whom women have no identity other than the sexual. Of course, Geschwitz's subsequent development shines back over *Earth Spirit*, but even so, the plays together suggest not only that the reduction of the female personality to fit masculine desire destroys Lulu, but also that emancipation is incompatible with female sexuality of a kind attractive to men. This has a strange proximity to the view that emancipated women are all lesbians anyway, and to that trend in the women's movement which argues for separation from men.

On economic matters Wedekind writes very much in the feminist spirit, yet finally fudges the issue. The singer Corticelli is an unseen figure from whom Lulu receives with evident pleasure a perfumed letter which she hides in her bosom (II, 1). The letter brings a breath of freedom into the constricted world of bourgeois marriage. Corticelli exemplifies a woman free from Lulu's dependence on protectors, a professional with a marketable talent who can preserve a professional distance between herself and predatory men. Schön's comments on professionalism are ambiguous (III, 10). Had Lulu been able to follow his advice she could have become another Corticelli, subject to market pressures like the male artists but freed from dependence on the whims of one man. At the same time, she would cease to be exclusively a sexual object and would recede into being an aesthetic object, a loss indeed to mankind. At this point, the humour at Schön's expense seems more defensive than satirically aggressive, an expression of the author's ambivalence, and of his bad conscience as a man and an artist who exploited women and the erotic female image. The female artist is finally reduced to absurdity in the motif of the ball for women artists, peopled by lesbian couples, to which Geschwitz invites Lulu (IV, 1). A cartoon in *Simplicissimus* in 1900 is similarly mocking. It shows a long thin lady standing behind a male painter who is saying: 'You see, Fräulein, women painters come in two types. The first want to get married and the others have no talent either.' In *The Marquis of Keith*, Anna is a singer without real talent who retreats into marriage. The fact that women work in areas other than the arts is completely ignored; from the audience's point of view, Lulu's maid, for example, is entirely faceless.

Earth Spirit is a fascinating blend of lucid critique and ambivalence, with a motif of role-playing that is endlessly suggestive. The fact that the play exemplifies its own theme of erotic art could either strengthen or defuse my criticisms, depending on whether the individual production is aimed at titillating a voyeuristic audience for whom Lulu is a sexy *femme fatale* or at unmasking the sexual exploitation of women. In the second kind of production, the audience watches a professional actress portraying Lulu's failure as a professional actress. A good actress will convey Lulu's sexual appeal, but she will do this on the stage for an impersonal audience, not including, one hopes, Jack the Ripper, and with an aesthetic control that avoids the pornographic. Similarly, an accomplished actress may introduce Brechtian distance in projecting Lulu as a sex object while not reducing herself. Such an approach could be taken beyond Wedekind's probable intentions to the point of an alienated presentation. On the other hand, to underplay the erotic appeal too much would rob the play of its vitality. The effect is comparable to the films of Max Ophuls, such as *Lola Montez* with its circus images, or *Madame de* . . . . While criticizing the exploitation of the erotic female image in the visual arts as an extension of male domination, these films themselves owe much of their success to erotic images.

The rest of this chapter will consider the theatrical language and the mixture of modes which both criticize and celebrate forms of sexuality and make *Earth Spirit* so difficult to place in any single dramatic mode.

Time, Sets and Costumes

Earth Spirit is structured differently from *Spring Awakening* with its suite of short scenes. Here is a much more overtly theatrical structure of clearly defined episodes marked off by act divisions, each act with its own set in the manner of the well-made play. A well-made play also has a dynamically developing plot, and up to a point this true of *Earth Spirit*. The central conflict, the struggle between Lulu and Schön just hinted at in Act 1, develops and deepens through the following acts to reach a horrific climax. In opposition to this dynamic structure is the repetitive quality of episodes as Lulu's husbands meet their gruesome ends, a series of dots demonstrating the same point which could be continued indefinitely and are continued in *Pandora's Box* until the end, the murder of Lulu. Thus *Earth Spirit* can stand on its own or as part of a continuing drama: underlying a symphonic structure are variations on a theme. Within each episode, dramatic time and audience time roughly coincide, but the pace varies considerably. Slow passages of intimate dialogue which do not advance the plot and which open vistas of past time or future hopes give away to frenetic farce.

The passage of time is mainly indicated by the comic motif of Schön's delayed engagement, followed by his delay in marrying his ageing child fiancée. The individual producer must decide whether Lulu too shows signs of ageing as she moves through the changing sets in her changing costumes. But at the end of *Earth Spirit* she stills looks like the portrait Schwarz was working on at the beginning of the play. Lulu does not seem to age, but remains, like her unchanging painted image, an image of youth: beauty like a dial-hand steals from his figure, and no pace perceived. The sense of time as a process of change and ageing is conjured up through the men, from the boy Hugenberg, through the young men Schwarz, Alwa and Ferdinand, through the mighty strong man Rodrigo, and through Schön, still in his prime but fearful of age, to Schigolch, an ancient of days – so ancient that he is almost in the underworld. The juxtapositions have a baroque quality, especially the tableau of Schigolch and Lulu, Death and the Maiden. Lulu, representing the fleeting moment of the *carpe diem* all the men wish to seize, seems to hold still, to be changeless. This stasis gives way in *Pandora's Box* to sickeningly rapid decline, which in retrospect intensifies the undertone of lyric lament in *Earth Spirit* where Lulu's seemingly changeless beauty only heightens the sense of the inevitable passage of time. Operatic comparisons suggest themselves. Hugenberg, a trouser-role, is reminiscent of that archetypal youth Cherubino in *The Marriage of Figaro* and of Octavian in another later meditation on time, *Rosenkavalier*.

Whereas the full effect of the time structure arises from the play as a whole and its relationship to *Pandora's Box*, the first feature to impinge on the audience is place. Wedekind specifies a great deal of detail, as in a Naturalist play, and the sets do convey milieu. But the anti-illusionism of the Prologue and the pervasive theatrical metaphors invite us to see the sets as an aspect of theatrical language: milieu is seen through a temperament; the sets are constructs which gain meaning from their place in the play rather than from exactitude of reference to a world beyond the play. The sets alternate between artistic and domestic interiors. The former promise freedom outside marriage, the latter offer security and luxury inside marriage. Both promises prove deceptive. The shift from nature out-of-doors in *Spring Awakening* to artist's studio and theatre dressing room as the realm of freedom means that the motif of nature given in the title becomes entirely metaphorical. Whatever human beings may be by nature they have to live in society. Schigolch belongs outdoors: he wanders with his accordion along roads we never see which lead, if not in straight lines, to the crossing to 'drüben', to 'over there'. He hopes that his asthma may help him on his way (II, 2). These exaggeratedly numinous hints are reminiscent of Mignon's mythical land of the South. But paradise or Hades, it is all the same: human beings may arrive trailing clouds of glory and depart across the Styx, but in the meantime even Schigolch needs money, and three hundred is the sum he requests.

The sets are full of significant detail. Schwarz's studio has a Persian carpet, an elaborate representation of flowers turned into abstract decoration. Schön's emblematic beast, the tiger, has beome a rug, suggesting the death of natural instinct. As a decorative artefact it shows too that natural images applied to human affairs are irreducibly metaphorical rather than literal: the meaning of nature is defined by culture. The dais on which Lulu stands for her portrait repreats in miniature the stage the audience watches as an actress plays Lulu playing Pierrot. The two doors, the ladder, easels and so forth provide the trappings for physical farce. The portrait is still coming into being, not yet framed, just as the figure of Lulu is developing dramatically in the exposition of the first act. In Act II, the elegant *Jugendstil* drawing room is full of decorative detail: the sinuous curve of a chaise longue, the black ebony writing desk, the twisting lines of gold and silver in the portrait frame, a touch of chinoiserie. To Schigolch it is all just another display of wealth, the delicacy replacing the heavy Gothic manner of his youth when people hung swords on the walls. The feminine style creates a doll's house for a beautiful puppet, a cage for the bored domestic animal enclosed in her household as her portrait now is in its frame. The mirror continues the theatrical metaphor and allows Lulu to watch her own performance, which her husband fails to appreciate.

There is less physical farce in this act – the incongruous figure of Schigolch in this elegant room is sufficent comedy in itself, while the comedy of the confrontation between Schwarz and Schön is primarily verbal. But again, the doors in the set allow for farce shading into melodrama at the end. The dressing room in Act III evokes an unseen audience, played by the real audience, bringing the theatrical metaphor to a climax. The mirror here is a practical aid to an actress putting on make-up, but it is also a metaphor for Lulu's conscious projection of a persona in human relations outside the theatre. The screen allows for the comedy of Lulu's costume change in the presence of Escerny. This is the one act from which the portrait is absent: here, Lulu makes her own image on stage. For a moment, she is the artist or producer herself, directing Schön's dismissal of his fiancée. In Act IV the portrait reappears in a golden frame: art is now a display of wealth in the household of a would-be Renaissance aesthete, as the name Schön (literally 'beautiful') suggests. The description of the set is reminiscent of the interiors of Franz von Stuck's villa in Munich, which is also an art gallery (Hager 1968). It evokes an eclectic bourgeois temple of the arts which mixes rich, dark neo-Renaissance with the chinoiserie of the screen. Here Lulu and her portrait are aesthetic objects and possessions. The staircase and gallery frame the lower stage, turning it into the set for a scene Schön will observe from above. Wedekind here anticpates Reinhardt's use of stairs to theatrical effect. The curtains and table are props for a farce which will turn to melodrama. The sofa on which Schön breathes his last is destined to play a part in Act I of *Pandora's Box*, when the son takes over as protector of his father's murderess.

The costumes too are overtly theatrical. In Act I Lulu begins as Frau Medizinalrat, appearing to the audience as a doll-like wife ushered in by her Doctor Coppelius. As Goll's wife she is his material possession, as Pierrot an emanation of his imagination. The collector of *objects d'art* risks losing his possession in creating such an image. The floppy costume allows Lulu freedom of movement which tight-laced, long dresses prevent. As she puts it on, the men wonder how she gets into it, no doubt secretly wondering how to get her out of it. In the costume she can run, climb ladders, smash the painting. After Goll's death Schwarz's helps to fasten her into her dress again, a premonition of his future status as husband. In Act III, Prince Escerny fails to accomplish an opposite task when he cannot undo a knot in the lacing of her corsette, clearly proving his unsuitability as a lover. She impatiently completes the task herself. Her competence in getting in and out of costumes suggests her freedom as an actress which contrasts with the restrictions of her situation as a wife. In keeping with the *Jugendstil*, which is characteristically adrogynous with homoerotic undertones, the Pierrot costume undoes the hourglass shape of a femininity associated with constriction. It does not so much turn Lulu into a boy as suggest an erotic freedom from socially constructed images of femininity; an obviously female body cannot signal freedom in this society. In Act III, Lulu is dressed appropriately as the young wife in a morning dress of green satin; but the cool colour and flowing material recall the nymph Melusine fresh from her watery element. Lulu's penchant for going barefoot on her rich carpets is a motif comparable to the loose unwifely Pierrot costume which recurs through to the end of *Pandora's Box* and looks back to her original barefoot entry into bourgeois society. Going barefoot suggests natural freedom – nymphs do not wear shoes – but it also suggests vulnerability and poverty. Act II is dominated visually by Schigolch's tramplike parody of male bourgeois dress and by the contrast between asthmatic age and Lulu's youthful beauty. As Lulu talks of the creams she puts on her skin, wrinkled Schigolch evokes the decay of the flesh with sepulchral relish. After the suicide Lulu assumes the disguise of coat and veiled hat as she tries to escape the scene of the crime, one of those rapid costume changes characteristic of farce, which are technically so difficult to achieve. In Act III, Lulu escapes from wifely dresses to the freedom of theatrical costumes, though these costumes, like the Pierrot outfit, are designed by a man. They recall Lulu as barefoot flower girl and sister to Alwa, and evoke the images of white angelic innocence and red sensual temptation with which the men associated her in Act I.

In watching Lulu put on a costume, the audience participates in the creation of an image and recognizes it for what it is, whereas the men in the play remain trapped in illusion: Schön for example, oscillates between seeing Lulu as a seductive temptress or as a model of innocence. Alwa, a man of the theatre, understands the power of clothes better than his father, who just wants Lulu to show off her legs. Like the Pierrot outfit, the costumes Alwa requires are designed as a subtle appeal to the erotic imagination rather than as pornographic aids to arousal. The balance between these two kinds of stimulation is delicate: Lulu senses both potential suitors and murderers in the audience. Similarly, in Act I the sight of Lulu gradually turning up the leg of her Pierrot trousers almost to the knee, invites sexual arousal rather than aesthetic contemplation: the erotic effect of the flesh is quite unlike the cool lunar magic of the painting. Eventually, Schwarz succumbs to lust heightened by thoughts of green underskirts, tightly laced *décolletés* and white overskirts as Lulu describes her Paris costumes. Similarly, Escerny is prompted to court Lulu, his desire heightened by the theatrical performance which turns her from a real woman into a noble savage. Such moments suggest the power of images and the uneasy balance between the erotic and the aesthetic. One wonders what kind of frame the portrait would have had in Africa and what costumes Lulu would have worn; a model might be the magnificent barbaric negress in Conrad's *Heart of Darkness*, another work of the period concerned with the primitive. In the last act, Lulu's feminine dresses, appropriate for the wife of a bourgeois sensualist, contrast with Geschwitz's faintly military appearance. Unlike the Pierrot outfit, Geschwitz's costume does not deconstruct sexual difference, but parodistically underlines it. Lulu's flowery négligé and the bouquet of flowers contrast with the dark tones of the furnishings, presenting an image of nature turned into decorative delicacy enclosed in oppressive wealth. Lulu finally appears in a ballgown, a grand costume *à la dame aux camélias* appropriate for the melodrama to come.

A producer will no doubt make much of Hugenberg, a piquant trouser-role, of aged Schigolch, of the circus strongman and the liveried Ferdinand to create comic effects, but once again no male costumes are specified apart from Alwa's conventional evening dress.

Modes and Perspectives

The sets and costumes underline the status of the play as a theatrical fiction. The succession of episodes is also overtly theatrical, with three of the four acts closing on increasingly noisy and violent death: a strangulated heart attack; a throat-cutting accompanied by gruesome

groans; a murder by five revolver shots punctuated by Schön's 'Und –
da – ist – noch – einer' (And – there – is – an – other: IV, 8); whether
another lover or another shot it hardly matters. The plot in brief
sounds like black melodrama; but in its intertwining of the comic with
the gruesome, of sustained verbal wit with evocative lyricism, *Earth
Spirit* resists categorization. Equally remote from Naturalist gloom or
the lachrymose sentiment of true melodrama, it combines tragic depth
with the ebullience of a Feydeau farce. Striking effects come from
sharp changes of perspective, generally towards the end of an act. Act
I begins as high comedy with a first hint of farce in Schön's startled
'Good God!' as he collides in the doorway with the incongruous
couple, Goll and Lulu. The pace quickens when Lulu and Schwarz
are left alone, and the ensuing scene of exuberant physical farce
culminates with the return of Goll who falls down dead after a second
or so of gasping and stick-waving. His demise, so rapid, puppetlike
and dramatically timed, induces laughter rather than horror. In pure
farce or melodrama the act would have closed on the frozen tableau of
surprised lovers and corpse, but here it modulates through still
farcical fussing over tumbled furniture to Lulu's eerily moving
monologue. The Arcadian dream withers in the juxtaposition of
Pierrot and a corpse; the exchanges between Lulu and Schwarz shatter
the traditional consolations of faith; while the final coda, as Lulu with
trembling hands begs Schwarz to do up her dress, suggests the
fragility of social arrangements which bring no real human contact.
The audience perceives Goll's death from at least three perspectives:
as the ludicrous climax of a sexual farce, as a melodramatic *coup de
théâtre* and as a grim *memento mori* of baroque intensity quite
dispersing the comic mood of the start.

Act II moves through a series of elegant *pas de deux* between Lulu
and Schwarz, Lulu and Schigolch, Lulu and Schön, and Schön and
Schwarz, each a comic vignette with Schwarz, the cuckold, as butt.
Berg's operatic transformation wonderfully catches Lulu's langorous
appeal in the first scene. Schwarz is proved a fool by the fact that he
answers not Lulu's sexual appeal but the doorbell, which will
contribute so insistently to the farcical close of the act. Schigolch sees
the brittle elegance of the drawing room through the eyes of a tramp
concerned with basic pleasures and necessities, an angle of vision
which renders the suicide absurd. Schwarz's death, precipitated by a
terrible revelation, could be the stuff of tragedy. But his death lacks
necessity: it is not truth which kills him but his evaluation of a set of

facts. Schigolch offers another evaluation of the facts of Lulu's life, as does Schön, the anti-moralist. 'That's fatal, of course', he says when Lulu remarks that Schwarz loves her, a pun which comes all too literally true some minutes later. The comment throws a cynical light on Schwarz's death. Cynicism is romanticism gone sour: on Schön's part, an apparently aggressive cynical attitude later proves to be the defence of the secret romantic. But for the moment the cynicism relativizes Schwarz's tragical self-image. Schön speaks in the bluff tones of a parent or parson trying to inculcate a bit of moral – here immoral – backbone into a rather weedy child, urging Schwarz to count his blessings and his money with the incantatory 'You married half a million', a sinister effect Berg splendidly translates into an insistently menacing rhythm in the opera.

So far, the act has moved on the plane of social comedy in the cynical mood. But soon horrific groans off-stage herald melodrama instantly turning to farce as Schön stamps then tiptoes, the bell rings, Schön rattles then hammers, the bell rings again, an axe is fetched and Alwa rushes in announcing Revolution in Paris. The fear of scandal, touched on briefly at the end of Act I, here swells to monstrous proportions, suggesting the power of Society, that huge audience which intrudes into apparently private lives, reducing them to farce. The act closes as the reporter repeats to Schön's dictation 'Ver – folg – ungs – wahn' (Pa – ra – noi – a) and the bell rings yet again. Like the repeated 'You married half a million', the long drawn-out sounds are a favourite device, echoed in 'Jetzt – kommt – die – Hinrichtung' (Now – for – the execution) and 'Und – da – ist – noch – einer' at the end of Acts III and IV. Such patterning devices suggest the impersonal workings of a mechanism. Schön's dictation to the reporter anticipates the way in which he will himself write to Lulu's dictation at the end of Act III. Act II is shaped by the jolting gear change from urbane comedy to melodrama and farce in a cruelly comic end which robs Schwarz's death of dignity or even pathos. An audience cannot feel for a prop in a farce. The greater cruelty of this close compared with the end of Act I indicates a more vicious attack on Schwarz's sentimental moralism than on Goll's consciously exploitative hedonism. Lulu's preference for Goll indicates that she shares her creator's judgement on this matter, and reflects the general thrust of Wedekind's attack on morality. The farce in Act II takes on a darker note, however, in the shadow cast backwards from the second play. When he has finished his encouraging anti-sermon and just before the groans start up Schön says with satisfaction 'Das war ein Stück Arbeit' (That was a hard job: II, 5), the words used by Jack the Ripper after butchering Lulu. This premonition opens up a tragic perspective. Mayhem is brought not by Lulu, but by the amalgam of male attitudes which come together in the cold fragmented banalities with which Jack accompanies his muderous task. In Goll, possessiveness turns to murderous violence when his possession seems to be escaping, and precipitates a heart attack. In Schwarz, the murderous impulse turns inwards, unleashed by the collision of romantic dream and economic fact. Schön cynically butchers Schwarz's dream, but himself falls victim to the conflict between convention and a profound attachment to Lulu which belies the cynical role.

While Schwarz was a self-deceiving moralist, Schön is a self-deceiving amoralist, his madness precipitated by an upsurge of bourgeois moral convention. But before the final act comes the interlude of Act III, where comedy is least distorted by farce or horror. It falls roughly into three sections. The first section recalls Lulu's meeting with Schigolch in Act II; here her partner is Alwa. Both scenes recall her girlhood and in both she finds relief with someone who is not currently a sexual partner: with a former lover turned friend and with the companion of her youth, a brother not yet turned lover. There prevails a shimmering mixed mood of friendly warmth, nostalgia and, towards the end, of creepy excitement as Lulu evokes the unseen audience with an icy shudder. But that remains a dark note in the lower register of what is otherwise a lyrical and moving scene. Alwa's monologue, the draft of a play within the play, forestalls any tendency towards sentimentality and reminds us that it is all fiction, not fact. As Alwa wonders what will happen next, Escerny's entry introduces a scherzo which is closely followed by the main movement of the act, the confrontation between Lulu the snake and Schön the tiger. This is the climax of the comedy the play might have been, as Lulu bends the *Gewaltmensch*, the Nietzschean man of will, to her will and dictates what he must do. His closing exclamations about death sentences and execution are the rhetoric of the protagonist in a high comedy, who has at last capitulated to the heroine. But Lulu's victory is pyrrhic, for the tiger's dreams of a bourgeois idyll re-emerge in the full flower of mania in the next act. Schön's words at the end of Act III thus appear in the twin perspectives of high comedy and tragic melodrama.

After the lighter mood of Act III, the forces of chaos reassert themselves in Act IV in a catastrophic heightening of farce culminating in black melodrama. The opening seems normal enough, until Schön responds to Geschwitz's question about the painter of the portrait with the sepulchral words 'er hatte genug' (he had enough). Traditionally, the mad are both funny and frightening, their thoughts and movements a caricature of the normal. The short, abrupt phrases of Schön's monologue are a mosaic of clichés conveying conventional attitudes, fragmented and magnified to become nightmarish. His madness colours the rest of the act. The logic of farce where every table, screen or curtain conceals another lover is the logic of the nightmare in Schön's head. Once set in motion, the force of this logic is inexorable. Schön's obsession, and his loss of rationality and control, exemplify what Bergson (1975: 29) called 'the incrustation of the mechanical on the living'. A decade or so later, Wedekind's farcical melodrama might have been turned into direct Expressionist exteriorization of Schön's inner frenzy, or else into surreal fantasy freed from all residual realism – in the first case at the cost of laughter; in the second with some loss of critical bite, though Buñuel's early surreal films, for example, do retain considerable direction. Here, the aggressive bite of farce makes us laugh at destructive social conventions unmasked as madness, conventions which equate goodness in women with asexuality and badness with sexuality, so that sexual Lulu can only be a mistress or an adulteress, but not a good wife.

Schön's view does not entirely engulf the action. The scenes between Lulu, Schigolch and company move initially in a childlike, nonsense wonderland, the innocent end of a spectrum stretching to destructive madness, a contrast skilfully captured in Pabst's film. They bring a breath of freedom into the oppressive ostentation of Schön's *bourgeois* palace. The ancient and disreputable Schigolch, the circus strongman who is the very acme of virility, and the charming Hugenberg are all clownish figures, representing three stages of man in comic juxtaposition, and standing as parodies of the three husbands: old Goll, Schön in his prime, and young Schwarz. Poor Ferdinand, trembling as he serves Lulu, is a comic parallel to Alwa, whose declaration of love is at first touching, then funny and finally depressing as the all too familiar images and words recognizable from earlier moments and other mouths interpose themselves. Lulu turns into Mignon: he idealizes her; he kneels to be destroyed by her. This depressing progression evokes in a different register the same distorted emotions which explode in the final destructive climax. Lulu's last terrified speech is full of love for Schön and naked fear. She kneels to Alwa as he had kneeled to her. Whereas he had pleaded rhetorically for destruction, she begs for her life, offering to pay for it with her body. The contrast is an indictment of the unequal commerce between the sexes. Neither sentimental nor self-deceiving, Lulu's speech arouses the tragic emotions of pity and fear. But once again the perspective shifts in the last few seconds. Voices off-stage herald the arrival of the police, and Hugenberg, son of a policeman, exclaims that he will be expelled from school. His exclamation, farcical in its immediate context, seems to be incongruous with Lulu's fear of the much greater horror of beheading, but it takes on a darker colour in the shadow of the second play, in which Hugenberg is indeed expelled from school into a penitentiary where he commits suicide.

Earth Spirit mixes comedy, farce, satire, tragedy and melodrama. Wedekind's peculiar humour is both an effect of the clashing modes and the element which holds them together. As in *Spring Awakening*, the humour acts as a weapon against fatalism. It turns tragedy into black farce in a play which could otherwise seem to demonstrate an inexorable chain of cause and effect. It is aggressive, expressing rage against a destructive sexual culture. But it is also a defence against the pain of contradictions recognized but not vanquished.

4
Pandora's Box

A Play and its Sequel

Pandora's Box opens with an exposition full of retrospective narrations. Immersed in memory, the characters speak in parallel monologues. But they also sketch continuations to their stories. At first, Hugenberg and Geschwitz do not look beyond plans for Lulu's escape from prison, for them an end in itself; later, believing Lulu dead, the boy Hugenberg looks forward only to going to the devil, an anticipation of his suicide. It is different with the three men. Alwa, identified as the author of *Earth Spirit*, means to continue his exploitation of the image of Lulu by making her the heroine of another play, but fears that prison may have rendered her unsuitable for his purpose. He is ready to surrender the flesh-and-blood woman to Rodrigo, who plans to make a living from Lulu's beauty, although, like Alwa, he fears that prison may have damaged the aspect of her he proposes to exploit. Schigolch has no plan for Lulu, determined only that his own life shall be better. Lulu herself combines retrospection and prophecy in recalling the dreams she had in prison of falling prey to a sex murderer. Towards the close of the act, however, the present asserts itself as Lulu and Alwa remain alone, accompanied only by the portrait, symbol of eros and timeless beauty. The dithyramb Alwa promises to write in the future, when Lulu has gone, becomes an erotic rhapsody in the present as he caresses her body. Lulu answers in the continuous present: 'Derweil ich vergrabe meine Hände in deinem Haar.' (Meanwhile I bury my hands in your hair.) Alwa's future plans give way to the present; Lulu can now dispose of him. The closing exchange also disposes of the past. The divan on which Schön bled to death becomes a couch for his widow and son. Alwa, the man of language, urges silence on Lulu and is himself silenced thereafter as a writer. Thus the urgency of *carpe diem* banishes past and future for an illusory moment of pleasure: by the beginning of the next act Lulu is Alwa's wife in name only, and Casti-Piani's mistress. But the erotic moment does mark a decisive break as Lulu and Alwa banish a dead husband and father. As the setting of the play is moved away from Schön's house, the world of *Earth Spirit* is seen in relative terms as part of a wider international world.

Alwa's authorship of *Earth Spirit*, written in the interval between the two plays, is a *mise en abyme*, to use André Gide's term for such Chinese box effects. It shrinks the first play to miniature proportions, like Matisse's painting of a room with a little picture of the same room hanging on the wall. The little picture shifts attention from what is depicted to the painterliness of the depiction. Here, attention is directed to theatricality with double effect. What *Earth Spirit* depicted is reduced in size and closed off; the second play follows as a sequel, a linear account of new events. As a metatheatrical intrusion, however, the reference to *Earth Spirit*, like the painting within a painting, points less to novelty than to analogy, repetition or even identity. But although there are striking parallels and hidden analogies between the plays, *Pandora's Box* is significantly different in kind from *Earth Spirit*. The *mise en abyme* places *Earth Spirit* inside *Pandora's Box*, which is larger and less introverted, setting the milieu of the earlier play in a wider context of international capitalism. In *Earth Spirit*, the marriage household or colourful atelier still offered an illusion of privacy. Schwarz struggles, if ineffectually, to express himself in his surroundings and in his work. At the end of Act I he longs to love and be happy. Schön is initially attractive in his amoral energy, so that his invasion by convention has tragic force. Alwa is a productive man of the theatre. Lulu is not just an image in the eyes of others, but retains some autonomy. In *Pandora's Box*, this lingering individuality of the characters has almost disappeared. We are not interested in the inner life of a Casti-Piani or in Dr Hilti's struggle to love and be happy. Removed from the cocoon of his father's wealth, Alwa is a burnt-out shell. The clownlike charm of Rodrigo turns to coarse brutality. Lulu is finally reduced to the condition of a terrified animal. The contrast is partly a result of the reworking of the *Monstretragödie* to which *Pandora's Box*, apart from the added first act, is textually closer than *Earth Spirit* is. But the sense of *Pandora's Box* is affected by its relation to the reworked *Earth Spirit*. Lulu's dehumanization is brought about by her loss of Schön, the effects of prison, and her criminalization. Conversely, as Alan Best (1975: 95) argues, the impersonal forces at work in *Pandora's Box* appear in retrospect as the hidden determinants of the catastrophe of *Earth Spirit*.

Social Satire or Existential Horror

Like *Earth Spirit*, the mythical title *Pandora's Box* suggests not unique historical events but a figural vision of unchanging archetypes re-enacted. It remains to be seen whether the title is misleading, whether the catastrophe is caused by social evils or by an unchanging human nature. According to Dora and Erwin Panofsky (1956) Pandora, the all-giver, was orginally a goddess of fertility. This interpretation is preferred by Ernst Bloch (1959: 389): Pandora is seen as the fount of all values; after their dispersal hope is still left that mankind may recover what has been lost. Following Bloch's interpretation, Pandora has recently become a feminist motif in East German literature (Reid, 1914). In Goethe's *Pandora* of 1807, on which one such work is based, Pandora brings love, beauty and joy; but man's reactions to the woman's gifts turn love to jealous possessiveness, harden beauty into a fetish and destory joy. In Hesiod's account in The Theogony, however, the *locus classicus*, there is no ambiguity; Pandora, the ancestress of all women, is a demonic temptress. When Prometheus stole fire, Zeus sought revenge and commissioned his son, the lame Hephaestus, to make a woman out of earth to whom the gods gave their choicest gifts. Zeus gave her a jar which he ordered her never to open; Hephaestus gave her a human voice; Aphrodite gave seductive beauty; and Hermes gave cunning and the art of flattery; Epimetheus, forgetting Prometheus' warning against gifts from Zeus, made her his wife. Pandora then opened the box releasing evil on mankind. Only hope remained shut in.

The myth has affinities with the story of the fall. Pandora was fashioned by a god and endowed with divine gifts, but is made of earth, suggesting fallen nature. Knowledge, especially female curiosity, and sex, especially female sex, are linked with evil. The conjunction is more evident in German, for the title of Wedekind's play is an obscene pun: *Büchse* is a vulgar term for the female genitals. In the gruesome *Monstretragödie* Jack cuts out Lulu's genitals, a mutilation practised in real life by the Whitechapel murderer, although according to Krafft-Ebing (1893: 64) he probably ate them, whereas Jack means to leave them to science.

The title of this play could presage a moralizing attack on the corrupting influence of the eternal feminine – woman's first disobedience of Zeus, the divine patriarch, as the origin of evil; man also guilty in falling prey to woman's seductions. In fact, however, preaching of obedience is reduced to grotesque parody in the mouth of Rodrigo, the state organs of law and order are excoriated, and the woman's fate at the hands of a man makes such a gross anti-feminist reading impossible. A more plausible implication is Schopenhauerian pessimism: human beings are driven on by desire for pleasure to misery and mutual destruction. Yet although some passages convey such general existential horror, the play emphasizes the peculiar unpleasantness of a specific culture, the world of late nineteenth-century capitalism. If existential horror is set in the foreground, then historical specifics become the accidentals of an essential figure: they body forth a timeless truth but are not in themselves the meaning. If the social structure is emphasized then the horror expressed by the characters becomes a psychological response to destructive social relations, itself compounding the destruction. If horror is more indirectly conveyed through motifs and patterns, it has expressive rather than analytic force as a rhetorical attack on social evils. Much will depend upon production.

The next two sections will consider the financial jungle of Casti-Piani and the urban jungle roamed by Jack the Ripper. The transition from one to the other might appear as a stripping away of illusions to uncover an existential truth: Act III reveals the beast beneath the civilized veneer of the moneyed classes and explains Act II. On the other hand, Act III may be seen as showing the end result of the social relations explored in Act II, as unleashed capitalism turns human beings into beasts, in which case Act II explains Act III.

The Economic Jungle

In contrast to *Earth Spirit*, nearly everyone in *Pandora's Box* is more interested in money than sex. Rodrigo, Casti-Piani, and Heilmann are attracted by the price on Lulu's head, not by her flesh, which is interesting only as a marketable commodity in the circus or a Cairo brothel. In Act II, two transactions proceed simultaneously: Casti-

Piani is trying to sell Lulu to a brothel, while the rest of the characters are buying shares in a funicular railway on the Jungfrau, a project threatening the purity of that virgin peak. The name of the shares – 'Jungfrau' – implies that virginity is a commodity, a motif echoed in twelve-year-old Kadidja, whose valuable virginity has been guarded in a convent school. But when the Jungfrau scheme collapses Kadidja will become a chorus girl, a euphemism for a prostitute; her virginity will be sold for money rather than bartered in marriage, unless she is lucky enough to find a man like Goll who is willing to make her his wife.

Female flesh is marketable because it is desirable; in the technical terms of Adam Smith or Karl Marx, it has value in use. But the characters lust after shares more than they lust after virgins. Money is the prime object of desire, and exchange-value overshadows use-value. Mountain railways and virgins both lose their substantial reality: all that matters is maximum profit. Casti-Piani is willing to hand Lulu over to the police for a reward, but would prefer to sell her for a higher profit to a brothel, though he has to win her consent, for this is not a slave economy but enlightened, liberal Europe. Lulu is therefore free to choose between prison or indentured labour in a more benighted part of the world.

The Marquis trades on a large scale. Rodrigo and Heilmann just want to make a quick buck by betraying Lulu to the police. Lulu pretends to offer Rodrigo a higher profit for sexual services to be rendered to Geschwitz, and in the meantime hires Schigolch to kill Rodrigo. Schigolch barters his services as assassin for the use-value of Lulu's body, rather than a fee. And so Rodrigo is murdered.

Structurally, this murder is one of a series of deaths punctuating the plays; temporally, occurring towards the close of an act, it marks off yet another episode in the career of a *femme fatale*. Thematically, however, it is significantly different from the other deaths, since it is the first for which Lulu, as client hiring an assassin, is unambiguously responsible. Whereas she killed Schön in self-defence, she now acts with malice aforethought. Nor is Rodrigo the victim of Lulu's fatal sexuality; he is the victim of his own lust for money, the only lust she arouses in him, and of her fear of incarceration, which turns her into a murderess. Lulu faces the twin threats of state power and her own exchange-value. To the horror of prison is added the horror of the brothel which would reduce her sexuality, the very foundation of her sense of self, to a commodity to be bought and sold. Originally criminalized through Schön's murderous possessiveness, she is plunged deeper into crime in opposing the combined power of the state and the market, united in the police spy and white-slave trader Casti-Piani. The police turn a blind eye to his dubious trade in return for his services in fighting anarchist threats to the state and private property. In Paris, the financial centre of capitalism, human relations are reduced to money relations under benevolent police protection. Without money Lulu is powerless, a commodity not a person; she resorts to brute physical attack by proxy in order to survive.

The primary activating force, then, is not sex but economics. Of course Lulu could have chosen prison or the brothel; but she is not a descendant of Goethe's Gretchen, doomed victim yet man's redemptress through her essential goodness. In Wedekind's play, Faustian amoralism resides in the woman; Lulu chooses liberty. To choose moral integrity might save the human spirit, but it would leave the actual person rotting in gaol or a brothel. The freedom she wins is illusory, however, for poverty exposes her to a terrible fate. An increasingly chilling aura of isolation surrounds Lulu; her freedom is not exercised through relations with others which would give it meaning. She does not rise triumphant over threats to her liberty, but is dehumanized by them. Rodrigo's murder is perhaps a model action against the enemy, man, but her indifference to the death of Sister Theophila, a victim of the escape plot, and her contempt for devoted Geschwitz are inhuman. The play subverts idealist belief in essential humanity and faith in the free individual. Freedom and individuality fall victim to the combined power of the authoritarian state and the free market where the fetishism of commodities extinguishes human relations.

The consequences for art of the primacy of the economic motive are symbolized in the fate of Hugenberg. In Act I, Alwa planned to base a play on the heroic Hugenberg, to be called *Der Weltbeherrscher* (*The World Master*), no doubt with mood music by R. Strauss. Hugenberg's little finger, Alwa says, is worth more than the whole of Rodrigo. Rodrigo is a parody of Nieztschean power and social Darwinist fitness. He is a strong man gone to seed, is unconscionably stupid and will never master the world of a Casti-Piani. Yet if Rodrigo is not a *Weltbeherrscher*, neither is the heroic Hugenberg; his preventive detention prevents him from taking action to save Lulu. The only heroic deed left to him is self-destruction. His act has the nobility of a classical suicide and is a defiance of patriarchal power (his father is a chief of police, the very power which holds him physically yet cannot bind his free spirit). But the heroic deed falls flat. The potential audience is not interested: Lulu is too caught up in her own worries; Alwa announces his death casually as a mere anecdote in the paper. In a world ruled by the market, heroic deeds are absurd. There is nothing left for a hero to do but disappear off-stage into the void. Alwa has lost interest in writing a play with a hero instead of the weaklings of Naturalism and is obsessed with the movement of shares. Hugenberg's fate is a wry comment on the Masked Man's vitalist message; heroic Hugenberg shares Moritz's fate, just as Ilse's successor Lulu meets an unhappy end.

The deepening of scepticism goes along with an attack (presumably in part directed at Wedekind himself) on the impotence of art and the artist in the world of commodities. Alwa becomes the very kind of weakling in the Naturalist manner he himself scorns, a decadent intellectual who cannot act. Sexually inadequate and physically weak, he falls easy prey to the brutal primitivism of Kungu Poti. Along with the Nietzschean symptoms of the decadent, too much mind and aestheticizing passivity, Alwa bears the Ibsenite mark of venereal disease, providing a mechanistic explanation for his weakness. A potential artist in *Earth Spirit*, he is now a dilettante comparable to some of Thomas Mann's early anti-heroes. Without his father's sub-aristocratic patronage, Alwa is flung into the full rigours of the market where the artist must sell his wares. Seduced by the stock market, he forgets his art. The intrinsic value of art, as of sex, is overshadowed by value in exchange.

Along with the corrosive effect of the market on sexual relations and art, Act II sketches the outer shape of capitalism. Casti-Piani trades with Valparaiso and Cairo. In the Cairo brothel, Scottish lords mix with Russian notabilities, governors of India and Rhineland capitalists. Lulu speaks French, the old diplomatic language; had she gone to the Cairo brothel she would have had to learn English too, the new world language. One of her colleagues would have been the ex-wife of a commercial traveller for a Hamburg company trading with the colonies. Women and French champagne are exported to the Cairo magnate, Oikonomopulos, who used to inhabit Ilse's bohemia, while in the endless circulation of commodities, the primary colonial products are imported through the great port of Hamburg.

Casti-Piani is an old-fashioned merchant capitalist, a seedy Buddenbrook with a dubious title. He does not deal in shares, accepting only

Reichsmarks or English gold. There is no nostalgia here as there is in Thomas Mann's *Buddenbrooks*, for mercantile community giving way to aggressive bourgeois civilization. Stock market capitalism differs from mercantilism only in its irrationalism, as paper fortunes are made and lost depending on the vagaries of confidence. The stock market is represented as a game of roulette in which, impossible as it may be, the punters and the bank are apparently all winning.

Puntschu, the banker, is a key figure in the new economics. He has been bankrupt thirty-five times and in his energy and frankness is more appealing than Heilmann of the hypocritical name, the money-grubbing representative of the fourth estate. Heilmann completes the picture of the free press begun in *Earth Spirit*. News is dictated by rich proprietors like Schön; those who have money can hush things up, those who have none are blazoned across the headlines. Heilmann is antisemitic: 'Jetzt kriegt er kalte Füße, der Saujude!' (Now he's getting cold feet, the Jewish pig!). But as Puntschu replies, he runs the same risks as the rest, who are only too ready to borrow in the hope of a fortune. The prime butt of Wedekind's attack is not the Jew, but Heilmann's irrational antisemitism. Arnold Schönberg took offence at the stage direction 'mauschelnd', speaking like a Jew, in Berg's *Lulu* (Cerha, 1979: 34; Perle, 1985: 287–8). Such a direction is necessary only in the opera, not in the play, for Berg has cut some of Puntschu's more stereotyped comments in joke Jewish German. But neither opera nor play has proto-fascist undertones, and Wedekind's loathing of antisemitism is clear from his diaries (Hay: 224–5). There is no anti-capitalist nostalgia for some earlier organic community, no sense of the Jew as an alien. The banker is just one of an international cast of cut-throat competitors, more appealing than the rest in playing the market as a game of snakes and ladders, with an enterprising adventurism which anticipates Keith. Puntschu strengthens the satirical attack on the free market as the road to freedom, adding a comic note to the grimmer overtones of Lulu's struggle, as he ruefully takes up the Sisyphean labour of pushing free enterprise up the hill for the thirty-sixth time.

The critique of the market is not in the ultra-conservative mould, nor does it anticipate National Socialist anti-capitalist rhetoric. But it is not socialist either. There are affinities with Marxist analysis: the market is irrational, and exchange-value obliterates use-value, resulting in the fetishism of money. But labour and primary production are distinctly absent: no navvies are plunged into misery when the Jungfrau scheme folds. Only the lumpenproletariat exists here, from which Lulu came and to which she returns in Act III. Attention is focused not on the working man with female and child dependants as extra items in the calculation of misery, but on the woman Lulu; not on production or class, but on sex. Economic relations between the sexes are highlighted by reversals of the stereotyped roles still prevailing in *Earth Spirit*, where the woman in middle-class society depends on men. In Act I of *Pandora's Box*, Rodrigo describes how he will train Lulu to work for him as if she were an animal. Like Goll, he will use a whip, but his aim will be to increase income, not pleasure: women are so practical that it is far less trouble for a wife to support her husband than the other way round. In Act II, Rodrigo boasts of his Cölestine who has savings in the state bank from twenty years as a prostitute. She has three daughters, from whom he also hopes to profit. In a grotesque parody of the love match to which the middle classes pay lip-service, he claims that Cölestine loves him for himself. In Act III, Alwa also becomes a kept man, albeit more reluctantly than Rodrigo: he is kept by Lulu who was once kept by his father. In the first play the men endeavour to secure a good match for the surrogate daughter Lulu; here the mothers Magelone and Cölestine have kept their daughters by their labour and are trying to ensure their future.

The motif of kept men among the lumpenproletariat becomes an alienation technique: the analogy estranges the situation of the kept wife in respectable society. This is no doubt designed to *épater le bourgeois*, but it also reveals how attitudes towards gender shape conceptions such as the dignity of man or of labour, or the holiness of motherhood. In the feminine role of a breadwinner's love-object Rodrigo is without dignity, as is the female labour of Cölestine, who supports three daughters. Cölestine's daughters were by an American bishop. Had the bishop married her to a husband, she would have entered the holy state of matrimony; as it is she is a bishop's whore. In the terms of political rhetoric, the female labour of sex and motherhood possesses little intrinsic dignity. The emancipation of women, always an item on the socialist agenda, has been overshadowed by the interests of male organized labour. Wedekind was neither a socialist nor a feminist, but his centring of a deadly interaction of economics and gender still today offers a challenge to traditional socialist priorities and class rhetoric.

The Urban Jungle

In Act III of *Pandora's Box*, the eclectic furnishings which have until now been present throughout both plays have almost disappeared. A petroleum lamp offers a dim artificial light, later replaced by moonlight; a basin catches rain from a leaky roof. The trappings of civilization are wearing thin; the forces of nature look set to reassert themselves. The rain and the moonlight are the first intimations of the outdoors since the long roads along which Schigolch the tramp trudged towards death, the outer darkness of poverty from which Lulu emerged barefoot, and Escerny's African jungle. These three earlier motifs suggest three ideas which mix ambiguously in this closing act. First, Schigolch's intimations of mortality return as a vision of the brief, senseless course of life enclosed in endless darkness. Secondly, Lulu's original poverty is recalled as she complains about her worn boots and returns to the streets from which she once escaped. Continuing the role reversals, Lulu is here literally a *bread*winner as she goes out to earn money for food, clothes and shelter, the basic use-values hitherto obscured by the luxurious households or tinsel bohemia of the sets. Man cannot live by bread alone, but he cannot live without bread either, and a number of moments in Act III convey a materialist argument. Finally, the jungle is evoked again through savage Kungu Poti and bestial Jack the Ripper: the dark heart of human nature is everywhere, in the jungle or in the city of London. The three elements presage three types of modern theatre: the Theatre of the Absurd, Brechtian theatre, and Theatre of Cruelty.

The motif of mortality begins when Alwa asks Lulu whether she means to embark on her pilgrimage on the streets with bare feet; and a few lines later, Lulu wishes she were at the end of her pilgrimage, lying where no kick can reach her, an anticipation of Jack kicking her on to her back before carrying her off to the slaughter. Alwa continues the metaphor of a pilgrimage towards death when he proposes with gallows humour that they should harmoniously starve to death together: 'Es ist ja doch die letzte Station' (After all it's the end of the road – literally 'the last station' as in Christ's ascent to Calvary). Lulu once had to choose between prison or the brothel; the choice here turns out to be between starvation or the knife. Just before the arrival of his murderer Kungu Poti, Alwa mourns his sunny youth, and Schigolch declares that the lamp is about to go out: 'Bis sie zurückkommen, wird es hier dunkel wie im Mutterleib.' (By the time they get back it'll be as dark as the womb.) In context, the simile presents life telescopically as an instant passage from the darkness before birth to the darkness of death, anticipating Pozzo's comment in *Waiting for Godot*: 'They give birth astride of a grave, the light gleams an instant, then it's night once more' (Beckett, 1965: 89). In her first monologue, Geschwitz sees life as a succession of disconnected moments as human beings pass from one desire to another with no continuity or identity or purpose. Only the body continues unchanged for a time; pursuit of pleasure brings only misery; we come closest to happiness when we are materially poor and can rejoice over the slightest morsel. Such pessimism measures life in terms of endings: even as we are born, the final end of death renders existence absurd.

Lulu's painted image stands in opposition to this grim litany. Lulu is at first horrified by the contrast between the portrait and her appearance, now ravaged by prison, disease and poverty, but cheers up when Alwa and Schigolch celebrate her past beauty and still childlike eyes. As Schigolch declares: 'Sie kann mit Selbstbewußtsein sagen: Das war ich mal!' (She can say with confidence: I was once that!) Roland Barthes (1980) writes similarly of photographs in the vocabulary of phenomenology. The *noema* of the photograph is 'That has been'; it testifies to the real existence *in the past* of its referent. To Lulu and to those who know her, the portrait acts in the same way as his mother's photograph did for Barthes. The *punctum* of the portrait is the eyes; they reveal an inner identity between the Lulu of the past and the Lulu of the present. They establish her right to 'Selbstbewußtsein' (literally, self-awareness), and testify to her personal continuity despite bodily changes. This is the opposite of Geschwitz's claim that only the body lasts for a while: the eyes symbolize a continuing self, Lulu's essence.

However, the testimony of past existence is double-edged. Photographs, and here the portrait, are a *memento mori*, for they say: this has been, is no longer so, and will cease to be. As a physical object too the portrait is marked by time: the paint is flaking round the edges where Geschwitz has cut it from its frame. Like a fading photograph, it exhales melancholy. At the same time, a painting, in contrast to mechanical photographic reproduction (for Barthes the guarantee of the past existence of the referent), testifies to the intentionality of a maker: this was made and someone saw thus. Geschwitz observes: 'Es muß ein eminent begabter Künstler gewesen sein, der das gemalt hat!'

(It must have been an outstandingly gifted artist who painted that!). She speaks before Wimsatt and Beardsley (1946) discovered the intentional fallacy and Barthes killed the author (1984), a deed he half undoes in *La Chambre Claire*. Geschwitz's comment has a double force. It recalls Schwarz's ghastly end – he is indeed 'gewesen', has been – but also the fact that he once had a vision fuelled by eros, and that the portrait communicates that vision through time. The existence of the portrait makes Jack's butchery more dreadful, as the extinction of a person who is more than a senseless succession of moods. At the end of Goetz Friedrich's Covent Garden production of Berg's *Lulu*, Jack slashes the portrait, losing something of the subtle last image: Geschwitz crawling towards her angel, at whose side she would stay for all eternity, dying under the childlike eyes of the portrait before she can reach Lulu. Her dying words are: 'O verflucht!' (O damnation!). Utopian innocence and beauty look down on inexorable division and blood-drenched horror. Depending on how we understand the horror, the juxtaposition may be seen as merely turning the baroque *vanitas* into secular *absurditas*, or as a black satire of an historical evil which has destroyed the human potential for freedom and happiness.

Interwoven with existential pessimism, but different in tone, is a series of motifs concerning basic necessities. The dripping rain, besides any metaphorical connotations, conveys poverty, as do the bare room, dim light and poor clothing. Alwa and Schigolch dream of food; Lulu worries lest her miserable clothes put off potential customers. It is cold, a cold the old man feels most keenly. The characters are bound together by need if nothing else. Alwa, whose intellectual decline began in Act II, is now physically incapable of earning a living, having caught venereal disease from Casti-Piani via Lulu: Pandora's most feared gift came to her from a man. In a scurrilous parody of 'chagrin d'amour qui dure toute la vie', Schigolch wishes that Hunidei should not forget Lulu until his dying day. For good or ill human beings affect, or infect, one another. After Alwa's murder, the scavenger Schigolch goes off downstairs to the inn for food and perhaps to share the landlady's bed. The view of life under the aspect of death leads him to conclusions different from Geschwitz's sense of empty absurdity: he cannot be disappointed in the search for spiritual communion or transcendent meaning, since he has never looked for them. To stay alive and enjoy what he can is his aim in life. To this end money in necessary, but he never makes a fetish of money. When Lulu was rich he asked for what he needed and, since she was not enthralled by wealth either, she gave. In Paris he was the only man more interested in Lulu's flesh than her exchange-value; even Alwa was so excited by stocks and shares that he was oblivious to all else. Schigolch has used his disreputable skills over the years to help Lulu wherever possible, and in a parody of an elderly parent he now expects his child to do what she can for him. Schigolch is not undignified when he asks women for money, food or comfort, for he has no pretensions to lose. He is a true amoral hedonist with no mask of respectability. He has been compared with Phorkyas-Mephisto in Part II of *Faust* as representing amorphous nature from which all comes and to which all must return (Rothe, 1968: 36). Like Phorkyas, Schigolch is clownish. His evening dress in Act II parodies bourgeois style, just as his 'yes-yeses' in Act III parody the English gentleman. He introduces what Bakhtin (1984) calls 'carnivalization', a subversive comedy which laughs at sex and death and the last things of life, offering a comic alternative to Geschwitz's disappointed idealism. The food he and Alwa dream of is festive: steak, champagne and cigarettes, and Christmas pudding. He would die happy, he says, after a portion of Christmas pudding.

In eating the wintry pudding, Schigolch would partake of his own funeral feast which also celebrates new birth at Christmas. The earthly cycle of fertility links food, sex and death in an older vision than the baroque elevation of death over life under the sign of a transcendent eternity. This earthy vision does battle with Geschwitz's pessimism and with her penultimate prayer for eternal union with her angel Lulu. For Geschwitz, eternity means personal survival and spiritual union with an individual. Because she starts from this individualist value, the failure of love seems grim, robbing life of meaning. Schigolch's talk of death and Christmas pudding, by contrast, subsumes individual death in a communal cycle of renewal. He lives on the edge of death, for his amoralism makes him as little fit to make money as Lulu is, whether in Schön's world where the mask of hypocrisy is essential, or in Casti-Piani's where money has extinguished all other pleasures. It is inconceivable that Schigolch might work for a wage: such an alienation is foreign to him and to the Lulu plays. This marks the limits of the realism and materialism expressed through Schigolch: human beings must reproduce themselves and produce their subsistence. The Lulu plays explore sex, but dissociated from reproduction, and they criticize the economic system of capitalism, but dissociated from basic production. Schigolch's vision is archaic; it belongs to a pre-class, agricultural world. But Schigolch does not speak from within a self-renewing community; he stands outside all community. His anti-heroic amoralism, like Hugenberg's heroism, is not a path to freedom and, like Hugenberg before him, Schigolch takes himself off-stage before the final catastrophe. Jack's disembowelling of Lulu delivers a fatal blow to the archaic life-cycle, a blow the detached Schigolch can and will do nothing to prevent. The plays offer no historical solution to the catastrophe, but neither do they integrate it into a timeless, earthly cycle.

Geschwitz, by contrast, fights to the end, inheriting Hugenberg's heroic role in a game with theatrical and sexual stereotypes: Hugenberg is played by a girl, while the lesbian Geschwitz takes over the masculine role of protector. Schigolch, not noted for his admiration of virtue, comments that she has guts enough for ten men. Unlike Hugenberg, however, Geschwitz is sophisticated and self-aware. She constantly undermines her own heroism by means of commentary on her actions similar to Melchior's view of morality in *Spring Awakening*: her unfailing aid to Lulu is not altruistic, for it is motivated by desire. Her first assistance involved acquiring cholera through an exchange of knickers, a deseased sexual contact at long distance, marking, like Alwa's venereal disease, the corruption of eros. Her thraldom to Lulu is shameful. In a terrible reduction of the self, all else fades before one obsession. Her condition is a sour post-script to the romance tradition. The ardent lover, the knight errant who would save the maiden, is here alienated as a lesbian woman. She is ludicrous to others and, more terribly, to herself. Heterosexual Lulu drags her by the rope she tried to hang herself with, as if it were a collar and lead, and says 'Kusch dich!' (Sit!). Heterosexual Jack pats her on the head and calls her a monster before killing her. Adopting the vision of heterosexual society, she sees herself as grotesque. In *Earth Spirit*, Geschwitz was seen externally as a parody of male attitudes; here we see her through her own eyes, that is, from the perspective of a self-proclaimed monster. The effect is a reversal of values: the monster is human and the 'normal' human beings are monstrous. Geschwitz may not be morally admirable, but her readiness to help, even at the risk of death and finally without hope of sexual reward, suggests a basic social faculty rooted in eros, which is a counterpoise to Lulu's isolation. Her intelligence lends weight to her anger and suffering. But Geschwitz's individual commitment to another individual, Lulu, cannot save her. For a moment she contemplates a move into the political domain:

DIE GESCHWITZ: *(allein, spricht wie im Traum)* Dies ist der letzte Abend, den ich mit diesem Volk verbringe – Ich kehre nach Deutschland zurück. Meine Mutter schickt mir das Reisegeld. – Ich lasse mich immatrikulieren. Ich muß für Frauenrechte kämpfen, Jurisprudenz studieren.

GESCHWITZ: *(alone, as if in a dream) This is the last evening I shall spend with these people – I shall return to Germany. My mother will send me the fare. – I shall matriculate. I must fight for women's rights, study jurisprudence.*

Lulu's screams disperse the utopian dream. The stage direction, 'as if in a dream', underlines the unreality. In Angela Carter's *The Bloody Chamber* (1979a), a reworking of the Bluebeard legend, the heroine's magnificent mother arrives as a *dea ex machina* to save her daughter. But there is no such help to hand here, and no sign that Wedekind would have welcomed a squad of educated mothers and daughters. The frail moment of political vision seems incongruous and puny beside what follows.

These various motifs continue to form a bleak and ambiguous picture. Archaic community is no more; Schigolch's earth gods have been overthrown by Christian faith in personal survival. But Christianity is tainted by a repressive morality. Modern secularism has not brought liberation, merely isolation and a corroding sense of absurdity. Return to Schigolch's archaic world is impossible; to attempt that would be to follow the path of Nazi mythology, a tendency quite absent from the play. The economic jungle of modern capitalism seems instead to have brought regression to a pre-cultural bestialized humanity. Only the portrait offers a fragile vision of hope, like the hope in Pandora's box. The question is, do the beasts who emerge from the London streets confirm such cultural pessimism, revealing a timeless horror and belying the hope?

Jack, a human beast from the urban jungle, fulfils the promise of the Prologue to *Earth Spirit*. He is preceded by three other clients, and the four of them recall in grotesque distortion many earlier motifs. People from all over the world walk the streets of the metropolis. The first and last clients are local, with a citizen of Basel and an African prince in between. The first three are associated with the spirit, the body and the mind. The Englishman Hunidei is hunnish in name and 'hünenhaft' (of giant stature) in appearance. His body suggests brute power, but he has eyes of heavenly blue and carries a religious pamphlet. The Englishman arouses only contempt in Schigolch because the brute power has been overlaid by soulful English hypocrisy. Hunidei is generous, capering about absurdly when Lulu expresses gratitude. In his overcoat and top hat, he recalls the rich men like Goll who pay for their pleasures but preserve the outer respectable facade of dead religious beliefs. His eerie silence cloaks the voice of a preacher, perhaps, a man of the word, and keeps the commerce with Lulu unnamed and unacknowledged. He wants no communion with a soul, only intercourse with a body. After the spiritual pilgrim comes the coarsely physical Kungu Poti, all brawn and little brain, who delivers the *coup de grâce* to Alwa, who is all brain and little brawn. To Kungu Poti, sex is a physical need in the same category as eating, to be satisfied with female flesh. His constant belching shows him to be as gross an eater as he is a lover. He recalls Monostatos in *The Magic Flute*, a savage with a simple way with women. Europeans seeking hidden depths in the jungle will find only a potentate who does not take baths and is even meaner with money than a Swiss university lecturer. This is no mythic embodiment of primitive passion, but a grotesque parody of European manhood, an African parading European clothes, a mockery of the imperialist fantasies of the primitive nurtured by Escerny. Kungu Poti is a vulgar racial stereotype, but his hissing African consonants are no more absurd than Hunidei's silence or Dr Hilti's Swiss German – guaranteed to raise a laugh from a German audience; and then there is Jack.

In such company the incipient racism in the presentation of Kungu Poti becomes part of a general attack on man's inhumanity to woman. Like earlier lovers, Kungu Poti too appropriates Lulu, by naming her Ragapsischimulara, the last of her names and as unpronouncable as Rumpelstilzchen. Kungu Poti and Hunidei, parodistic embodiments of man's physical needs and spiritual aspirations respectively, cast a grotesque shadow over all the male characters. Dr Hilti, the man of mind, a University teacher and scion of the Basel patriciate, has lived frugally, as scholars do. Like Rodrigo and Casti-Piani, he is more interested in money than sex and has better things to do with his pocket-money of two florins than spend it on women. When Lulu asks if his fiancée is pretty he replies 'Yes, she's got two million' – even prettier, then, than the bride Schwarz once found who was worth only a quarter of that. A virgin, he has come to Lulu to prepare for his wedding night as for an examination. Dr Hilti recalls Schwarz and the baneful connection between money and marriage; and, like the other two, he strengthens the social satire rather than evoking eternal human nature.

Jack the Ripper has the animalesque features of a powerful, low-set physique and springy gait. When he follows Lulu after his first attack on her, he bends low to avoid Geschwitz's gun and runs a knife into his victim, like an animal which has been worrying its prey and is ready to spring again. His deep breathing and staring red-rimmed eyes suggest animal growling and the hypnotic gaze of a beast of prey. His hands are fiery red when he first arrives and later drip blood, reminiscent of a human butcher rather than an animal. Instead of claws he has the bitten nails of a neurotic human being; and other banal features conflict with his animalesque attributes. Unlike Hunidei and Kungu Poti, Jack is not dressed as a wealthy bourgeois, but could be a small shopkeeper, a butcher perhaps, in his overcoat and bowler hat. The meanest of the clients, he bargains with the skill of a shopkeeper and talks Lulu into paying *him*, the culmination of the financial role reversals. (In his Paris diaries Wedekind tells of trying to avoid having to pay for a cab when going home with a prostitute; of girls who offered a night for nothing; of an animal trainer whom the prostitutes paid for sexual services rendered.) The surface banality of his appearance is more frightening than a savage from Uahubee: he could be anyone from the drab London streets, the man next door, the shopkeeper from down the road. In the manner of an artisan he washes his hands after a job well done, drying them on Geschwitz's underskirt. The pleasure he takes in his good fortune has the ring of someone who has had a bit of luck in business. His contempt for the miserable attic and lack of towels suggests a decent well-kept household back home.

All these features place Jack among the ranks of small businessmen, down-market of the rich men in *Earth Spirit* or the would-be shareholders in Paris. The earlier financial dealings are here reduced to a client screwing money from a prostitute for his bus fare home. Schön was also a man of commerce and wanted a decent, clean household. Jack repeats his words: 'Das war ein Stück Arbeit', linking Lulu's slaughter to Schwarz's end and suggesting that masochistic self-annihilation can turn into sadistic annihilation of the other. The flight and pursuit look back to Schwarz chasing Lulu round the studio, and his fantasy of a reluctant virgin. This is Lulu's first time as a prostitute, she tells Jack, who thus has the pleasure of slaughtering a virgin-prostitute. Jack is something of a connoisseur of female beauty. Despite dim street lighting and Lulu's poor clothes, he can tell from her walk that she is well built, a detail which recalls the aesthetes at the beginning of *Earth Spirit* and Lulu in the theatre illuminated in stage lighting in the first poor costume Alwa specified. Jack is drawn by her mouth, never mentioning the childlike eyes. The second time he attacks her, when his hands are dripping blood, the mention of the mouth, a passage into the body, takes on an especially obscene undertone. To Jack, Lulu is not a person at all but purely genitalia. In Notebook 5 (p. 14; 40v), Wedekind notes Casanova's association of mouth and genitals. In a study of male fantasies, Klaus Theweleit (1983: 189–209) documents this association horrifically and queries Freud's view that the female genitals arouse fear because they look like a castration wound; in his view, the fear comes rather from the threat of engulfment or castration by the *vagina dentata*. When Lulu persuaded Schön to marry her he cried out: 'Jetzt – kommt die – Hinrichtung' (Now – for the – execution). The cry expresses fear of engulfment by Lulu and by his own love and desire for her. The cry is doubly prophetic. Lulu is indeed the death of him, but her act is precipitated by his own murderous impulse which comes to fruition through Jack. Jack does not wait as long as Schön before trying murder; in murdering Lulu on their first meeting and her first night as a prostitute, he asserts the right of possession and destroys any threat of engulfment, whether physical or emotional. Jack's excision of Lulu's genitals in the *Monstretragödie* suggests hatred combined with possessiveness. The prostitute accessible to all men is contemptible, but also frightening, for she suggests that men are interchangeable, thus threatening masculine power and identity. In killing a prostitute, Jack destroys the threat of being reduced to a cypher, one man who might as well be another. This is the horror which grips Schön in his mad vision of multiplying lovers, echoed also in Kungu Poti's and Dr Hilti's horror on discovering that they are not alone with Lulu.

If Jack sees Lulu solely as genitalia, Lulu reduces both herself and her partner in the same way. The men are interchangeable; all that matters is their sex, through which she seeks confirmation of her sexuality. Lulu began as a dream women who would be whatever men desired; but the dream culminates in nightmare as a man with a knife confronts a woman with a broken-off bottle. But in this battle of the sexes the odds are in man's favour. Lulu's career began in hypocritical bourgeois society where women are bought and sold: a transaction decently obscured by marriage or the secret liaison; more openly revealed in the free world of Paris; quite overt in London street-prostitution. At the close of *Pandora's Box* the commercial relation is reversed, as Lulu tries to buy Jack's services. But like the other reversals, it leaves untouched the real power relations, physical and social, between men and women. In this world men win the battle, turning to monsters in the process. Though the pessimistic strain of existential horror is strong, the bleak vision of regression to bestiality is intimately linked with more specific social and economic critique. The many parallels linking Jack and the clients with Lulu's earlier lovers bring to a culmination the social and commercial relations explored previously; they suggest that *Earth Spirit* and Acts I and II of *Pandora's Box* explain Act III, rather than the reverse. It is not male or female sexuality as such, but the depersonalized forms they assume historically which are destructive. In a society of institutionalized male power, the thought-experiment of a woman free of sexual inhibitions but in every other way subject to male domination can only end badly. The very object of desire, the sexually free woman, is in her freedom a threat to male power, but in her weakness a threat which can be destroyed. Lulu is crucially subject to male domination through her exclusively sexual (and heterosexual) nature. She has no other interests than intercourse with men, and her sexuality is a mirror of masculine fantasies. Even Geschwitz scarcely escapes a reductive vision of woman defined through the perspective of masculine desire, which makes her a monster. Lesbian fulfilment, in contrast to homosexual fulfilment in *Spring Awakening*, is not only absent but irrelevant. The next section will consider Lulu, the sexually liberated woman who is really a reflection of masculine ideas of freedom.

Freedom and the Social Animal

In *Spring Awakening*, the city promises freedom. In *Earth Spirit*, the promise proves illusory. The issue is posed anew at the beginning of *Pandora's Box* as the characters plan Lulu's escape from a German prison to an international world free of the moralizing hypocrisy of German society. Freedom, descended from the emancipatory thought of the Enlightenment, is the core value in nineteenth-century liberalism. It has a double aspect in the economic doctrine of free trade and in moral and political ideals such as those enshrined in the American Declaration of Independence – the right to life, liberty and the pursuit of happiness. Liberty, the political aspect of freedom, designates the rights of the citizen against external threats of *force majeure*. But there are other threats. Lulu, lacking social conditioning, is initially inwardly free to pursue happiness, which she offers as a gift to men. But they fail to be happy because they cannot bear her freedom and are themselves psychologically unfree. The Masked Man's mask of bourgeois respectability invades the mind, destroying autonomy. The would-be free individuals meet external barriers such as the legal and financial inequality of the sexes and the internal effects of social conventions threatening the rational exercise of free will.

Lulu's imprisonment evokes *force majeure* ot the most obvious kind. The same fear she felt under Goll's dead gaze attacks her alone in prison until she is able to see her image reflected in the shiny surface of the shovel she is given to clean out her cell. A Narcissus communing with herself, her reflected image confirms her sense of identity. But such self-nourishment is difficult to sustain. Lulu is hungry for freedom and human contact. An operatic genre of the Romantic age, close to theatrical melodrama, was the *Rettungsoper* in which a hero is saved from unjust imprisonment. In Act I, Lulu's ringing exclamation: 'O Freiheit! Herr Gott im Himmel!' (O freedom! Dear God in Heaven!) is worthy of the prisoners' chorus in *Fidelio*. Operatic prisoners greet release into the open air: 'O welche Lust, in freier Luft/ Den Atem leicht zu heben!' (Oh what joy to breath freely in the open air!: *Fidelio*, I, 9). Lulu longed for curtains, armchairs, pictures; deprivation of the cultural artefacts with which human beings define themselves is as painful as lack of fresh air. Operatic prisoners are full of fraternal feeling. Lulu is hungry for union with anyone of the male sex; even the inadequate Alwa will do. There is no trace of sisterly feeling for the symbolically titled Sister Theophila, nor for Geschwitz, a Leonore to her Floristan, languishing in prison in her stead. Sociability is reduced to the sexual drive. Lulu's reactions anticipate the hero of Döblin's post-Expressionist novel of 1929, *Berlin Alexanderplatz*, whose first deed on being released from prison is to confirm his masculinity by raping the sister of the woman for whose murder he went to prison. Lulu confirms her femininity by seducing the son of the man for whose murder she went to prison. The pain of sexual deprivation is less openly acknowledged for women, so Wedekind's play may shock the prudish more than Döblin's novel. The shock effect expresses condemnation of the penal system; encaging the human animal dehumanizes. But it is also a proto-Brechtian mockery of Schillerian or Beethovenian idealization of the human spirit in adversity. Act II goes on to show what happens to the values of German classicism and European liberalism in the free market economy.

The threat posed to the male psyche by the fear of loss of freedom is a perennial topic, but the freedom-hungry woman is more ambiguous. Ibsen's Nora has to throw off the role of the caring female; but at least she does not abdicate in response to mere sexual urges. Wagner's Isolde, a great romantic heroine, follows a sexual urge, but one which is legitimized by an alternative morality because it is focused on a great romantic hero. Lulu's is a more radical freedom from moral constraint. In *Earth Spirit* there is little sign that Lulu betrays Schön, except to his order before marriage and in his imagination afterwards. In *Pandora's Box* she is retrospectively transformed into a fully fledged libertine, in Alwa's words, a latter-day Catherine the Great. She has female predecessors in an operatic tradition I shall discuss in the next chapter, but the closest parallel is an illustrious male ancestor, Don Giovanni. In Act I Rodrigo presents a catalogue of Lulu's husbands and lovers and tells how he and Schigolch, Leporellos to her Donna Giovanna, roamed the cafés to find a male Zerlina, the virgin Hugenberg. In the original play from which *Don Giovanni* is derived, written in 1630 by Tirso de Molina (1982), the Don's crime was less the ruin of women than the murder of a father, an act flouting patriarchy and an irreligious assertion of Man's freedom in the face of Divine Law. The seduced women are cyphers in a drama between Man and God the Father. In murdering Schön, Lulu disposes of a father-figure, her husband, and the father of her next lover and husband in a clean sweep of the patriarchy. Her deed might seem to turn the tables in revenge for all the faceless cyphers ruined by men, whether seducers or tyrannical guardians of patriarchal law. But the role reversal also highlights the chilling coldness of Don Juan; the kind of freedom which reduces others to a cypher brings with it terrible isolation. Exploits which may seem bold, even admirable in a man, as in Mozart/da Ponte's ambiguous handling of the theme, are estranged when committed by a woman.

Happiness, the pursuit of which is the third right in the American Declaration, is close to the libertine value of pleasure. Like freedom, pleasure without reciprocity brings isolation. In Jack, Wedekind's Donna Giovanna meets a sadist at the extreme end of libertinism; but there is a possible hint of a secret identity between Jack and Lulu, who treats Geschwitz sadistically. In his novels *Justine ou les malheurs de la vertu* and *Juliette ou les prosperités du vice*, de Sade divides women into innocent Justine and her sister, the libertine Juliette. To the men around her, Lulu is both: she is ever innocent and ever voracious. Justine, the forbidden object of a repressive culture, is entirely subject to the male will as it asserts its freedom in desecrating innocence. The victim must remain innocent (that is, must never feel pleasure) in order to be subject to ever renewed, ever more extreme desecration. For Justine, the culmination is her destruction by God, as a bolt of lightning passes through her mouth and out of her vagina – the passages of the body Wedekind's Jack is also drawn to – to the delight of the audience of libertines male and female, like the audience in the Prologue to *Earth Spirit*. With Justine's destruction, the reign of evil is complete, as it is at the end of *Pandora's Box*, signalled in Geschwitz's 'Verflucht!'.

Juliette is the antithesis of Justine. Freed of all vestiges of femininity and humanity, she asserts her unbridled will in a series of ever more appalling abominations which culminate in her throwing her daughter into the fire. Commenting on Sadeian logic, Angela Carter (1979b: 78–9) writes that being a woman is like being poor, but is more easily remedied; the woman who abandons 'the praxis of femininity' can enter the class of the rich, the men, on the terms of that class. In *Pandora's Box*, the condition of being a woman is not so easily remedied, for the men cannot bear Lulu's freedom from the 'praxis of femininity'. Jack's deed is a double slaughter: he destroys Juliette in order to preserve virginal Justine, but Justine simultaneously falls victim to the same brutal assertion of power. If Lulu is a descendant of Juliette, unlike her predecessor she remains powerless.

Lulu's affinities with Juliette, stronger in the *Monstretragödie*, are strictly limited in the final version of the plays, and her sadism, as far as it goes, is directed at another woman over whom she has power. Female sadism towards men is liable to lack conviction. Women rarely have the power or physical strength to carry out the sadistic programme for real rather than as a game while the double morality persistently defines man as agent and woman as acted-upon forbidden object. Nonetheless, it remains a recurrent fantasy, as Andrea Dworkin (1981) documents. Fantasies of female sadism generally take the form of strictly controlled role-playing such as Escerny's dream in *Earth Spirit*, an example of that 'most delicious titillation, of compensating but spurious female dominance' (Carter, 1979b; 20). Escerny's fantasy is just a Rococo game, a chapter of soft porn from *Fanny Hill*, for the true power relations are too obvious. A more full-blooded version is the murder or unmanning of an aroused male or a male in love with the murderess. Polanski's *Repulsion* or Oshima's *Empire of the Senses* are modern examples. Several Biblical prototypes were popular at the turn of the century. The Biblical Judith, Delilah, Salome and her mother Herodias did not murder or unman for sexual gratification, but that is how they are presented in voyeuristic fantasies. The implied observer of Klimt's exultant Judith, with her sexy come-on look and a gold collar round her neck, is male; fresh from the kill, she is ripe for subjection herself. Wilde's *Salome* is a theatrical example of the same kind of presentation.

Early productions of *Earth Spirit* in the ambit of the Strauss opera provoked Wedekind in his Prologue to complain about overheated playing of his heroine. Lulu does not murder for sexual gratification; this is quite clear when she murders Schön. But when she orders the death of Rodrigo, the sinister obscenity of her repeated 'Besorg es ihm' (Take care of him) allows a double meaning to the voyeuristic audience. The whole episode is imbued with a sexual aura as Schigolch swears on her ankle (in the *Monstretragödie* on her genitals):

SCHIGOLCH: (*legt seine Hand an ihren Fußknöchel*) – Bei allem, was heilig ist! – Heute nacht, wenn er kommt. –

LULU: Bei allem, was heilig ist! – Wie das kühlt!

SCHIGOLCH: Wie das glüht!

SCHIGOLCH: (*lays his hand on her ankle*) – *By all that's holy!* – *This evening, when he comes.*

LULU: *By all that's holy! – How that cools!*

SCHIGOLCH: *How that glows!*

Schigolch speaks for a male audience in implying Lulu's sexual warmth as she envisages the murder of a man in a state of sexual readiness – Rodrigo believes he is to render sexual services to Geschwitz. The episode offers the illusion of female blood-lust combined with an even cruder Roman-circus motif, a terrified woman forced into the male role of killer but doomed in the end to be rent to pieces. The theatrical effect comes from the thrilling spectacle for a voyeuristic audience of a woman who is killer and terrified victim in one. But unlike Schigolch, Lulu is moved by fear rather than lust, as her indifferent response to his sexual proposal shows: 'Wenn es weiter nichts ist?' (Is that all?). The play, then, re-enacts for the audience of the Prologue the very fantasies it excoriates. The double appeal of sadistic killer and masochistic victim in one is a theatrical shadow looming behind the foreground of solid critique of male exploitation and cruelty. The extent to which the shadow obscures the critique will depend on production and on how far the mentality of a real audience corresponds to the mentality of the audience of the Prologue, or to that of the London audience Wedekind describes in his diary, baying at the spectacle of a virginal heroine with her hands tied behind her back (Hay: 315–16).

A similar double effect pervades the murder of Lulu. Here de Sade's schematic rationalism is modified by nineteenth-century Romanticism. According to de Sade's rules, Justine cannot reciprocate. But in order to fulfil all the latter-day fantasies Lulu must respond physically and emotionally; she must be at once innocent, predatory and ecstatically yielding. Yet the Romantic sadist's dream is ever-receding: it is impossible to enforce the maximum of forbidden pleasure in the innocent yet yielding object while simultaneously subjecting it to the maximum of pain and fear, so achieving the maximum destruction of the taboos. The black-romantic *Liebestod* requires a coincidence of death and orgasm in the object: Lulu's screams as she is disembowelled should be ecstatic. At least three critics have treated Lulu's death as a *Liebestod* (Rothe, 1968: 57; Hahn I: 45; Fritz: 1977). David Midgely (1985: 224), however, argues convincingly that Rothe's textual argument is unsound. To be sure, even as a child Lulu loved to read the story of Tristan and Isolde, but any echo of the legend at the end of the play can only be a parody, like Thomas Mann's *Tristan*. In neither case is there a union in death; the lover remains all too alive, Jack complacent at a job well done, Spinell downing a comforting swig of brandy, the water of life.

Such asymmetrical outcomes travesty the Wagnerian *Liebestod*. But the final version retains a number of sufficiently ambiguous motifs, suggesting if not a *Liebestod* at least an analogy with the consummation of a love match: Lulu is the virgin prostitute; her broken-off bottle recalls the scratching with nails and feigned reluctance of the Rococo nymph; Jack carries her across the bridal threshold; her screams recall initial reluctance and the pain of deflowering, followed by the ecstacy of consummation. But such echoes do not show that Lulu embraces death or that female sexuality is masochistic and death-directed. Rather, they recall in parody Schwarz's sentimental dream and uncover the sadistic undertones in the cult of virginity. The epithalamium turns to gruesome horror as the blood-rite of deflowering, the act of possession, becomes a bloody excision. Lulu may have dreamed of falling victim to a sex murderer, but faced with the reality she resists violently.

As with Rodrigo's death, the voyeuristic spectators of the Wedekind circus are offered a double image: in the foreground, terrified woman facing ravening beast; in the background, masochistic victim embracing the knife. But the pornographic thrill offered by either image is undermined by Geschwitz's way of seeing, so different from that of an implied bloodthirsty audience, and by the many features of Jack which rob him of aura, making him ludicrous as much as horrific. Such mockery is detumescent. It demystifies, saving the play from that characteristic of high-class pornography Andrea Dworkin pinpoints, 'death is the stunning essence of sex' (1981: 175). As Midgley (1985) shows, Lulu's sadism and masochism in the *Monstretragödie* are toned down in the published plays and largely placed as the outgrowth of masculine fantasies. Nonetheless, to achieve full theatrical and indeed critical effect, the pornographic thrill must not be entirely absent, nor is it possible to control what happens to that thrill in the minds of actual spectators and critics.

Masculinity and Femininity in the Lulu Plays

The focus in *Earth Spirit* and *Pandora's Box* is primarily masculine, and Lulu plays her multiple roles for men. But the female spectator can also construct a perspective on typically feminine fantasies. The role reversals work in both directions, for if Lulu is a Donna Giovanna, Schwarz's typically feminine dream of ideal marriage to an ideal partner in an ideal home is unmasked as ludicrous when transferred to a man. Similarly, virginity, which many women think proper only in a woman, becomes absurd in Schwarz and his alter ego Hilti; the plays subvert such ingrained attitudes. Women dream of being fascinatingly seductive, and girls educated in convents long, like Kadidja, to go on the stage. Women, possibly more than men, dream of the one true lover, after whom life can never be the same, a Heathcliff complex touched on in Lulu's feelings for Schön. Such a relationship is bound to be a battle unresolved in the truce of marriage, since marriage is the death of romance and equality. Schön's unseen, sick, first wife is the equivalent of Cathy married and dying in child-birth, or the mad Mrs Rochester banished to her attic. The gentler versions of masochism may be attractive to women, though generally we would prefer a Sheikh of Araby to an ugly old roué like Goll. The Sheikh dream, the feminine equivalent of Escerny's imperialist masochism, is less appealing, however, if the harem is a Cairo brothel. Geschwitz's masochistic revelling in unrequited love, fuelled anew by every humiliation, is an all too familiar pattern of feeling among men and women alike. To judge by the work of Genet or Fassbinder, such power rituals are as prevalent among homosexuals as heterosexuals. Just as women's imagination is imbued with a predominantly masculine culture which imaginatively heightens or reverses real power relations, so the games between the sexes extend into homosexual experience. Neither is Lulu alone in being fascinated with her own image; the multiple images of women in the visual arts, the cinema and advertising appeal to men as objects of desire, to women as objects of identification. The self-alienation is caught at the close of Mankiewicz's *All about Eve* as star struck Eve holds the leading lady's dress to her body and watches her own image multiplied endlessly in mirrors. Men are also depersonalized, turned into faceless observers of the all-powerful image. As the multiplying mirror-images suggest, Eve will leave the stage for Hollywood. Although they focus on theatre, the Lulu plays strikingly anticipate cinema's debate with itself about the power of the image.

Thus the plays capture both feminine and masculine fantasies; but they also show the differences between them. The most brutal assertion of power and the extremes of sadism, the realm of hard porn, are shown to be male and only fleetingly tinge Lulu's assertion of freedom. The plays show how dreams rooted in a long tradition of sexual morality falling unevenly on men and women are modified in a society where sex has become a commodity. This is the main critical thrust. The fantasies of *Earth Spirit*, measured in Act II of *Pandora's Box* against the brutal reality of the market, return in grotesque fragmentation in the last act and culminate in Jack's destruction of the object of desire. The female genitals become literally depersonalized possession as Lulu is destroyed, and with her the initial dream of sex freed from ancient taboos on female sexuality. The plays demonstrate the way in which the reification of female sexuality robs men of autonomy in robbing men and women alike of free interaction with one another. If Lulu initially represents a dream of liberated sexuality, by the end of the play the dream is deconstructed.

The deconstruction of the dream gives the plays bite in our time, when the sexual revolution has apparently freed women to be sexually active, but in many cases has actually freed them to be sexually available. The kept woman in the Lulu mould is no longer a contemporary figure, and Geschwitz's vision of rights for women has been partially realized. But the imagination lags behind changing social structures; though the cult of technical virginity has weakened, the other fantasies still haunt relations between the sexes, while sexual revolution in a consumer market has intensified a reification of sex which mixes possessiveness and depersonalized rapacity. In sum, the plays contain much that is in line with feminist attack on socio-economic inequalities, but foreshadow current disillusion with the liberal programme as merely freeing women to become like men. Liberal and socialist feminism oppose sharp differentiation between the sexes, arguing that, basic biology apart, men and women share the same human potential and that gender differences are culturally induced; the supposed inadequacies of the emancipatory programme are simply a sign that it has not yet been fully achieved. Radical feminists, by contrast, stress sexual difference. When women ape men they do violence to their essential female nature. Just as the plays deconstruct the initial liberal programme, they are similarly ambiguous about the female essence. Lulu is addressed in the Prologue to *Earth Spirit* as the 'Urgestalt des Weibs' (the primal form of woman). She has some of the qualities which anti-feminists like Nietzsche or Weininger and sexual theorists like Simmel, with no anti-feminist intent, attribute to women: they are close to nature, ruled by bodily instinct rather than intellectual and moral rationality. But it is difficult to disentangle the 'Urgestalt' from the images imposed by men. In the last act of *Pandora's Box*, Alwa lightly offers a weighty comment on sexual difference:

ALWA: ... (*Leicht hinwerfend.*) Das Weib blüht für uns in dem Moment, wo es den Menschen auf Lebenszeit ins Verderben stürzen soll. Das ist nun einmal so seine Naturbestimmung.

ALWA: ... (*Carelessly.*) *Woman blossoms for us just at the moment when she is doomed to plunge human beings into lifelong ruin. It's her natural destiny.*

Alwa distinguishes 'das Weib' (woman) from 'den Menschen' (human beings) as if women were a species apart. Woman blossoms for us, that is men, in whom humanity is located; though another reading could be that sexuality in woman ruins humanity in both sexes. Some radical-feminist separatists posit a fundamental antagonism between the sexes, arguing Alwa's claim in reverse: men are fatally destructive of humanity and all potential Jack the Rippers. The plays might seem to bear out such a view, for in context Alwa's comment is absurd; by that point it is all too evident that the ruin is brought about by men. But the destructiveness is linked to social and cultural influences rather than maleness, suggesting that it is not an inevitable doom laid on mankind. The plays use essentialist vocabulary only to undermine it.

This was perhaps not Wedekind's intention; elsewhere he insists on the unbridgeable and fascinating difference between the sexes (Notebook 5: 9; 19r). Yet rather than female sexuality, Lulu embodies a masculine ideal of freedom. To that extent sexual difference is undermined; although the partial dismantling does not bring pansexual liberation, but leaves Lulu entangled in masculine visions. The portrait evokes a utopia transcending the gulf between the sexes, but it does so by obscuring Lulu's female shape, by drawing her back to childhood, by alienating her as an image on canvas. In person, she turns up the leg of her costume in a reassertion of difference and as an object for male eyes. Whereas Lulu, visually the 'Urgestalt des Weibs', is psychologically liberated from femininity, the lesbian Geschwitz bears the traditional feminine value of devoted love. Hugenberg, who loves generously, is still close to childhood and is played by a girl. Alwa, who stays by Lulu to the end, is robbed of masculinity: he is an inadequate lover, not a real man like his father. Schigolch, so old he is almost asexual, stays with Lulu for a while, but finally deserts her for sex with the landlady. Thus humanity, stunted in the sexually active characters, survives better in those distanced from the sexual norms: a lesbian, a boy played by a girl, unmanned

Alwa, and to a degree ancient Schigolch. Emotional attachment leads finally to death for Hugenberg and Alwa in solidarity with Lulu, the fate Melchior escaped in escaping from Wendla.

The division of humanity from sexual pleasure is most striking in Geschwitz. Walter Benjamin (1974: 666–7) suggests that the emergence of lesbianism as an issue was symptomatic of a percieved threat to femininity from the involvement of women in capitalist production, and cites Baudelaire's cult of lesbian love as an ambiguous example. Unlike the theorists who worried lest women become denatured, Baudelaire affirms the subversion of femininity, but the resulting image is almost as reductive as the feminine stereotypes: Baudelaire's lesbians are a voyeuristic spectacle of purely sexual women and, as Benjamin notes, though the writer glorified an imagined Sappho, he disliked the real George Sand. Wedekind's lesbian is ambiguous in a different way. Geschwitz's intellect brings her closer than Baudelaire's *femmes damnées* to the conventional mocking image of the masculinized lesbian; but she has feminine emotions. Thus mind and emotion in woman, which Wedekind otherwise attacks, are half affirmed in the sympathetic presentation of Geschwitz – in the lesbian, they pose no threat to masculine freedom but are alienated in this monster who is not an object of desire. Lulu's manifest cruelty to Geschwitz is an attack on those aspects of femininity which in a desired woman would threaten freedom. The ugliness of Lulu's attack – a woman attacking femininity – dramatizes the bad conscience of an author who, like his creature Schön, is torn between Nietzschean amoralism and a longing to love which can only be admitted in the heavy disguise of Geschwitz, who is neither a man nor a woman. She is a man with a woman's body and feelings, or a woman with a man's mind and manner. Her love is dissociated from the social concomitant of heterosexual love, the happy marriage mocked so unmercifully through Schwarz. And she is remote from the ultimate anathema, the mother, the original source of imprisoning love.

Together, Lulu and Geschwitz convey a deep contradiction of sexual attitudes. Both in their different ways deconstruct sexual difference: Lulu in her masculine freedom; Geschwitz in her man-woman mixing of intellect and feeling. The sympathy with which Geschwitz is portrayed suggests a longing to break down emotional differences between the sexes, yet fear of love and of an assimilation which might destroy pleasure rooted in difference. Conversely, Lulu remains desirable to the end as a feminine image of bodily difference, yet frightening in her unfeminine freedom. Thus differences between the sexes are at once denied and asserted. In texts which so vigourously deconstruct their own terminology there is ample room for producers and spectators to extract readings in line with their own beliefs, though some positions are clearly excluded. There is no hankering for an organic community in the past or in some other culture. Nor is there any plea for a decentring of sexual pleasure; the plays are anti-puritanical. What they do show, if inadvertently, is that sexual liberation is inseparable from social liberation of the whole person. Beyond that it must be for the spectator to decide what conclusions to draw. Though there is no political programme, the plays present the calamity of Lulu's career not as grim tragedy leaving no room for change, but as comic and grotesque melodrama, a theatrical effect which modifies the sexual argument.

Theatrical Language: Time, Costume, Set, Mode

In the course of the two plays Lulu passes through life-stages of many years, from Goll's child bride, to young married woman, to actress at the height of her beauty, to long-term mistress promoted to wife, to adulterous wife no longer in the first flush of youth, as Casti-Piani cynically comments, to a *demi-mondaine* doomed to become an ageing street-prostitute. But there is no illusion of long, slow evolution. The juxtaposition of episodes foreshortens and denaturalizes time, high-lighting structural analogy rather than character development. Lulu is the focus of a changing cast of male characters who appear less and less as individuals and more and more as vessels of an abstract montage of motifs which shift about kaleidoscopically in different combinations. Whether as child bride, wife, actress, *demi-mondaine* or prostitute, Lulu is the object of the same confused dreams and the same structure of male power. Her emergent autonomy, most evident in Act III of *Earth Spirit*, is crushed. Jack is a product of the same culture which shapes bourgeois marriage and is deeply hostile to the sexual woman. Thus the dramatic time conveys a patch of history, the late nineteenth century, in terms of social structure. To that extent, the plays avoid the presentation of human nature in fatalistic terms. But the traces of autonomy in Lulu, and Geschwitz's brief dream of emancipation are the only explicit signs that the structure might be open to change. In themselves, they scarcely rescue the plays from a fatalism rooted in social structure if not in nature. No programmatic way out of the dead-end of Lulu's destruction is offered.

However, the rhetoric of theatrical effects offers a kind of anti-fatalism in corporated into the structure of the play. The juxtapositions which create the sense of repeated structure also produce highly theatrical shock effects. The major shock is the transition from Lulu in *Earth Spirit* to Lulu after prison in *Pandora's Box*, repeated in miniature as she blooms after the departure of Rodrigo in Act I, initially blooms then withers under the threats of Act II, appears in miserable poverty in Act III after the glitter of Act II, blooms again when the portrait reappears, only finally to be destroyed. The portrait draws the beginning of *Earth Spirit* together with the end of *Pandora's Box* in a final temporal condensation, so that the whole time-span of the plays is present simultaneously to the imagination: Lulu as Pierrot and the butchered corpse. Such a juxtaposition resists fatalistic closure. It is provoking and enraging. It is also thought-provoking, for rage is mixed with detachment. While the plays condense life-stages of many years, the production time remains long compared with a standard play: the two plays can scarcely be put on in full as a single performance. Thus, within the overall hectic effect of Lulu's career there is space for variation of pace and a whole range of emotional colour of the kind already noted in *Earth Spirit* and in Act I of *Pandora's Box*. In the closing act, provocation is mixed with melancholy or lyrical retrospection. Comic talk about food, and the stasis of Geschwitz's philosophical reflections slow the pace. The action proceeds with the entries and exits of the clients who bring a mix of the comic, the grotesque, and the horrific in rapid succession. The sheer suddenness of the transitions is shocking, as when the grotesquely comic Kungu Poti brutally clubs Alwa. Time effects, then, avoid a monochrome gloom and are crucial to the mixing of modes.

From *Earth Spirit* on through *Pandora's Box* the shock effects are heightened by Lulu's costume-changes from gay variety to drabness, to splendour, to miserable shabbiness. Lulu's costumes for her roles, and the mythical bare feet, have already been noted. In *Pandora's Box*, male clothes are important too. In Act I, Rodrigo describes his circus costumes; he was fined in Germany because his *décolleté* revealed hair on his chest, which he now shaves. In France, there are fewer restrictions, and he has ordered blue-green tights and little pants so dainty that he can scarely afford to sit on the edge of a table.

(Rodrigo is highly reminiscent of Dürow, an animal-tamer in the Paris diaries who wore paste jewellery (Hay: 235).) The groom, Bob, in his red jacket, tight white leather trousers and high top-boots is as pretty as young Kadidja and of roughly the same age as her: Puntschu the banker clearly cannot decide which of them he fancies most. Bob shares with Lulu the dubious distinction of being renamed: Bob instead of Freddy. Like Lulu, he is an object of desire. Lulu escapes in Bob's clothes, a transvestite costume like the Pierrot suit, if more vulgarly sexy, recalling also the trouser-role of Hugenberg and Geschwitz's hussar costume. Such motifs offer a *frisson* of pederasty and transvestism. They also alienate woman as sex object by offering male exemplars, especially the grotesque Rodrigo. Stereotyped gender roles dissolve in a haze of ambiguity. In Act II, Schigolch's parodistic evening dress highlights the costumes of the other men as a sign of status; in Act III, the customers' clothes link or contrast with earlier characters. Rather than building up the illusion of a milieu caught in exact detail, the costumes overtly demonstrate the cultural fashioning of gender and social status. The exaggerated vulgarity of the costumes in Act II is a perspectivistic effect. We see the new wealth in France through mockingly satirical eyes. The fact that the *nouveaux riches* are a collection of pimps and prostitutes heightens the satire.

Pandora's Box is both more gloomy and more garish than *Earth Spirit*. The sets, like the costumes, create strong contrasts, as the glitter of Act II is sandwiched between dim lamplight in Act I and Act III. The lamp shines throughout Act I, but in Act III it goes out as Lulu and Jack disappear into the cubbyhole. The portrait, first painted in the light of an artist's atelier, recedes into advancing shadows, but as part of the whole set should still remain fully visible. Jack wants moonlight instead of the lamp, apparently heightening the suggestion that he is an emanation of nature. Moonlight is cool, silvery and diffuse; it is associated with romance and magic, effects exploited by Reinhardt in his famous productions of *A Midsummer Night's Dream*. But the stage direction here calls for a quite different effect: the two harsh squares of light, the source unseen, provide a stagey illumination not for an emanation of nature but for a human murderer in a long overcoat and a little round felt hat. The geometrical shapes denaturalize and depoeticize the moonlight. It becomes overtly theatrical, an abstract pattern against the dark tones of the set. In combining sinister expressiveness with artificiality, Wedekind's moonlight stands somewhere between the blood-red moon in

Büchner's *Woyzeck* and Brecht's parodistic moons in *Drums in the Night* or *The Threepenny Opera*.

The sensational action of the play has affinities with melodrama, while the gory end is close to its later black outgrowth, *Grand Guignol*. In France, melodrama originated in the aftermath of the Revolution, with roots in the sentimental literature of the Enlightenment. Peter Brooks (1985) defines it as a genre which made the world morally legible again in a new democratic and post-sacred age when the traditional social and religious order no longer held; it uncovers a Manichaean drama of good and evil, of unrecognized or despised virtue set against villainy; the characters are without depth, pure signifiers of good and evil; the action is emblematic of the ethical drama and the language is essentially hyperbolic. Brooks goes on to consider Balzac and Henry James as social melodramatists who reveal the moral drama implicated in everyday existence in a melodrama of manners. *Earth Spirit*, full of hints and portents of Manichaean forces, has something of a melodrama of manners, though comedy of manners and farce still predominate: Goll, Schwarz and Schön are not purely evil, while Rodrigo belongs in a comic farce. At the end of *Earth Spirit*, however, Lulu assumes the features of a heroine of melodrama – but a Nietzschean melodrama in which virtue has been revalued. Her virtue remains despised or unrecognized and she is doomed to languish in prison, echoing the predominant motif of innocence held captive.

Pandora's Box shifts massively towards melodrama. Rodrigo, Casti-Piani and Jack are without depth, signifiers of pure evil. Lulu continues her perilous journey aided by Schigolch in the role of the comic man, a mysterious, often conventionally immoral figure who always turns up to save the heroine in her hour of peril. As David Hirst (1984: 73) puts it: 'The comic man is another reincarnation of the Vice: a character who disturbs the smooth flow of the plot, interfering with the action to comic effect though with serious results.' An unmotivated comic intrusion, he diverts tragedy and saves the black and white moral universe by ensuring that villains are thwarted and the virtuous saved: melodrama must have a happy ending, and the virtuous are too guileless to save themselves. But Schigolch, who does intervene in Act II, abdicates his task in Act III, leaving the way free for the villain.

The Lulu plays, which undermine the liberal faith of post-revolutionary Europe, subvert the stark simplicities of melodrama.

Lulu is a hopelessly ambiguous heroine hovering between innocent victim and wicked villainess. Yet the echoes of the genre remain potent, and heighten the play's accusatory power. Whereas melodrama satisfies the moral imagination by revealing an essentially ethical universe, by celebrating 'the sign of the right' (Brooks 1985: 42), the Lulu plays refuse such satisfaction: the true signs of the afflicted heroine's essential nature do not become manifest; it remains unknown, dissolved into a series of conflicting images. Denied easy identification with a conventionally moral heroine, the audience is forced to identify with a villainess and to rethink the terms of the Manichaean battle, to recognize the features of Jack the Ripper in the innocent face of Schwarz, to question the origins of Lulu's fatality. Refused escape into an essential universe, they must re-examine quotidian life in the bourgeois society which gives birth to Jack the Ripper.

Pandora's Box uncovers sadistic undertones beneath the moralism of melodrama. French melodrama reached a highpoint in the first three decades of the nineteenth century. Its black undertones emerged fully at the end of the century: in 1896, Oscar Méténier opened the *Théâtre du Grand Guignol*, which became a vehicle for horror plays full of shock effects exploiting sensational events of the day. The *Monstretragödie* belongs squarely in the same genre; the seed of Wedekind's idea for the play was the London murders of 1888–9, which became instantly notorious throughout Europe. *Grand Guignol* is melodrama turned upside down, as villainy triumphs. Brooks (1985: 41–2) claims that melodrama presents a spectacular victory of 'the sign of virtue' over initial repression and so satisfies basic moral sentiments in a public who desire a universe free of moral ambiguity. The claim rests on redefinition of the repressed as the sign of virtue. Yet as Brooks himself notes, though virtue triumphed it was evil which fascinated: the *boulevard du Temple*, the centre of melodrama in Paris, was known as the *boulevard du crime*. In conventional Freudian terms, melodrama is a direct combat between id and superego with no intervening reality principle. The superego must win spectacularly in order to hold down a scandalous subtext, the potent desires of the id, which citizen de Sade might have recognized in this democratic genre. In the gory outcome of *Grand Guignol* the id emerges spectacularly, but the superego just holds the line, for the sheer blackness of evil displayed confirms moral discourse, like the moral tacked on at the end of the related genre of crime ballads, the *Moritat*. *Grand Guignol* is the negative to melodrama's positive. Melodrama, strongest in Act II of *Pandora's Box* where Lulu is an afflicted heroine, becomes *Grand Guignol* in Act III.

Grand Guignol was generally interspersed with farces to jolt the audience from one theatrical shock to another, a device known as *douches écossaises*. The temperature changes in Wedekind's plays are even more rapid and disconcerting, as at the end of Acts I, II and IV of *Earth Spirit*. In *Pandora's Box* melodrama and *Grand Guignol* are so intermingled with comic or satirical farce that the audience can scarcely tell what the temperature is. Pure, crude effects are disrupted by subversive laughter. The grotesque image of the fat strong man setting off for a rendezvous with the gauntly elegant aristocrat interferes both with the image of Rodrigo as cruel villain and with the horror of his end. Kungu Poti producing a club he just happens to have about his person, with all the suddenness of Punch laying into Judy, leaves Alwa's demise poised uncertainly between farce and horror. Even his corpse becomes comic when addressed in Swiss German as 'Ä Todtnige! – Ä Liach?' (A dead body! – A corpse?). Jack's petty meanness, his banality, the grotesque incongruity of his complaint about the lack of towels alongside the monstrosity of the murder, make it difficult to judge whether he is horrific or ludicrous. The final effect is a withering mockery, shrivelling the power of such ridiculous villains to instil terror. The plays offer no programmatic answers; but the theatrical shock effects, as farce clashes with the moral simplicities of melodrama and the horror of *Grand Guignol*, deny fatalism.

5

Berg's *Lulu* and the Operatic Tradition

The Operatic Transformation

Alban Berg attended the performance of *Pandora's Box* staged in Vienna by Karl Kraus on 29 May 1905, in which Wedekind played Jack the Ripper and his future wife Tilly played Lulu. Berg began work on the opera in 1928; at his death in 1936 it was complete except for the orchestration of the last act, a task completed between 1962 and 1974 by Friedrich Cerha, with final revisions in 1976–7 after the death of Berg's widow, who had opposed the project. This completed version was premiered in Paris in 1979 with a first London production in 1981. In his magisterial study, George Perle (1985) places *Lulu* 'among the uniquely significant, uniquely original, and supremely important musical creations of our century' (p. 280), and judges that 'Berg has transformed Wedekind's Lulu plays into a work that is simultaneously more complex and more coherent, a supreme masterpiece of the lyric theatre' (p. 67). I am deeply indebted in what follows to Perle's formal analysis of the opera and its relation to the plays. I shall concentrate on the opera as a transformation of the plays rather than on its intrinsic qualities, and then comment on a literary and operatic tradition to which both plays and opera belong.

Berg reduced Wedekind's seven acts to three, but retained material from all seven, bracketing the close of *Earth Spirit* and the opening of *Pandora's Box* in the middle act. The fundamental division, however, is into two parts: Act I and the first scene of Act II, then the second scene of Act II and Act III. In the centre is the orchestral Interlude accompanying a silent film of Lulu's escape from prison. The Interlude is palindromic in structure, intensifying the symmetry of the two parts. Thus the opera retains the division of Lulu's life into phases before and after Schön's death, corresponding to the two plays. The fundamental musical principle is recapitulation, culminating in the last scene which is imbued throughout with reminiscence of earlier material. This corresponds to the patterned episodes of the plays, a dramatic effect Berg intensifies by doubling of roles. Personal names are retained for Lulu, Geschwitz, Schön, Alwa, Schigolch and Jack, but the rest become impersonal types: the Painter, the Medical Specialist and so on; the Professor combines Hunidei and Hilti. The same singer plays the equivalents of Schwarz and Kungu Poti, of Goll and Hunidei/Hilti, of Schön and Jack and of the Prologue animal-tamer and Rodrigo (although these pairs have sometimes been altered in production). The emphasis on musical recapitulation and the double roles mean that everything after Schön's death takes on what Perle calls a quality *déjà vu* until 'the staged events seem to be accompanied by a shadow of themselves in which the first half of the opera, culminating and concluding in the death of Dr Schön, is reenacted in a nightmarish distortion' (p. 60; p. 84). Berg thus intensifies the anti-illusionist handling of character which, along with other features such as the film, makes the opera a more Expressionist work.

Perle (p. 67) suggests that the structural symmetries binding the characters give them a puppetlike helplessness. On the other hand, the overt doubling of the husbands with their alter egos creates a strong contrast between them and the non-doubled characters, while the relationship between Lulu and Schön is emphasized as the centre to which all leads and from which all flows. This means that Lulu, Geschwitz, Schigolch and Alwa are signalled through contrast as unique identities and that the depth of the central relationship is stressed. The technique of recapitulation extends the Wagnerian leitmotif into *Leitsektionen*. The two most important recurrent musical themes, Perle suggests, are Lulu's Entrance Music and the Closing Theme of the Sonata. The first is introduced in the Prologue, appears in II, 1 when Lulu is Schön's wife and mistress of his household, recurs after her imprisonment and is heard for the last time when Jack carries her off. The second motif is first heard in I, 2 when Lulu replies to Schön's demand that she cease visiting him with a declaration of the bond between them. The nobility of the theme makes Lulu's depth of feeling unmistakable. I have argued that this is a possible reading of the play too, but in the opera it becomes the necessary reading. Her aria as Schön's wife in II, 1 is an assertion of selfhood which is repeated when she responds to Casti-Piani's brothel proposal. The orchestral commentary and expressive power of her singing in such passages create an indubitable personal identity and convey unambiguously the value of erotic love. The horror of her end bears no suggestion of merited punishment. As Perle (pp. 127–8) notes, Schön's madness in II, 1 is associated with a tremolo figure which reappears at the end with Jack, marking him as the embodiment of that madness, rather than an avenger of moral values. The music signalling Lulu's love of Schön returns with Jack's entry but gives way to horror, so that Jack does not appear as a sadistic embodiment of eros, but as its destroyer.

Two further structural features are a succession of orchestral forms such as the sonata or the theme and variations, and a succession of numbers in the traditional operatic manner: arias, duets and ensembles which recall Mozart's *Don Giovanni* whose hero was seen by Berg as Lulu's operatic forebear. This rich musical language creates brilliant dramatic effects, as powerfully expressive passages alternate with grotesque or parodistic moments achieved by playing against the springboard of traditional musical forms. Thus Berg wonderfully translates into music the plays' patterning and games with modes. Just as in *Wozzeck* the humanity of Wozzeck and Marie is contrasted musically as well as dramatically with the grotesque doctor and captain, here too the material conveying the value of eros and Lulu's individuality contrasts with parodistic passages. In addition to the basic strict series of the whole opera, each character has an associated twelve-tone row and there are subtle correspondences between them. Geschwitz, for example, is linked with the Acrobat, and the musical mix of like with unlike, intensified by the instrumentation, sets her suffering abnormality against his brute normality so that the music queries the conventional judgements. Berg's own sister was an unhappy lesbian, which may be one reason why *Pandora's Box* so appealed to him. Besides such parodistic echoing, there are moments of pure comedy such as the graveyard wheeze that Berg, himself an asthmatic, has given to Schigolch. Theatrical self-commentary becomes musical: the opening chords of *Wozzeck* are played as Alwa imagines composing an opera about Lulu; his rhapsody on Lulu's body complements Wedekind's musical metaphors of *cantabile* and *andante* with a quotation from the *Lyric Suite* which had a secret programme referring to Berg's mistress, whom he also identified with Lulu. The most startling quotation of all is the tune which is the basis of the Act III Interlude. It first appears in the duet between Lulu and Casti-Piani, but emerges as unambiguously tonal in Variation I of the Interlude and through each Variation until the fourth, when it is played on an off-stage barrel-organ as the curtain rises for the last scene. It is the melody of Wedekind's tenth lute song, dedicated to Gertrud Eysoldt who played Lulu in the first Berlin production of *Earth Spirit* in December 1902 in Reinhardt's Kleines Theater. The song is the confession of a prostitute defiantly asserting the joy of sex:

Lieben? – Nein, das bringt kein Glück auf Erden.
Lieben bringt Entwürdigung und Neid.
Heiß und oft und stark geliebt zu werden,
Das heißt Leben, das ist Seligkeit!

To love? – No, that brings no joy on earth./ To love brings only indignity and envy./ To be loved hot and strong and often,/ That is life, that is bliss!

Such a quotation, occuring just as Lulu is about to be slaughtered, could have been searingly satirical. But the reference is musical rather than verbal, and is poignant in the extreme as the heart-rendingly simple tonality of the tune emerges in its barrel-organ setting and then is lost before the engulfing orchestral horror of the end. It is most touching too as Berg's tribute to a fellow music maker.

Expression and Projection in Opera and Drama

The opera is more coherent than the plays, and as a musical structure is highly complex yet powerfully expressive. Whether it is more complex in dramatic terms is another matter. Berg's masterpiece is less ambiguous than the plays, with fewer resonances in Lulu's multiple roles. The intellectual distance of the plays gives way to intenser emotional expression. The possibilities of varied production are greater in the plays than the opera, where the music interprets the action and sets mode and mood. The actress who plays Lulu can ironize her roles more readily than the singer, who is bound by the music. In the opera Lulu is a more unambiguously human and positive figure; she is less of a shifting image, more of a powerful presence. As a result, the opera is a less varied exploration of sexual feeling, if a more vivid evocation of it. Berg's musical dramas are particularly subtle. But even here the flamboyant skills of the singer, so evidently skills of projection at a great remove from ordinary communication, produce a relation between player, role and audience different from that in the theatre. Opera tends to be less mimetic of the person, to project purer expressions of emotions in the abstract. The audience response is a paradoxical simultaneous yet separate sense of the singer's performance and of the emotion in quasi-detatchment from the plot. One is moved to tears more easily than in the theatre, not by the plot nor even by the emotion, but by its projection. Wedekind's *Der Kammersänger* (*The Singer*) of 1899 is a tragi-comic farce about a woman who falls in love with both Tristan and the tenor, a double image remote from the man seen afterwards in the dressing room.

Lulu is more sophisticated, less rendingly moving than *Wozzeck*, but even so, compared with the plays, effect is more prominent than analysis. As Jack Stein (1974) notes, the cynical dimension is lacking and Berg has omitted Geschwitz's last bitter 'Verflucht!'. As an opera about a woman who draws men to their doom and herself suffers, *Lulu* stands in the tradition of *Carmen*, *La Traviata*, *Manon Lescaut* or *Turandot*, whose happy ending Puccini found himself unable to complete. Such heroines are played by great singers, heroines in life fêted by the public, whose massive vocal powers stand in much more startling discrepancy to the role of victim than is ever apparent in the theatre. Wedekind's mother and aunt were singers and his sister a celebrated soprano. Though the singer in his farce is male, his plays are full of coded references to the real divas who play the often pathetic heroines of operatic plots. Operas, more strikingly than plays, convey a double image of woman: the role and the triumphantly powerful singer. Triumphant power is not otherwise typically feminine, and the glories of the female voice mean that female performers are as central as men. In the novels Manon, Carmen and Marguerite are seen through the filter of a male narrator; in the opera they are there in the flesh. Nineteenth-century opera was a ritual enactment of sexual tensions, less by way of analysis than as a showing forth. Berg's opera is structurally remote from French or Italian opera; it is a through-composed work with an overarching musical structure. But the retention of numbers means that the link with tradition is not entirely severed.

Operatic and Literary Forebears

The affinities between *Lulu* and the earlier operas are legion. Don José murders Carmen because, like Lulu's lovers, he cannot bear her freedom. While Carmen's freedom comes from her exotic provenance as a gypsy, Wedekind was thoroughly familiar with the non-exotic Parisian *demi-monde*, as Ronald Peacock (1978) notes, though the prostitutes he met were not courtesans at the level of Manon or Violetta. In opera, the sexes humiliate and torment one another: threateningly free or excitingly vulnerable heroines suffer and die terrible deaths to the delectation of the audience, while the men writhe with pain or remorse. Patriarchal power wreaks pleasurable havoc as we thrill to the erotic force of Puccini's villain Scarpia or Verdi's patriarch Germont confronting Violetta. In *Turandot*, the sado-masochistic ritual is overt, with a chorus as internal audience, while Ping, Pang and Pong introduce a note of travesty. In *La Traviata* Violetta's humiliation is a public ritual performed for the audience of party guests, just as Carmen's death is achieved in the shadow of the bullring as a greater consummation for the opera audience than the off-stage slaughter of the bull. The spectacle continues in the *Lulu* circus. But *Lulu* travesties the tradition in cutting away sentimental redemption through suffering and love. More clearly than its analogues, it unmasks the patriarchal morality which twists the men's feelings and destroys the women. More than the plays, it still stands in the tradition through the force of the love music of Lulu and Schön, but the shift from beautiful singing to a harsher vocal idiom stretching from speech, through *Sprechgesang* to full singing voice produced an effect remote from pleasurable delectation.

The affinities of the plays with the literary texts of the operas I have discussed are if anything more striking. Mérimée's story is altogether a more powerful attack on convention than the opera: Carmen's assertion of freedom is not set against the sentimental sufferings of a tenor. With Prévost's *Manon Lescaut* and Dumas's *La Dame aux camélias* it is tempting to see direct links. Wedekind mentions *Manon Lescaut* in Notebook 5 (p. 6: 9r) in a list of female types, and Frau Kadidja Wedekind-Biel assures me he would have known both Dumas's novel and Verdi's opera. *Manon Lescaut* is a leitmotif in *La Dame aux camélias* and the Lulu plays read almost as a commentary on both, though the common motifs may result from the theme of the kept woman. Des Grieux, the hero of *Manon Lescaut*, is a theology student, like the hero of Wedekind's early play *Elin's Awakening*. He is locked up by his father and then by the police, like Melchoir or Hugenberg. Mannon becomes the mistress of a father, G . . . M . . . , a Goll-like figure, and later of his son, recalling Lulu's passage from Schön to Alwa. The endlessly devoted Des Grieux is reminscent of Alwa and Geschwitz in combination; like the Countess he is a nobleman, a chevalier. In helping Manon escape from prison he gives her his breeches, whereas Geschwitz gives Lulu her knickers, and finally goes with her to America, a proposal Geschwitz makes but Lulu refuses. During his own escape from prison a minor character is killed whose fate is a matter of complete indifference to him, just as Sister Theophila's is to Lulu. Like Alwa, he reluctantly lives off Manon's gains from her clients which, like Alwa, he tries to augment by gambling. Like Schwarz, he cannot accept her profession while his Schön-like longing for married respectability precipitates the final catastrophe.

In *La Dame aux camélias* the father-son complex is less explicit, but it is the father Marguerite strives to please and whom she asks to kiss her, a moment with even more ambiguous sexual undertones in the opera. Duval's innocent daughter corresponds to Schön's child fiancée. The financial relations with the son recall Alwa as kept man and Lulu's payment of Jack: Armand is a courtesan's kept man. Like Lulu, Marguerite is a succession of images. Her elderly lover loves in her the image of his dead daughter, a motif recalled in travesty in Goll's child bride. Armand puzzles over how 'sa vie ardente' (her ardent life) left untouched 'l'expression virginale, enfantine même' (her virginal, even childlike expression: Dumas 1983: 36). She was still 'à la virginité du vice . . . on reconnaissait dans cette fille la vierge qu'un rien avait faite courtisane, et la courtisane dont un rien eût fait la vierge la plus amoureuse et la plus pure.' (a virgin in vice . . . one recognized in that girl the virgin whom so little had turned into a courtesan, and the courtesan from whom so little might have made the most loving and purest of virgins: pp. 109–10). Marguerite complains of the man in love who wants to dominate and possess, unlike her other clients, while Armand desires the victory of making her love him with an immaterial love, like Schwarz after Lulu's soul. But it is the body which is possessed. Armand cannot even leave the corpse in peace, but has it dug up to gaze upon the horror of its corruption before moving it to a grave of his choosing in emulation of his forebear Des Grieux who buried Manon.

In both novels the men recover and are reconciled with the patriarchal order. The consummation is even more grotesque in Verdi's *La Traviata*, as father and son sob over Violetta's corpse. It is as if Schwarz, Alwa and Schön were to gather round Lulu's agony, which of couse they do. Wedekind's work makes overt the sub-text of the two novels: the deadly effects of possessive love and the sadistic attraction to the woman's agony. The deadly love of Des Grieux and Duval, their insistence on binding their mistress with love, brings about the catastrophe. Lulu is not killed by consumption or in a wilderness; she is killed in the midst of civilization by the grotesque embodiment of all her lovers. Wedekind destroys the ideology of redemption through suffering which both novels still purvey and which allows for the protracted female agony the audience so enjoys. Geschwitz's last 'Verflucht!' pronounces its end.

6
The Marquis of Keith

All the world's a stage,
And all the men and women merely players:
They have their exits and their entrances;
And one man in his time plays many parts . . .

(As You Like It: II, 7)

In *The Marquis of Keith*, the metaphor of life as theatre, introduced in the children's role-playing in *Spring Awakening* and developed in Lulu's many names and roles, becomes all-pervasive. The building blocks of names, costumes, props, lighting, timing, plot and dialogue, and the actorly techniques of accent, appearance, gesture and gait all become anti-illusionistic. As the performance proceeds, the audience grows aware that the actors on the theatrical stage play actors on a social stage; we see with a double vision actors playing actors. Accordingly, this chapter will begin with a discussion of theatrical effects before moving on to consider the theme of personal identity in a world in flux.

The Social Stage

The programme for *The Marquis of Keith* – the first thing the play-goer sees – sets the action in Munich in the late summer of 1899. The cast list suggests a cross-section of Munich society. It includes a local writer, Sommersberg, and the exotically named Saranieff and Zamrjaki, a painter and a composer respectively, who can be seen as the equivalent of a Wedekind and a Kandinsky or a Kokoschka. There is an aristocratic widow, Anna, Countess Werdenfels; police commissioner Raspe; businessmen and their wives with Bavarian names, one in the Bavarian trade of beer-brewing; a couple of divorcees from the minor aristocracy; and a chorus consisting of the butcher's boy, the woman from the baker's shop, a porter and guests at the *Hofbräuhaus*. Two characters are unplaced by job or title: Ernst Scholz and Molly Griesinger. Their names are obtrusively ordinary when sandwiched between the Marquis and the Countess. Two further characters have decidedly extraordinary names, Sascha and Simba, the former to be played by a girl. Surprisingly, the list is not headed by the eponymous hero, but by Consul Casimir, a wholesale merchant, and his fifteen-year-old son Hermann, another trouser-role: the decorative young are played by women. Only in third position comes the Marquis von Keith. His title looks suspicious: *Marquis*, usually pronounced in the French manner, is not a German title, yet is coupled with the German aristocratic indicator *von*, while *Keith* looks English or even Scottish – Keith is a small town in Banffshire, Scotland.

The cast list is the first of many theatrical jokes in the play, and is not to be relied on. Reflecting the idea that all this world is a stage where men play many parts and bear many names, the list designates only roles; it does not tell us who the person behind the role 'really' is. Keith's title is indeed fishy. His father was the tutor of his childhood friend, one Graf von Trautenau, now Ernst Scholz. We never discover the real name behind the impressive title which Keith claims to have inherited from his adoptive father, an English Lord. Keith plans to build a palace of the arts to be funded by business money. The key figure in this scheme is Consul Casimir, the most powerful business-man in Munich, whom Keith fails to win over. In the end, the businessmen assume control of the project, excluding Keith, its author, because he does not keep proper accounts: his ledger contains only a description of the Parisian dress worn by Countess Werdenfels at the grand concert to promote the project. The Countess, once Anna Huber, assistant in a hat shop in the Perusastraße, will become Frau Consul Casimir, deserting art and her lover Keith for money and marriage. Consul Casimir's position at the top of the cast list reflects the power of money over art and sex alike. Then come the four main characters, men before women. The order otherwise sets artists above policemen and beer-brewers, and divorced aristocrats above servants, again male before female, though Simba is a more important character than the divorcees and her male counterpart, Sascha.

Social status and dramatic status do not coincide, and the cast list is misleading on both fronts. Keith's mistress is Anna, but he lives with Molly Griesinger, who appears as his wife. (Since they are not in fact married, she really is Molly Griesinger.) Unable to stand Keith's life-style, and fearful of losing him, Molly drowns herself, one of the blows which precipitate his business failure. Women regularly change names, of course, so that the fact that Molly has not changed her name is as surprising as that the men have changed theirs. Ernst Scholz, once Gaston Count Trautenau, decided to become a useful member of society, a civil servant with the railways, but through an excess of conscientiousness caused an accident, killing several people. He has taken a middle-class name appropriate to his middle-class guilt feelings, and arrives to seek Keith's help in becoming a hedonist, leading Keith to hope for aristocratic patronage. But after sexual failures with Simba and later Anna, he departs to a lunatic asylum, leaving Keith in the lurch. Keith's evil genius is his old buddy, police commissioner Raspe, who once had a French name, spent two years in a French gaol, and studied theology before taking first to crime, then its policing. On becoming a useful member of society, he abandoned French names, just as Scholz dropped 'Gaston' in favour of 'Ernst'. In revenge for Keith's failure to help him when he was in prison, Raspe spreads rumours which undermine Keith's credit. Sascha and Simba, a servant and a waitress, turn out to have broad Bavarian accents and alternative broad Bavarian names, Sepperl and Kathi.

In realist literature, names are appropriate to milieu. They may discreetly hint at individual character, like 'Casaubon' or 'Heathcliff' or be overtly satirical like 'Gradgrind'. 'Molly Griesinger' is a discreet indicator. 'Molly' sounds unassuming, and the first stage direction tells us that she is exactly that, 'unscheinbar'. Her surname indicates that she is *griesgrämig*, a sour type, and she comes from oppressive-sounding Bückeburg (*bücken*, to bow, and *Burg*, a fortified castle). Countess Werdenfels (*werden*, to become; *Fels*, a rock) is fluidly changing, yet has a core of strength. Sommersberg (Summerhill) grows into his name; initially a miserable creature in an overcoat, he becomes more summery in mood and costume as the play goes on. The two *Freifrauen*, Ladies, are literally free women, divorcees. Freifrau von Totleben (Lady Livingdeath), is clearly to be avoided. The other, Freifrau von Rosenkron, (Rosecrown) is dubious, her name a hybrid containing elements of both *Rosenkranz* (rosary) and *Dornenkron* (crown of thorns). 'Consul Casimir' sounds impressive if faintly exotic, dimly recalling the many Casimirs who were kings of Poland. His son is an ultra-German 'Hermann', suggesting determination to put down secure German roots. Even the Consul does not stand on firm ground: with bad luck he could end up in prison.

So far the names conform to the realist or comic traditions, but the names of the painter and composer sound so exotic that one wonders whether they really are foreign, or whether, like ballet dancers with Russian names, they are trying to cultivate an 'artistic' image. In this case, the foreign accent may be just an act. This slight doubt about Saranieff and Zamrjaki introduces a different note into our interpretation of the cast list. Pseudonyms show how people wish to appear, not who they are. Characters choosing their own names echo an author – who is lord of the fictional world and creator of the characters peopling it – choosing fictional names. In naming themselves, Keith, Scholz and Raspe all try to create themselves and determine their place in society, rather than having it determined for them by birth or reputation. They know the importance of reputation, however, and stage-manage themselves to produce the desired effect. Each tries to escape the fatality of past history, leading his life as a series of discontinuous adventures. Each new beginning starts from a *tabula rasa*, marked by the death of an old name. The new names show artistic flair. 'Scholz' sounds decent and solid, especially combined with 'Ernst'. 'Raspe', from *raspen* (to grate), suits a hard man and helps to counteract Raspe's angelic appearance, which is fine for a theologian but far from appropriate for an ex-criminal policeman. Keith wants to build a *Feenpalast*, a magic palace of the arts, floating high above the mundane and *mesquin*. Keith's cosmopolitan cocktail of a name is appropriately free-floating and without foundations. He has also named his servant 'Sascha'. As Sascha kneels in his decorative livery to do up Keith's splendid button boots, the boy and the boots alike are accessories enhancing his image.

The names are a first indication of the kind of play *The Marquis of Keith* is: a comedy of manners (at least, almost a comedy), set in a recognizable milieu at a specific point in history. At the same time, it is a speculation on the abstract theme of identity and social determination. Keith lays claim to be a Nietzschean *Übermensch*, emancipated from social determination or heredity, who can constantly recreate himself, setting the values by which he lives and the name by which he is known. He is an aspiring world master, like the hero of Alwa's unwritten play. But he rejects Zarathustra's advice to shun the flies of the market and the crowds. You cannot master the world by shunning it. His magic palace will be in Munich, not on top of a mountain. Art is communication; it can be practised alone, but not very satisfactorily. The central theme of art and its role in society is thus intimately connected with the broader issue of social threats to freedom and self-determination.

After the cast list, physical appearance is the next clue to character. The actor produces a body language of appearance, movement and gesture which we read as an index of character; our impressions may then be modified by the plot, as the characters are developed through the action. The directions on appearance fall into three categories: there are unchanging features such as eye-colour (though this is imperceptible, of course, and is a sign to be interpreted by the actor); there are easily changed features such as dress or hair style; and there is the more indefinable aura or manner. The three categories signal a major argument. The unchanging features suggest a fixed inheritance which, like fingerprints, may identify without signifying anything further, or may be a constant disposition inherited from parents or acquired in childhood, the modern version of fate. The inheritance can be combatted or reinforced by choice of style, and the first two kinds of feature in combination produce the third, the manner or mien. As the players have their exits and entrances, the audience must constantly decide whether the part each plays adds up to a character in the round, a deceptive mask, or just a succession of appearances. In normal circumstances, an actor might play Othello one night and Iago the next, but we would not judge his character from the two performances and his height and eye-colour; here it is doubtful if anybody is there between the performances. This doubt is compounded by the difficulty we have in deciding whether the characters are like one another despite surface contrasts, or unlike one another despite surface similarities. The metaphor of surface appearance and inner self becomes confused because we are not sure what counts as superficial and what, if anything, as essential. Apart from the performances on stage, there are several narrations of past episodes, extra fictions which create a peculiar temporal effect. They place the action, which unlike the action in the Lulu plays is fairly unified – Keith's plan, its success and his failure – as nothing more than an episode without finality for most of the characters, but as The End for at least one, perhaps two. Thus the time-structure also leaves the audience puzzling.

Let us consider appearance then plot, first with the men and then the women. At first sight, Keith and Scholz look unalike. Keith's eyes are a piercing grey; Scholz's are large, watery-blue and helpless. Keith's straw-blond hair is cut so short it bristles; he has a little moustache and strong features. Scholz has black curly hair and a full beard which hides his chin. In a cartoon, Keith would be all straight lines, Scholz curves. Scholz looks aristocratic whereas Keith has the coarse red hands of a clown or butcher. But Keith is elegantly dressed and lean, 'schlank', whereas Scholz is excessively slender, 'schmächtig'. Both words designate a slim build; the difference concerns posture rather than anatomy: Keith's slimness reveals a strong bone-structure; in Scholz, gait and posture produce weak curvature. Both men's eyes and Keith's coarse hands are fixed, the other differences are more of style and manner. And each has a feature which does not quite fit: Keith's face, though hard, looks nervous, and Scholz has powerful eyebrows. Both men are aged about twenty-seven. One last difference between them is Keith's marked limp, an ancient symbol of postlapsarian man. *Homo claudus* displays the wound of concupiscence, the chief *vulneratio* of original sin.

Scholz, the moralist, has come to concupiscent Keith to take lessons in pleasure. At the end of Act III, during the firework party to promote the magic palace, Scholz undergoes a visual transformation. He seems to turn into a hedonist. The mortar for the big fireworks explodes, a fragment hits him in the knee and he returns indoors limping; as a rocket goes off in the garden he is bathed in lurid red light. Keith, confronted with a limping alter ego, exclaims he would scarcely have recognized him. The lurid light comes from stage lighting and the moment demonstrates its transforming power. Scholz hops about like a red demon shouting that his ten years of misery were all illusion. 'Nichts als Einbildung!' (All imagination!) are the closing words of the act. The stage effect of lighting becomes a metaphor for self-transformation, or else for illusion. At this point it is not clear which, or what the illusion is: Scholz as he seemed or as he now seems. His amazing resemblance to Keith means that the uncertainty envelops Keith too. The audience, used to reading theatrical body language, is here left uncertain as to its meaning. The undermining of the outer sign also undermines the sense of inner continuing selfhood. The point is emphasized in the minor figure, Raspe, who looks like a Guido Reni angel, and claims that his appearance was to blame for his criminal past: he inspired too much trust. Had he had Keith's gallows-bird appearance he would have had no problem in being honest. Had he looked like Raspe, Keith retorts, he would have married a princess by now (Act II). The exchange explodes any simple equation of appearance either with truth or with illusion. Raspe's eyes, windows of the soul, offer no help; whenever anyone looks at him, he puts on a pair of blue pince-nez; the colour suits his angelic blond curls. Rather than character in depth, we see surface images, and remain uncertain whether there is any reality behind the image.

Keith and Scholz are alter egos or diametrical opposites. As young Graf Trautenau, Scholz acquired his moral fervour from Keith's middle-class father, who turned him into a spiritual son. The actual son has an aristocratic contempt for middle-class morality. They are changelings, the personality of each according with the other's origins. Both narrowly escape death by the bullet. Keith faced a firing squad in the Cuban Revolution, feigned death and since his resurrection has been beyond good and evil. Scholz is also resurrected after trying to shoot himself following the railway accident. The threat to his survival came from inside, to Keith's from outside. Keith sought change by revolution, Scholz by reform. Keith has turned to aesthetic hedonism, a path Scholz too now wants to follow, though as part of a dialectical zig-zag towards a synthesis of morality and pleasure. Keith also dreams of synthesis: he will make of Anna a great singer and the mother of his children in a synthesis of art and life. Both Keith and Scholz are bathed in red light at the height of their vision. Similarly, Raspe, the theological student turned criminal, has now synthesized theology and crime as a police commissioner and is still only in his early twenties.

The surreal details of Raspe's career highlight the erratic nature of the life histories. They are not shaped as in a *Bildungsroman*, which ideally follows the plantlike evolution of personality from an original seed which is affected by the social soil and fed by educative influences; instead, they proceed as a series of theatrical melodramas, involving revolutions, catastrophes and fantastic turns of luck. Scholz, born an aristocrat, turns into a middle-class civil servant devoted to reform, and causes disaster. He even considered marrying a woman of low origins, not in the spirit of his counterpart Count Werdenfels who used his status to buy a decorative wife, but as part of his reformist programme. He now wants to change direction again and become a man of pleasure. Keith, born of a contemplative scholar and lackey, a *Hofmeister*, becomes a revolutionary activist. Having almost died in a revolution from below, he tries, an aristocrat of the spirit, to create an aesthetic world rising above the material. He leaped from his grave as a Marquis, whereas Count Trautenau crept from his as Ernst Scholz. The plot we see, just one of a series, asks through Scholz whether it is possible to escape *Bildung*, the spiritual education visible in his watery-blue eyes; through Keith, who seems to have escaped the origins visible in his plebeian hands, it asks whether freedom can be realized in social practice. Thus the men do battle with the fates of origins and conditioning and with a recalcitrant society.

The women start off with nondescript names acquired from their fathers: Huber and Griesinger. Both move beyond their origins, Anna in marrying a count, Molly in running away to America with Keith. Molly's step, for all her mousey manner, is the bolder: in physical terms, it is a journey to the land of the free; in moral terms, it is a step beyond the pale with a man with no papers who cannot or will not marry her. The women do not directly choose a name but acquire one through men, Molly from a father, Anna from a husband. But there is one exception, a rare female Keith who chooses her own name. This is an unseen character reminiscent of Lulu's correspondent in *Earth Spirit*, a singer who lives in Paris and is called Marquesi, an Italianate version of Keith's adopted title. It is a fortunate coincidence that there really was a singer called Marquesi. Yet perhaps Anna did choose her name too, for it is clearly the name she married, not the man.

Visually, Anna is paired with Keith and Molly with Scholz. Anna's bright eyes correspond with Keith's piercing eyes, and both fit gender stereotypes: a woman with piercing eyes would be disconcerting. Soulfulness gives a woman depth, but makes a man weak; accordingly, Molly's large eyes are soulful, whereas Scholz's are helpless. Keith's masculine leanness is paralleled in Anna's voluptuous femininity. Her turned-up nose is a more appealing sign of low origins than Keith's coarse hands; in reality aristocrats may sometimes have turned-up noses, in theatrical iconography they never do. Scholz's unmanliness corresponds to Molly's lack of feminine sex appeal. Her nondescript domestic clothes reveal her origins, as does Scholz's aristocratic expression. Neither looks appropriate to their roles as Marquis's wife and civil servant.

The differences in the two women's appearances are significant. Molly first enters with a tray of breakfast things, looking like a servant; Anna looks like someone to be served, though she was once a shop assistant. Molly is a plain brunette whereas Anna has rich chestnut hair. Any woman who remains a plain brunette has only herself to blame, and the hair is the clearest signal that the difference between the two women may be a matter more of projection than of essence, though the image may correspond to an essence. 'Unscheinbar', unassuming – the German root means to appear or present an image – is repeated of Molly's appearance and her clothes. In her movements too she is self-effacing, scurrying on and off unobtrusively, setting tables and admitting visitors, as if she were an unnamed bit part in a comedy. On several occasions she tries to introduce other people to one another, but her own name is of no consequence. Yet her manner and look gradually take on an emphasis which positively shouts at the audience. By the second act we are not surprised when she brusquely refuses to play the Marquis's wife and have her hand kissed, or stalks off in a rage when Anna, who clearly often takes her place in bed, for a moment takes over the domestic role too and offers to clear the table. Not that she lifts a finger.

The women's appearances also convey tne themes of origins, conditioning and self-transformation. Anna moves in society as to the manner born, suggesting that in fact, ladies are not born but made. The plot asks whether she can transform herself further into a singer, and escape the female destiny. Molly stepped into the abyss of freedom from determination, but also of definition by milieu. She now wants to find herself again by reverting to her origins. She tries to pull Keith back with her into the small, safe world of Bückeburg. Her dress, manner, and gait all assert loudly that she is not Madame la Marquise; she even tells young Hermann directly that she is not married. Yet she obsessively acts the part of somebody's wife, an ordinary wife, anything but the wife of the Marquis of Keith.

A minor character again reinforces the logic of similarities and contrasts. Simba, so named by Keith, was once Kathi. She is a petty redhead further along the line from Molly's mousey brown through Anna's glowing chestnut. She plays many parts as maid, waitress and bohemienne. Her childhood recalls Molly's: Molly enjoyed skating as a girl; Simba spent her summers in the Tyrol among cherry trees and her winters sledging. This is exactly the kind of carefree youth Molly now regrets, for it led to her step into the abyss: she wishes she had been conditioned for a hardworking life as a good wife in Bückeburg. Simba may follow Molly into rootless bohemia, for she sometimes works as an artist's model and has lovers; on the other hand she sometimes earns her living as a waitress, like Anna Huber in the hat shop, and she could marry Count Trautenau as Anna did Count Werdenfels. Simba's role as waitress recalls the self-cast waitress, Molly, but Simba has none of Molly's resentment: according to Keith she is honoured to work at the party; she does not disdain bit parts as a training for the social theatre.

Like Raspe, Simba does not add up to a defined character. She looks like a typical Munich lass, but there is no knowing what she might become. Keith sees her as a female alter ego, outside the social order as he is, but like him determined to operate inside it, for there is nowhere else to go. She will act the part of waitress if need be, as he acts the part of Marquis. In a punning exchange in Act III, Simba questions the fatefulness of origins. Saranieff, jealous of Sommersberg, calls Simba a born whore. She makes him repeat the insult twice then retorts that she was not born a whore but a Käsbohrer, her family name, punning on the double meaning of 'geboren' – both 'born' and 'née' – and making it clear that one need not remain a born anything. The exchange recalls Anna's accusation in Act II that Keith is using her as a whore to get money from Scholz, which he indignantly denies. She claims to have talent as a whore and challenges him to use it and see what she will bring him – a whore is not something one is, but a part one may play if one has the talent. In the end, Anna uses her talent not to help Keith but to become Casimir's wife and Hermann's mother, parts she also has talent for. Who is really a whore or really a wife when both trade sex in exchange for their keep? Poor Molly, technically Keith's whore, is by repute his wife; yet he fails to provide her keep and sleeps with Anna whom he would make his wife and the mother of his children.

Voice and costumes reinforce the shifting images. The play offers a panoply of accents: foreign, regional and standard *Hochdeutsch*. As soon as Simba and Sascha open their mouths they are recognizable as Kathi and Sepperl; but as Anna's chambermaid, Simba can produce formal *Hochdeutsch*: accents are the stock in trade of the social as of the theatrical stage. The opposite extreme from Molly's inconspicuous domesticity is the dress Keith buys in Paris to launch Anna's career. It is a magic dress to transform her into a great singer; her appearance will cast a spell to make the audience hear a beautiful voice in harmony with the beautiful image. Molly, by contrast, is a Cinderella who refuses transformation by silk stockings or a *décolleté* and tries to draw Prince Charming down to the dust and ashes of the household hearth. In the party in Act III, the two brown-haired women with their secret affinity of origins and their contrasting appearance demonstrate the power of projection. The point is underlined at the opening of the act by Sommersberg, last seen in his miserable overcoat and now undergoing a visible transformation. His evening clothes, though still shabby, are decidedly elegant, and he has become Simba's sweetheart.

Molly wants to return to her origins, Anna has moved on and may go further, and Simba is a quicksilver creature who could become anything. In keeping with the schematic opposition of aristocratic pleasure and middle-class morality, Scholz also wishes to reappropriate his origins, though not by simple regression but by an upwards-spiralling dialectic which unites the apparent opposites in a higher synthesis. The characters engage in a complicated tussle with Keith as kingpin. He strains to launch Anna and himself upwards like a rocket, and lends a helping hand to heave Scholz out of his grave. At first Scholz strives to climb, but eventually he starts to pull downwards, the direction in which Molly has been pulling all along. Thomas Mann (1977) writes vividly of Wedekind's performance as Keith in the final confrontation with Scholz. As the insinuating, devilish voice tries to draw Keith down, he climbs up on to the writing desk and clings spreadeagled to the windowframe. Mann says he had never experienced anything stranger in the theatre than this eerily prodigious confrontation. His character Krull, the confidence trickster, is a direct descendant of Keith, as is Sternheim's Christian Maske, another player of roles, as his name indicates.

The play explores the idea of the free personality not through studies in depth but through cyphers and masks. The cyphers gain momentary definition through interchangeable masks, costumes, stage lighting and tricks of movement such as a stage limp. The plot is not grounded in an illusion of embodied life but starkly displayed as a decorative game of lines: the rising curve of a rocket, the zig-zag of Scholz's dialectic of virtue and pleasure, the downwards plunge of a body falling into water. As the rocket rises, the audience waits to see whether Keith, an Icarus flown too near the sun, will plunge down to a watery grave as Molly does. In Keith's closing words, life is a slide; not a dialectical upwards spiral, but a downwards swoop after the rising zoom of the rocket. The play is a fireworks display of contrasting motions of bodies. It is for the audience to decide whether there is a predominant trajectory, a unifying vision, and whether it is tragic, comic or something else again.

Archetypes and Aphorisms

The archetypal echoes in the *The Marquis of Keith* are travesties which never threaten to obscure the historically specific social and economic relations the play explores. Along with the aphoristic dialogue, they create an effect of patterned artifice. Fairy-tale motifs abound. Molly remains a stubborn anti-Cinderella, but Keith dreams of being the poor child who turns out to be a king. Anna will be his queen and they will dwell in a royal palace with Sascha and Simba as elfin servitors (Act IV). The magic palace of the arts is to be borne on the shoulders of the caryatids, as Keith calls them, the pot-bellied, bleary-eyed giants of the business world, in a scurrilous echo of Wagner's giants and Nibelungs and the lofty palace of Valhalla (Act II). Alas, it is the all too solid caryatids and their lord Casimir who triumph. Keith and Scholz recall the transformations and *Doppelgänger* of the Romantic *Märchen*. The changeling is a soulless substitute for a human baby and the *Doppelgänger* a soulless other self. As Karl Miller (1985) suggests, the motif is associated with social mobility and escape from the bonds of traditional morality. Comparable works in English literature are Stevenson's *Doctor Jekyll and Mr Hyde* (1886) and Wilde's *The Picture of Dorian Gray* (1891). Doubles may be alter egos or a split self (Tymms, 1949). In *The Marquis of Keith*, good and evil are parcelled out into two characters with secret affinities; Stevenson makes the division within the one person; in Wilde's story the portrait shows forth the evil alter ego invading Dorian Gray. Stevenson, like his predecessor Hogg, author of *The Confessions of a Justified Sinner* (1824), belongs in the tradition of Scottish Calvinism: by God's grace the chosen are exempt from the law and can act as they will; but no one can know who is chosen; the double may be one of the elect or else the Devil incarnate.

There is a theological flavour in this play pervaded with Biblical tags. The changeling Keith, alter ego to Scholz, claims to belong with the elect. He is certainly a sinner, but by the end we are bound at least to doubt if he is justified. Neither does Scholz find any grace in good works, and as he tries in the name of virtue to drag Keith off to the hell of the lunatic asylum he closely resembles Hogg's Calvinist possessed of the Devil. Further literary motifs with a theological flavour identify Keith as satanic as well as demonic and bind him to Scholz as a brother. Keith claims that he is a bastard, son of a mathematician and a gypsy, or of a philosopher and a horse-thief (Act I).

It is a good story for a man beyond good and evil, like Christian Maske's claimed bastardy in Sternheim's *The Snob*: better a bastard than a bourgeois; better the aristocratic bend sinister than respectable middle-class origins. Illegitimacy sets the bastard outside the law which he then claims to stand above. Keith is a bastard Edmund to the Edgar, Scholz, the true spiritual heir to Keith's father. Keith's escape from the firing squad recalls Dostoevsky, and the doubling of brothers, good and evil, looks back to *The Brothers Karamazov*, which looks back to Schiller's *Die Räuber*, which in turn echoes *King Lear*. In an explicit reference to Shakespeare's *Richard III*, Molly recalls Keith in Santiago shouting 'A dollar, a dollar, a Republic for a dollar' (Act I). Like his wicked predecessor, who was also a master of roles, Keith was born a cripple. Such echoes recall the archetypal association of freedom with evil. Lucifer himself is the prototype.

But the reverberating tradition is travestied in Wedekind's play, for Keith does not rise to the sublime heights of evil his predecessors attain. Nor is evil so sharply defined here as in Christian tradition; echoes of the Old Testament story of Jacob and Esau complicate matters. Richard III was a crippled usurper who seized a title not his by birthright. Keith's concupiscent limp also recalls Jacob, another usurper who wrestled with God and wrenched his thigh. When Anna sells out to Casimir, Keith accuses her of selling her birthright for a mess of pottage, as Esau did, while the aristocrat Scholz, who has inherited the goods of this world, laments the loss of his birthright which he calls human rights, a new-fangled notion remote from the Old Testament. Keith is a Jacob who would inherit the world not by descent – he flaunts his illegitimacy – but by virtue of his power to enjoy. His vision of philoprogenitive bliss with Anna recalls Jacob the patriarch. Like Jacob's Leah and Rachel, Keith has Molly and Anna. The fact that Jehovah, not the most just of gods, loved the usurper and made him prosper is in keeping with Keith's confirmation motto, 'We know that all things work together for good to them that love God' (Romans 8, 28; Act IV). The motto poor Scholz received was 'Many are called but few are chosen' (Matthew, 22, 14; Act IV). Anna is astonished when Keith claims to love God. But God, he says, is self. Keith has chosen himself and is justified by self-love. Hence his faith that he will inherit the promised land: in Act I he echoes Peter on a high mountain with Christ when Moses and Elias appear to them: 'Hier laßt uns Hütten bauen', ('Let us make here three tabernacles': Matthew, 17, 4), a common tag in German, meaning 'here is the place to settle'. Keith's self-promised land is here on earth and he mockingly tells Molly, 'Thy kingdom is not yet come.' Scholz is fleetingly Christ to Keith's Satan. He would have like to take up Satan's offer of 'the world in all its glory' (an echo of Matthew, 4, 10), but bitterly recognizes that it is not to be. In their final meeting he plays the Devil to Keith's suffering Christ, as Thomas Mann's description of the scene implies. Anna ignores Keith's taunt about messes of potage and opts for Casimir's world in all its glory, following the precepts Keith/Satan/one-of-God's-chosen has hitherto proclaimed. When Scholz tries to take Anna from Keith, he is branded with the mark of Cain, introducing another pair of brothers (Act IV). This time Scholz is the would-be usurper. Finally Scholz, instead of thanking God, complains that he is not as other men are, playing the anti-Pharisee to Keith's publican (Act V). Keith, like the Pharisee, thanks God that he has never doubted his difference from other men, but in being worse than them, rather than better.

All these references to changelings, *Doppelgänger* brothers and pairs decoratively connect Keith and Scholz as protagonists. To some extent, they can be ordered as good Scholz and wicked Keith, but this moral distinction continually breaks down. It does not work very well with Jacob and Esau, still less with Cain and Abel, and when it comes to the Pharisee and the publican we lose sight of which is which and who is who. Different orders of values clash in post-Nietzschean combat. Neither Scholz's moralism nor Keith's revaluations emerge in a very favourable light, while the Bible seems to support both positions. Scholz's motto says that only a few are chosen of God, and Keith's that those who love God will prosper. If God is self, the message offered by the two mottoes together is that if Keith chooses and loves himself, he will prosper. By sheer intensity of egoism he will bend the world to his will: my will be done and I shall inherit the earth. But such Nietzschean faith is undermined, as the social barriers to freedom and threats to selfhood close in. The archetypes only compound the social confusions in turn-of-the-century Munich.

Goethe's *Faust* is a major source of reference in *The Marquis of Keith*. Scholz seems to be Faust and Keith Mephistopheles. Faust had two souls, and so has Scholz, the moralist who wants to be a hedonist. As Keith says, 'Seine eine Seele heißt Ernst Scholz, seine andere Graf Trautenau' (One of his souls is called Ernst Scholz, the other Count Trautenau: Act II). This makes him a monster in Anna's eyes; she does not like people who are neither one thing nor the other. Scholz's career follows Faust's in reverse. He starts off with a humanitarian project which results in the death of the beneficiaries, like Faust's disaster with Philemon and Baucis. Only then does he turn to Mephistopheles/Keith and the pursuit of pleasure, moving with disgraceful rapidity from Simba, most unlike Gretchen apart from her simple origins, to Anna/Helen. His career reaches a climax in the concert party with its dancing women echoing the *Walpurgisnacht*, the nocturnal festival of witches. But rather than being saved by a mystical choir he ends up in a lunatic asylum.

Apart from his two souls, Scholz is not a very convincing Faust. When he tries to take Keith with him to the asylum to save him from his evil ways he has become Mephistopheles dragging Faust for his own good off to hell. The secret affinities of the doubles, Faust and Mephistopheles, have often been noted. Keith is both rolled into one. He is a spirit who denies traditional pieties, and he tries unsuccessfully to play Mephistopheles' games with paper money. But he has to be recast as Faust because of his relationships with Molly/Gretchen and Ann/Helen. At the end, Mephistophelean negation denies Goethean metaphysics; there is no sign that everything earthly is but an image, and no upward-soaring close, only a bumpy ride here on earth. Molly tries to draw Keith down rather than onwards, and does not disappear into the mystic collectivity of the eternal woman, but remains an untransfigured corpse. The audience is left in the historical world where human beings often die premature and meaningless deaths.

The echoes of the Bible and *Faust* merge easily with the aphoristic dialogue. Keith is a master of the pithy formulation: 'Sünde ist eine mythologische Bezeichnung für schlechte Geschäfte'; 'Die Wahrheit ist unser kostbarstes Lebensgut, und man kann nicht sparsam genug damit umgehen'; 'Das glänzendste Geschäft in dieser Welt ist die Moral' (Sin is a mythological expression for bad business: Act II; Truth is our most precious possession; we can't be too economical with it: Act II; The best business in this world is morality: Act V). Keith declares the last of these aphorisms to be the philosopher's stone. 'Es gibt keine Ideen, seien sie sozialer, wissenschaftlicher oder künstlerischer Art, die irgend etwas anderes als Hab und Gut zum Gegenstand hätten' (There are no ideas, whether social, scientific or artistic, concerned with anything other than property: Act I). An expert in *Ideologiekritik*, Keith believes he can manipulate the power of money to his own ends. In this he anticipates Brecht's Mother Courage, another witty exponent of the cynical aphorism and deluded devotee of free enterprise. Aphorisms sound like quotations; they have a proverbial air that says: we speak with authority; these are not private opinions but truths universally acknowledged, like Holy Writ or the works of Goethe. In form Keith's aphorisms sound timeless, but their content attacks hallowed pieties. Their subversive quality comes more from the disparity between form and content than from the actual cynicisms; they subvert the form of timeless truths and all the archetypal echoes and quotations.

The aphorisms are not the only feature which recalls *The Importance of Being Earnest*, first produced in 1895 and published in 1899, the year Wedekind completed *The Marquis of Keith*. Wilde's eponymous hero shares a name with Ernst Scholz, and both are worthier than their respective companions Algernon and Keith. Jack, who is earnest, turns out really to be Ernest, whereas Ernst, who is earnest, is really Gaston Count Trautenau. The German play is a more bitter attack on the surviving cult of origins in money-worshipping liberal society, and a more anxious reflection on identity. But Wilde, the Irishman, and Wedekind, nominally American with long years in Switzerland, men of talent both fêted and abused, launched a barbed wit against the pretensions of a society to which they did not quite belong. The travestied archetypes and the pervasive aphorisms, which deny the timelessness of truth they appear to assert, give the audience no firm basis for judging the roles the social actors play on the historical stage of Munich at the turn of the century.

Collapsing Structures

The Marquis of Keith has close affinities with *Spring Awakening*. Keith is an older Melchior in the mask of a Marquis. Moritz has emerged from his grave, transmogrified into Ernst Scholz, who eventually reverts to type and joins with Molly/Wendla in trying to draw Keith down. Simba is another Ilse, Anna possibly so, but in the end she withdraws from childish transformation fantasies into an adult role. The Masked Man's programme for survival in bourgeois society is explored through characters of parental age, though memories and minor figures like Hermann or Sascha preserve the child's-eye view. The play shows a world in flux. The landed aristocracy are no longer dominant; whether they have gambled away most of their money like von Werdenfels or are still wealthy like Scholz, power resides with the bourgeoisie, the Consul Casimirs. Not rank or land but capital seeking investment outlets determines what gets done. The class distinctions of the past have weakened, as aristocrats marry actresses or shop assistants, while Casimir marries a Countess, albeit née Huber, to add lustre to his household.

But the sense of flux comes less from socially mobile individuals changing positions in the class structure. Rather the whole metaphor of structure is wobbling dangerously. The collective equivalent of the uncertainties surrounding the individual characters – who and what are they 'really'? – is the imminent disintegration also of institutions and classes which have hitherto preserved some continuity between generations. The link between private self and public image has become tenuous not only because characters move away from their origins but because that very process undermines the public categories of definition. If men like Keith or Raspe can play the marquis or the policeman, what value or meaning do such categories retain? Consul Casimir, the public embodiment of patrician power, knows privately that he could be thrown into a gaol at any time, yet he acts the part of the paternal fountainhead of moral authority. The metaphor of actors playing shifting parts subverts both individual identity and the parts played – the aristocrat, the husband, the wife, the whore – leaving a sense of all-pervading fraudulence, a dance of masks behind which there are no clear features. Nor do the masks represent anything, for where only masks exist there is nothing to represent. Fraudulence loses meaning without the authentic as a measure. Take Raspe, the theologian–criminal–policeman: if religious and worldly laws are a sham, then 'criminal' loses its meaning, for there is no order against which to define transgression.

The sense of flux inheres in many details. Keith has no papers, possibly no nationality; he has moved about from Cuba to Munich to Paris. It remains obscure why Raspe was in a French gaol, or how he comes to be in Munich. Hermann cannot wait to set off for Africa. Just as Molly has left Bückeburg, von Trautenau has moved from Trautenau and become a rootless wanderer across continents. Blood and earth, whether peasant or aristocratic, offer no hold. Two motifs of physical transport symbolize social movement on a large and a small scale respectively: railways and bicycles. Germany's industrial growth in the nineteenth century was founded on railways, and the network almost doubled in size between the mid-sixties and the mid-seventies when nationalization began (Stolper, 1967, p. 41). The top rank of the civil service, as of the army, was still the preserve of the aristocracy, but the middle rank, consisting of people such as railway officials, was manned by the educated middle class, whose education was far from practical. Such men enjoyed high social status if not always high rewards (Sagarra, 1977, p. 263ff). Scholz's desire to do good is in keeping with the reformist ideology embraced by the state in competition with the rising socialist movement. But Scholz brings mayhem, not safe efficiency, when his efforts at technical improvements cause a terrible accident. As with Raspe, this is less a satire on an incompetent or criminal bureaucracy which ought to be reformed, than a grotesque image of collapsing social categories: the reliable servant of civil society who kills men, women and children; the opposite elements of the hybrid criminal–policeman, which cancel one another and destroy the concept of law.

Whereas the railway is a juggernaut beyond the control of well-meaning reformers, the bicycle is a wholly positive symbol of change. *The Marquis of Keith* is set in 1899 at the very height of the cycling fashion, before the motor car took over. The decorative posters of the time convey the exhilaration of wheeled motion and the charm of new fashions. Some citizens, however, were less than enthusiastic about the new trend, as we see from the following item from the *Münchener Zeitung* in 1900 (quoted in Rauck et al. 1979: 76):

Yesterday, at 12 o'clock of a Sunday morning, the public strolling in large numbers along the Maximilianstraße were offered a disgraceful and shocking spectacle. A young couple drove rapidly along the street on a bicycle built for two. The couple consisted of a person of the male sex and his inamorata, the latter in a flowered silk skirt through which her pounding legs propelling the vehicle forwards were clearly apparent to all who wished to see. Proud as an Amazon the fair lady shamelessly displayed herself to all and sundry, travelling on quite unconcerned. It remains to be asked: is this the latest fashion in cycling? Is public decency to be thus flouted with impunity? Finally: is this the newest kind of advertisement for a certain type of female? And last of all: Where are the police . . .

Hermann appears in Act I of *The Marquis of Keith* in an elegant cycling outfit. In the early days, women went cycling disguised as men, and the young cyclist, a boy played by a girl, dramatically evokes the changing female image which conservative spirits saw as a threat to social order. Cycling helped liberate women from petticoats and the corset. As a doctor and cycling enthusiast of the time points out, the corset deforms the rib-cage and weakens the muscles, turning women into the delicate creatures so beloved of chivalrous men. He advocates divided skirts and bloomers, invented in America in 1849, as well as rather large knickers and the *Reformkorsett*, a kind of liberty bodice (Lessing 1982: 408–424). In the 1890s, cycle production rose over tenfold and by the end of the decade prices had dropped spectacularly so that they were not beyond the means of girls like Simba, whereas earlier in the decade, as we learn from Wedekind's Paris diary, the prostitute Kadudja had to pawn her jewellery to buy a second-hand bicycle (Hay: 201). In *Three Men on the Bummel* (1901), Jerome K. Jerome (1983: 205) writes of the New Woman on a bicycle:

> If anything can change the German character, it will be the German woman. She herself is changing rapidly – advancing as we call it. Ten years ago no German woman caring for her reputation, hoping for a husband, would have dared to ride a bicycle: today they spin about the country in their thousands. The old folks shake their heads at them; but the young men, I notice, overtake them and ride beside them.

Scholz cycles to Schleißheim with his inamorata, the fair Simba, who tells of his mad laughter amidst the flashing lightning of a thunderstorm (Act III). His transfiguration seems to confirm Jerome K. Jerome's view. But Simba's fear that he might be struck by lightning later comes true, when the fragment from the fireworks canon enters his knee. The concupiscent demon in lurid red lighting is an illusion; the limp becomes an excuse for cancelling a cycling trip with Anna, and then disappears: Scholz remains untransformed by the New Woman.

Cycling marks women's growing freedom from physical and psychological constraints. Young Hermann is also representative of the new youth culture of open-air activities. The youth culture of late adolescence was an outgrowth of the middle-class childhood as a distinct stage in life with its own fashions and rituals. Middle-class women with all the urban services at their disposal had greater leisure than in the past, a trend intensified by the movement of work out of the home into the office or factory. The result was the two spheres: the private realm of the household to which women were confined, and the public male realm. Such developments produced the isolated woman with too much leisure, but they also engendered a complex domestic culture and the craft of mothering set in the nursery with its children's games, stories and toys – the toy industry was particularly successful in Germany. The expression 'aus guter Kinderstube' (well brought up, literally 'from a good nursery') evokes a prosperous household where children had their own realm, like Melchior's study in *Spring Awakening* (Weber-Kellermann 1982: 108). Frau Gabor shows traces of mothering craft and Wendla's pretty dress exemplifies the kind of children's fashions and freedoms which create the adolescent crisis as the constricting adult clothes and roles begin to bite. In the later play, the picture is less of a straightforward generation conflict between lively children and dead adults. All the references to childhood – picking cherries, sledging, skating – suggest freedom, but Molly's complaint that she was not made to work enough suggests that too much freedom can be harmful. Bückeburg is at once a realm of happy childhood and a fate worse than death to the adult Keith. Hermann cannot be too oppressed or he would not have his cycling gear. His mother, dead for three years, no doubt indulged him so that he now jibs under his father's direct rule unmediated by the mother. The nuclear family with its mix of maternal indulgence and paternal authority contains the seed of its own instability. It stimulates individuality in children, yet binds them under the rule of the father. The two factors together create the adolescent crisis for which peasant or proletarian children, who have to work from an early age, have no time. The sense of flux stems in part from such centrifugal tendencies in the family: the very foundation of social order seems to be crumbling.

Relations between parents and children and between spouses or quasi-spouses like Keith and Molly or Anna are most at risk. Motherhood is as strikingly absent here as it is in Lulu's roles. Mothers are either dead like Hermann's or invisible like Molly's. The latter is a mother-in-law, part of Keith's fate worse than death. Molly, past the daughterly age, ought to be a mother. In this new mobile world her desire to go back to her mother in Bückeburg is a regression even beyond the nuclear family, towards extended obligations to the older generation. The fact that her author does not make Molly a mother is an anomaly, for her agonized concern for practical survival is quintessentially motherly. The lack of children strengthens the values upheld by Keith: were his behaviour to threaten the survival of children, not just of an adult woman, the value of free self-development would be harder to uphold. But Molly does have a surrogate child. Just as Frau Gabor's love of her son had undertones of feeling for a lover, so Molly's feeling for Keith has maternal undertones. Her obsessive and possessive concern recalls the mother in the nuclear family, whose life is narrowed exclusively to private relations. Such a mother displaces her own selfhood into her child and is left empty, a non-entity, if the child breaks free. This is the logic ordaining Molly's death; without Keith she does not exist. Molly is the dead weight of love; it scarcely matters whether the love she represents is that of the mother or of the good woman. Both are a threat to the masculine psyche in pursuit of freedom, masculine because the focus of the play is male and because economics shape the issue of freedom in these gender-specific terms. Unlike Molly, Keith goes on living, but how far he has selfhood other than mere physical identity is unclear, stripped as he finally is of all relations with others.

In losing Molly, Keith loses a surrogate mother and a quasi-spouse at one fell swoop. His life is a series of adolescent crises. He was estranged from his father an an early age. A break with Molly, a more traumatic casting-off of a mother figure, is pre-empted by her death, when he feels that rush of love and guilt children often feel on the death of neglected parents. Keith had thought of leaving Molly to marry Anna: serial marriage is serial adolescent crisis. Divorce is a more substantial threat to the family than adultery. Here it seems to liberate women rather than men, for the obvious exemplars are all free women, 'Freifrauen'. Scholz's proposed marriage would have been one of duty on his part and convenience on his fiancée's. Instead he settles money on her, a case of pre-marital divorce. His fiancée is only too glad to be rid of him.

Divorce weakens patriarchy if women can break the marriage contract without risk of penury. The play shows divorce only among the well-off and childless who can afford it. But Molly's situation is different. The horror she contemplates, of loss of Keith and total penury, recalls the situation of the divorced wife bereft of children, of husband, of the means of subsistence and of social identity grounded in family and marriage. Scholz defends Simba, whose free life-style, he remarks, has never caused pain like the hell that was his parents' marriage. The settlement with his fiancée pre-empts the fate of partners bound by duty and financial constraints. But if there is no money to settle and women cannot earn their living on a par with men, divorce is less of a liberation. Simba might offer a model as hetaera in a utopia when marriage has withered away; but her fate in this world is more sordid: she has to earn her living by means of waitressing and a bit of prostitution. This may please bachelors and husbands, but it is scarcely ideal for the divorced wife. The *Freifrauen* hope to become dancers, but women cannot all be dancing hetaerae even in utopia.

Besides finance, there is the problem of stigma. The milieu depicted is ambiguously located between respectable society and the *demi-monde*. Would Casimir have married Anna had she been divorced, as Raspe thought, rather than respectably widowed? Anna preserves the outer facade of respectability in maintaining her own household even though she is Keith's mistress. The phenomenon of the mistress, her status decently cloaked, is compatible with patriarchy. Divorce, by contrast, threatens social structures, but apparently without bringing a new freedom to relations between the sexes because women remain economically dependent. Wedekind remains caught in a vision of women as exclusively sexual beings, while at the same time showing the disastrous effects of such a reduction combined with economic inequality.

Children are crucial in any change of partners. Keith is not the only surrogate child in this play devoid of mothers. Hermann is on offer to a motherly heart, but Molly fails to rise to the challenge. In their exchange in Act II she lives up to her sour name; too immersed in her own worries, too inwardly dependent, she cannot play mother to anyone other than Keith. In any case, a woman who so obsessively seeks definition through another would be a bad mother. It is different with Anna. Casimir's main motive in proposing to her is his perception of how well she will play the part of mother. The role of the mother is alienated by being played by a woman who is not a biological mother. The social function of the mother becomes clearer when it is cut off from a relationship going back to pregnancy, which could make it seem a fact of nature. The little scene in Act II when Anna teaches Hermann how to behave towards his father is analytic rather than mimetic, like Brecht's Azdak in *The Caucasian Chalk Circle* playing the part of the Grand-duke. Anna teaches Hermann to become like his father rather than like Keith. She directs him away from adventures in Africa, the equivalent of the Cuban episode; he should stay in Munich and learn to make his mark here, as his father has done. The obedient child of today is the patriarch of tomorrow. The mother must mediate between father and son so that the child will neither rebel against paternal authority nor be so crushed by it as to be incapable of assuming power in his turn. She teaches the child to observe the forms of obedience; those who would rule must first obey and respect the hierarchy of power. This is like the old wisdom of dissimulation taught to women: the clever woman does not nag like Molly; the clever child does not rebel. Hermann's shift from indignant rebellion to sobs is as theatrical as Scholz's transformation from moralist into hedonist: the first is achieved by means of a histrionic show of tears, the second by the actorly trick of a limp. If he can learn this lesson, Hermann will avoid corrective detention in contrast to his predecessors, Melchior and Hugenberg, and be rewarded with money for a trip to London. Nor will he make Keith's mistake of trying to stand above society only to end up outside it. Anna herself decides not to rise like a rocket; she chooses the path of accommodation and draws Hermann with her.

Anna also annexes two other surrogate children, Sascha and Simba. Simba reverts to Kathi and becomes Anna's maid, and Sascha also moves into Anna's household where, unlike in Keith's, he will get a decent meal every day. Keith names Sascha as a father names his son. The extra stab of pain he feels on losing him echoes the pain of divorce when there is a parting with children too. But Keith, with no papers, no money, and no social position, is unfit to be a conventional father, while his treatment of Sascha, whom he fails even to feed, also contradicts his ideal of the free self, his rejection of family conditioning: he reduces the child in his household to a lackey who must kneel to do up Keith's boots in a costume of Keith's choosing, in a parody of the obedient son of an authoritarian father. But lackeys and children have to be fed, a responsibility Keith refuses: as a result, he loses Sascha to Anna, and both will enter Consul Casimir's household, one as wife, the other as servant.

Hermann kneels to his father as Sascha kneels to Keith, postures conveying power-relations between father and child, or employer and servant. The relations bring their own logic independently of the will of individuals. In the theatre, the logic is an inconography of roles. The actors must follow the rules of the part. As on the stage, so in the world: a son kneels, a waitress carries trays and does not have her hand kissed by visitors. Because the characters so overtly choose to play parts and change roles, the social institutions the roles represent – nationality, class, marriage, the family, gender, the state – take on an air of arbitrary factitiousness. The person fragments into a series of masks; the institutions are canvas-and-paste scenery. On the other hand, the roles once assumed exert an iron logic. An actor who cannot or will not observe the rules will be dropped from the play and excluded from society. The theatrical metaphor is ambiguous: it is unclear whether all the changing of roles represents liberation from the fatality of origins, or serves merely to prop up rickety social institutions which are an ideological surface overlying real power-relations.

Power and Money

The power of money is a real force at work in four sorts of relations: between generations; between the sexes; between classes; and between would-be artists and patrons or the paying public. The first three are constantly interwoven as one complex. The power of the old over the young, of men over women and of those higher in the social hierarchy over those lower in it is brought out through visual and postural patterns and repetitions. Sascha, the peasant, might once have knelt to a marquis because he was a marquis, especially had he been a Russian serf as his pseudonym suggests. Here in progressive Germany it does not matter whether Keith really is a marquis; Sascha kneels to an employer whom he leaves as soon as possible when he fails to pay the wage; Keith inspires no feudal loyalty. Hermann might once have honoured his father out of filial piety; now, having failed to get money to run away, he honours a father whose money and mantle of power he will one day inherit, provided his father has not gone to gaol. Molly's movements as wife – servant are echoed by Simba's as waitress. In both cases women serve, and receive wages from men. Again, Keith fails in all respects to fulfil his role, and in response, Molly nags him for money, struggling to buy food and hold off the local tradesmen. Anna's future position in Casimir's household is veiled. She will be the wife of a rich man, the part Molly refuses to play when she crassly exhibits poverty and servility. But the lesson with Hermann clearly demonstrates Anna's instrumental function in reproducing the power of wealth. Her elegance will decorate the household of a rich man who can pay, unlike Keith who fails to pay for decorative Sascha. Whether or not Casimir ends up in gaol is immaterial. The power he wields is not a birthright attaching to him and his heirs personally, as to the long generations of feudal landowners; it is the impersonal power of money. The individuals who wield such power may keep changing, but the power remains active.

Because the play focuses on upwardly mobile Keith and down-wardly mobile Scholz, transition between classes at first seems easy, and the opportunities available to young people endless. But other details conflict with this impression. Simba's conversation with Saranieff in Act III is a telling moment. When Saranieff exclaims on hearing of the bicycle trip with Scholz that Simba might have become a Countess she retorts:

> I dank schön! Sozialdemokratin hätt i können werden. Weltverbesser-ung. Menschheitsbeglückung, das san so dem seine Sozialdemokraten. Noa, weißt, ich bin fein net für die Sozialdemokraten. Die san mir z'moralisch! Wann die amal z'regieren anfangen, nachher da is aus mit die Champagnersoupers. – Sag du, hast mei Schatz net g'sehn?

> *Not a chance! I'd have become a social democrat. Improving the world, uplifting humanity, that's him and his social democrats. No, I can't be doing with social democrats. They're too moral. Once they start laying down the law there'll be no more champagne suppers. – I say, have you seen my feller?*

Her rejection of Scholz looks like a refusal to barter herself for marriage to a man she does not fancy, even if he is a count. But what she opts for is the world as it is, and the power of money to buy champagne suppers. There are few possibilities for Simba in the world as it is, however. She can sell sex in return for champagne suppers in a *chambre séparée*. Any money she earns will be controlled by her 'feller', a euphemism for 'pimp': Sommersberg boasts that he dictates her love letters, but whoever dictates the letters holds the power. She cannot leave the *chambre séparée* and enter society in her own right. Even Keith, the man of masks, can only smuggle her in as a waitress. She will play that role well and cause no embarrassment, for she understands class differences, as Keith assures Scholz. She may appear a lively, beautiful person behind the scenes in the interval, but on the social stage she is a waitress, as Raspe makes clear in scolding her for keeping the guests waiting. Raspe, the policeman, protects the social order and ensures that Simba, née Käsbohrer (literally Cheeseborer), serves the cheese promptly. If Sommersberg can acquit himself well, he could become her *entrée* to society; Simba fears that he will get drunk and blow his chances in Keith's venture. Simba's only hope of improving the quality of her life rests on a man, and he in turn is dependent on the power of money. When Keith fails, Sommersberg fails, and Simba's modest ambitions crash. She finally turns into

Wedekind as Schön and his wife Tilly as Lulu in Earth Spirit.

Wedekind as the Masked Man in Spring Awakening, *Vienna, 1908.*

Wedekind with his lute, which he played to accompany his songs in the Elf Scharfrichter *cabaret in Munich.*

Wedekind in 1917.

A cartoon of The Marquis of Keith *and caricatures of Wedekind and Tilly from* Simplicissimus.

Tilly in the trouser role of Hermann in The Marquis of Keith.

The idyllic Schloß Lenzburg in Switzerland where Wedekind spent his youth.

Comic cartoons of Strindberg, Wedekind and Shaw from the Deutschetheater-austellung of 1927. Photograph in Das Theater, *1927, VII, Heft 11, p. 253.*

Louise Brooks as Lulu, Alice Roberts as the Countess Geschwitz and Fritz Kortner as Schön in Pabst's film Pandora's Box *of 1928.The film combines the two Lulu plays.*

Kathi, the maid in Casimir's household, where she will serve champagne to others as she serves cheese now.

Measured against historical reality, the position Simba and Sascha are in at the end of the play is still rather rosy. Social historians paint a grim picture of life for domestic servants at the turn of the century. Young people from rural areas did not commonly find employers like Anna, filled with motherly protectiveness. Weber-Kellerman (1982: 122) writes of the social gulf between employers and servants in the hard shadow of capitalism, and quotes the following ordinances laying down the duties of servants and employers:

The Employer's Duties: The employer must pay the promised wage punctually and provide good, nourishing food.

The Servant's Duties: The duty to work according to the will and orders of the employer; the servant should devote himself at all times to serving not just the employers but all members of the family and guests; the servant is subject to the training and supervision of the employer, may not go out without permission and should the occasion arise may even be punished by the employer. The servant should be faithful, diligent, attentive, respectable, of good character, cleanly, respectful, godfearing, virtuous, and well-behaved; the servant should not be extravagant and should be loyal, that is should not gossip, eat too much, or steal.

As an employer, Keith imposed few of the conditions to which servants were normally subject – Sascha is required only to kneel and look decorative – but he fulfilled neither of his own duties; and if Kathi wants to keep her position in Casimir's house, she will enjoy no more champagne suppers.

Art as a Commodity

The crumbling of caste exclusivity and the consequent apparent freedom for enterprising individuals is, to quote Scholz, 'illusion, all illusion'. Behind the illusion is the reality of money and power relations bolstered by a hypocritical culture of appearances. The only difference from the past is the greater turnover of actors playing the top parts, now that power flows not from birth but from money. In the *Communist Manifesto*, Marx asserts that the defining relationship of bourgeois society is the naked money transaction, a reality clothed in appearances, in lip-service paid to family duty, sexual decencies, respectability, but also to freedom, individual talent and enterprise. Among the professed values is art, the supreme expression of the emancipated individual, and hence the very spirit of bourgeois society. Keith's palace of the arts should have a double aspect. It will be a free realm where the individual can unfold his gifts: Saranieff will no longer have to paint fake Böcklins, but can join the *avant-garde* along with Zamrjaki, who need no longer starve with integrity; there may be a corner for Sommersberg and the private art of poetry, the distilled quintessence of the inner self. At the same time the palace will be a shrine where the bourgeois public may worship its own essence of freedom. Feuerbach argued that God was man's alienated essence. Keith is high priest of the cult of art elevated above material reality as the alienated essence of bourgeois society. His magic palace should reconcile two claims: first that art flows from individual genius; secondly that it is at the same time the supreme value of society and its highest expression. The palace will be the meeting place of genius and the public; poets will come together there, emerging from isolation yet preserving their artistic freedom. According to Kutscher (1970, 2: 64) Wedekind had the new *Deutsches Theater* in Munich in mind, opened in 1896, in creating Keith's Magic Palace. Peter Jelavich (1985: 115–25) records how the *Deutsches Theater*, orginally conceived as a centre for theatrical modernism, quickly declined into cheap commercialism. Other prototypes are the *Glaspalast* or the palatial Stuck villa. Stuck was the son of a miller and no doubt had red hands like Keith (and Wedekind). The idea might also have been inspired by Wagner's Bayreuth, a shrine in which the master realized his revolutionary *Gesamtkunstwerk* and which became a national institution.

From a less flattering perspective, art can be seen as opium offering the illusion of spiritual freedom to profoundly unfree and materialistic bourgeois society. The illusion is not even very powerful; it is little more than an empty sham, like going to church as a social chore. The businessmen backers are not thrilled by Zamrjaki and are more moved by the soprano's bosom than her voice, as Keith well knows. Their concern is with building contracts and restaurant facilities. Nor will the palace unite society in communal ritual; just as the mass of people evoked in the last scene of *Die Meistersinger* have no *entrée* to Bayreuth, so the Kathis and Sepperls in Wedekind's play will have no *entrée* to Keith's palace, unless dressed in fancy livery, selling programmes.

Keith knows that the edification of the public is as spurious as the freedom of the artists who, as he says, are completely free as long as they draw the paying public. Released from the tyranny of individual patrons like the Bishop of Salzburg, who proverbially kicked Mozart down the stairs, the artist is free to die a pauper if the philistine public will not pay.

When art is a commodity, the impresario becomes a key figure. In creating Keith, Wedekind had his friend Willy Grétor in mind, an art-dealer and faker of paintings. Keith foreshadows the rise of impresarios like Diaghilev or Reinhardt. In bourgeois society, the artist no longer deals face to face with a patron, but with the faceless collectivity of a public stretching beyond local and national boundaries. The impresario heralds specialization and division of labour in a more complex market. He is the go-between, the investment and marketing manager. The good impresario incorporates the public within himself, presenting the product effectively so as to conjure up the appropriate response, truly a task for a magician with plenty of scope for fraud. Wedekind, the mere author, was not entirely pleased with Reinhardt whom Thomas Mann, an expert on fraudulence, celebrated as the old magician. Kafka's artist stories such as *A Hunger Artist, First Sorrow* and *Josefine the Singer* or *The People of Mice* are fascinating explorations of alienation in modern art production. The performing arts, with their division between artist and impresario, become a metaphor for the self-divided artist split between free expression and projection for a public. The Janus-faced work of art is not an icon complete in itself, but is shaped by the impresario inside each artist through whom a ghostly public, not the flesh-and-blood patron of the past, exerts its power; it only comes to life effectively – recreated or distorted, always modified – in the minds of the receiving public. The impresario, literally the businessman of art, is also a metaphor for essentially aesthetic matters of presentation and projection – the literal can affect the metaphorical when the need to sell affects aesthetic form. One may draw optimistic, pessimistic, or mixed conclusions from all this. At one extreme Brecht, a master-impresario, saw the relation between work and audience as one of mutual transformation, as audiences actively participate in making the work and in so doing are themselves changed. As an artist, he identified with a potentially revolutionary public. In *A Hunger Artist*, Kafka tends towards a pessimistic view; in *Josefine* he offers a wry mixture of attitudes very much akin to Wedekind's.

For all his ruthlessness, Keith fails to manipulate the market. After Cuba he has no interest in revolutions and no ambition to transform the public. He tries only to project the illusion most liable to appeal to his target public of businessmen, and for a while he succeeds. Anna, however, does not believe that the illusion can be sustained. She does not have a great voice, and fears the Munich public schooled in opera. Art does not just consist of *trompe l'oeil* effects of lighting and costume; a great performance rests on years of training and long rehearsal. After all, it has taken Keith himself ten years to produce his current dazzling performance as a rich marquis, and he has had to strain every nerve. Anna is not a singer and has no faith that she can become one. The Parisian dress exemplifies the intrusion of the impresario into aesthetic form, creating a vulgar spectacle based on sex-appeal. In his efforts to raise money for the arts, Keith debases art into mere show and Anna into a thing to be manipulated. By 'show' I do not mean the popular arts such as circus or variety for which Raspe (here the mouthpiece of his creator) thirsts. The acrobat and tightrope walker in Wedekind's work, as in Kafka's *First Sorrow*, symbolize a perfection of skill beyond the categories of high or low art. In Kafka's story, the anxious impresario protects the tightrope walker from mundane necessities, to leave him free to practise his art. Keith's activities *vis-à-vis* Anna are not like that. As she comments bitterly, he treats her like an animal to be marketed, 'wie ein Stück Vieh', the phrase Raspe uses to describe Casimir's treatment of his son. In both cases the phrase designates a power-relationship. Keith's concern with marketing reduces the putative artist to a well-packaged commodity or an advertising gimmick. He is the pimp of the art world who makes Anna into a meretricious spectacle. This vicious circle develops quite against his will, as his anguished protests at Anna's complaints show. He needs money to liberate art, but debases art to gain money. He is a victim of the logic of money. The market flows through him in his capacity as impresario. The relationship between two people, Keith and Anna, becomes a relation between the market and a commodity. Anna retreats from exposure to the faceless market into marriage, where she can use traditional female skills to manage one man. In so doing, she escapes the illusion entangling Kakfa's circus artiste in *In the Gallery*, driven on by the ringmaster, an impresario-pimp, and the pounding hammer-blows of the audience's applause.

Keith's best efforts are at self-presentation and have lasted for ten years. Composing, painting, poetry, and singing are touched on explicitly, but playwriting and acting pervade the whole play. Keith writes his own script, and directs and markets his performance. But this does not make him free; he is subject to the logic of his role, even though he has written it himself, because he has to project it to his audience of hangers-on and businessmen, and is bound by their expectations. His role of brilliant, ruthless entrepreneur is the ideal figure of the age. Ruthlessness is justified, he claims, because his project will provide a living for all the workers employed on it, an argument heard as often now as in 1899. As a result, no private sentiment for women or children can be allowed to intervene. His project belongs to the decorative facade rather than the manufacturing base. He needs a touch of grandeur to dazzle the beer-brewers, hence the aristocratic flourish of his title. But grandeur is not enough. To sustain confidence he must appear to have capital. Hence life-style is all-important, with caviare and champagne in the public rooms while Molly and Sascha hunger off-stage.

Among characteristic gestures, such as children kneeling or women carrying trays, are Keith's repeated, ostentatious gifts of money. This gesture is ambiguous: it is done for show, but Keith clearly also likes giving money away – to artists if not to women and children. That is why he launched his project in the first place. The gifts are also comically self-defeating; an impresario is supposed to raise money, not give it away. Like Scholz's limp, which suggests that he has succeeded in becoming a hedonist, Keith's gifts of money look like success but signal imminent failure. Keith's project succeeds, but he personally fails. The magic palace is taken from him, to become a symbol of wealth and power as palaces have always been, decorated by the arts the rich and powerful pay for.

Social Dilemmas and Theatrical Responses

Like the Lulu plays, *The Marquis of Keith* shows human beings in pursuit of freedom. Lulu and Keith are compulsive actors who enjoy their skills. Both enjoy giving pleasure, and both genuinely like the practice they engage in. But neither of them is good at selling. They finally debase sex and art, and are themselves dehumanized by the market. Both play a part in causing the death of those who love them. But neither of them is ruthless and dehumanized enough: desire for sex or art is not sufficiently displaced by desire for money. Keith's self-destructive pleasure in giving money to artists is like Lulu paying her clients for sex. As with Lulu, so with Keith the question posed at the beginning of this chapter arises once again: has he any authentic self or is he just a series of masks?

For Keith, as for Lulu, role-playing is not *per se* a sign of inauthenticity or alienation. It is a metaphor for self-awareness and sociability, for the capacity to develop and change through relations with others. Keith acts what he wants and feels himself to be, a free agent unenslaved by his origins. He displays what Nietzsche's Zarathustra calls 'die schenkende Tugend', the giving virtue of those whose love of themselves gives them the power to love others. As much a would-be philanthropist as Scholz, Keith tries not to reform but to exploit the new wealth to a good end: universal pleasure, a gift not unlike Lulu's. The act becomes spurious not because Keith does not genuinely feel free and want to give pleasure, but because an agent under capitalism is not free, however much he might wish to be so, and because success entails ruthless disregard for others that brings them the antithesis of pleasure. Though he knows all along that money is what counts, he plays his role in good faith at first, apparently at one with it. His ebullience reflects faith in his power. But in the last two acts a gap opens between the role and his knowledge of impending disaster until he ends up, like the clown in *I Pagliacci*, with a breaking heart behind the mask. He is no longer the author of his role and no longer at one with it; he who sought to manipulate others has been a puppet directed by power and money. By the end of the play Keith has developed a split personality: behind the social mask of ruthless entrepreneur is a suffering, isolated creature in an environment which threatens his very existence. He is an image of the effect of free-market capitalism on the human gift of acting, or, to use a metaphor from the play, of fluid adaptability or elasticity. Keith is the image both of free-enterprise man and of individual and social alienation.

In spite of this, Keith clings to the mask to the end. He refuses to admit that he is schizophrenic and retreat with Scholz to a lunatic asylum; he refuses to despair and follow Molly into the river; and he refuses Anna's way, the happy ending of reconciliatory comedy. His last facial gesture is neither the upwards curve of comedy nor the downwards droop of tragedy, but a grin close to the snarl of an animal undecided between attack and flight, as inconclusive as the play as a whole appears to be. It is tempting to seek closure and argue that

Keith and Scholz together could produce a solution. Scholz's efforts at reform fail twice over, in the railway accident and in Simba's failure of class consciousness, her preference for champagne suppers over social democracy. Keith experiences equal failure in his attempt to exploit capitalism. Perhaps Scholz's moral fervour together with Keith's free spirit could usher in utopia. The devotees of pleasure must learn that the wealth produced by enterprise must be socialized for all to enjoy. The advocates of justice must try, as Scholz briefly does, to be less crabbed and grey, and to take account of the fact that human beings are sensuous creatures driven by desire. Too often justice looks puritanical and socialism bureaucratic, diminishing instead of enlarging personal autonomy. In short, champagne suppers for the workers might be a more effective slogan than nationalization of the means of production. Those so inclined can ignore Keith's grin and Scholz's abdication and go off to redefine socialism in the light of what actual people want as distinct from what that abstract entity, the working class, ought to want. The political agenda cannot ignore desires that have arisen with vastly increased productive forces and the market economy.

Tempting though it may be, the play resists such closure. It is too heavily focused through Keith on a specific set of desires and too narrowly placed in a wealthy and a bohemian milieu. Politics are presented only in a scurrilous light, as conveyed through Scholz, formerly Count Trautenau, who has to represent *noblesse oblige*, the reformist middle class, the civil service and an unspecified brand of social democracy instantly rejected by Simba, the genuine Munich lass and the only person in the play attracting the adjective *echt* (genuine). Her verdict has the ring of authorial authority. Given such various burdens, it is hardly surprising that Scholz retreats to a lunatic asylum to play billiards, a step which devalues what he represents and shifts the balance further towards Keith who, apart from a corpse, holds the stage alone at the close of the play. Politics are undermined by being equated with morality, always an inauspicious word for Wedekind. The play is full of resonances in our neo-liberal times of mass consumerism and a shrinking industrial working class. But at the turn of the century the Social Democrats had just become the biggest party in the Reichstag, and a great many people hotly desired justice rather than champagne. Simba's answer to Saranieff is faintly obscene in the face of the horrors of the city slums in 1899. Like Keith's palace, Wedekind's play stands on a rather lofty niche. The stage sets are symptomatic of its narrowness. We are imprisoned in the drawing room; the wider world of exotic names, of Cuba and of Paris, remains abstract; even the city of Munich lacks definition. The plebeian chorus which arrives with Molly's corpse quickly becomes a timeless mob baying for revenge. Only skating or sledging in the Tyrol or Bückeburg brings a breath of air, but it smells of country backwardness or the idyll of childhood, gone forever. The focus on art and the reduction of social democracy to an abstraction sustain a false dichotomy between morality/politics and pleasure, as if no one had ever desired anything but caviare, champagne and the latest modernist painting. That being said, the play does convey the inhuman bondage of life on that lofty niche.

The play offers no solutions to the problems it exposes, but it does present three responses to them. The classic masks of tragedy and comedy fall to the women, Molly and Anna. Molly has the characteristics of a tragic heroine in ambiguous distortion. Though she longs to sink into the obscurity of Bückeburg, in Munich she stands emphatically apart, invested in her assertive isolation, her determination to be what she wants, her refusal to bend to Keith's will and be defined by him. So powerful is her presence that her absence in the last two acts is felt even more strongly. In keeping with a tradition which presents comic heroes as flexible, the tragic hero as hubristically unyielding, Molly stands pitted against the world of Munich to the last. Her suicide is a final defiant act in the struggle with Keith. At the party in Act III she appears incongruously enveloped in a shawl, straying from a melodrama into a comedy of manners. Come to rescue the hero from the forces of evil, she plays through all the tones of a distraught heroine. In her last appearance as dripping corpse she leaves Keith to choose between being hero in a tragedy or villain in a melodrama. Keith's grin denies the tragic role; whether it confirms his villainy for the theatre audience as well as the plebeian stage-chorus is for the audience to decide. A failed heroine of melodrama, Molly also fails to turn the play into a tragedy, for no old or new order is restored or established.

Anna, by contrast, is a comic heroine. Like the sensible woman in a Molière comedy, she opposes male eccentricities, refusing the part of heroine in utopian fantasies in favour of wise reconciliation with society. Keith's dreams reach a climax in Act III when, bathed in lurid red light like Scholz at the end of the act, he imagines a future with Anna as great singer and mother of his children, children endowed with his brains but with aristocratic hands. He will be omnipotent and fulfil her every desire. Like Scholz, Keith here envisions dialectical synthesis. Whereas Scholz wants to combine morality and pleasure in marrying Anna, Keith dreams of uniting art and parenthood in a kingly home, 'ein königliches Heim'. Not surprisingly, Anna opts for Casimir rather than a pipe-dream. The tragic hero does battle with nature, the comic hero is the cultivator who manipulates nature to make her fertile. As Anna points out, Keith has no children; nor has he provided for Molly and Sascha. Anna's comic accommodation is designed to assure survival not just of herself but also of children: of Hermann, his sisters, Simba, Sascha and any offspring of her own. She accepts the social order as nature to be manipulated and made fruitful, not transcended as Keith would do or reformed as Scholz wants. But Anna's comic accommodation fails to integrate individual and social values; it is capitulation rather than integration. It will reproduce the power of money, and of men over women and fathers over children.

The women are a conservative force. Molly's downward drag, Anna's retreat and Simba's scorn of social democracy all deny the visions of the men. Keith's synthesis would have appeared unreal even to many feminists who, as Richard Evans (1978) documents, accepted that women could have careers but had better be wives and mothers, though the arts were a special sphere where exceptionally gifted women might be emancipated from conventional norms. But Anna, the realist, knows that she is not exceptionally gifted. The women are conservative if measured against the radicalism, however absurd, of Keith or Scholz, because they have no sphere of action independent of men or even in equal partnership with them. They are not potential historical agents. Unable to make history, they sink back into the status quo as into nature. Anna *qua* artist is a commodity. In Keith's glowing vision of their future she produces children for him, the male: 'Die schenkst du mir' (You will give them to me: Act III). Anna's contribution appears to stop at parturition – the children will have Keith's intelligence. The home will be 'königlich', the normal German word for royal, which in English is less evidently gender-loaded. But in context, the adjective contributes to the overweeningly masculine bias. Anna is to be the passive recipient of gifts; she will not even have a voice – Keith says he will read her wishes in her great dark eyes. But what men read from a woman's eyes are their own wishes. For an energetic, accomplished woman this sounds just as much a fate worse than death as Bückeburg does to Keith. Casimir, for all the power of his money, offers a little more breathing space, if only because he is not an overwhelming personality and he sees the craft of motherhood in larger terms than Keith. But the idea that mothering skills might become a historically active force rather than bolstering the status quo, just hinted at in Frau Gabor and in Geschwitz's brief mention of her mother, is always put aside as the burdens of parenthood threaten a masculine vision of freedom.

That women might be active in some other sphere (unless as opera singers) remains inconceivable. The play shows women caught between the power of money, largely in male hands, and masculine visions of change in which women are objects of bounty rather than active subjects. From this arises the paradox of Molly's tragic status. Her self-assertion is an emphatic denial of self. She lays tables and refuses silk stockings in a heroic assertion of servility, denying the spurious aristocracy Keith would thrust upon her. Unwilling to be Keith's shadow or to lose herself in the role-playing of Munich society, she has nowhere to go but Bückeburg or the river. To go alone to Bückeburg would be to concede defeat. In choosing the river she might still wring a pyrrhic victory. Whereas Anna capitulates to the male world, Molly holds out, but at the cost of self-extinction. And Keith denies her even the pyrrhic victory.

While the women don the classic masks and strive to bring the play to a clear end, Scholz and Keith combine to produce an absurdist close which is not an end. When the world is mad, the only place to stay sane is the lunatic asylum. Scholz of the mad peals of laughter and the demonic limp walks off, his transformation reversed, unlimping and rational to his haven of sanity in the madhouse. Such sanity is a living death, as far removed from the world as Molly has become, but without the finality of her act; it is an absurdist modulation of her tragic suicide. Keith decides with a grin to stay in the mad world, the absurdist modulation of Anna's comic ending. His decision is as cool as Scholz's. After picking up a revolver and moving towards Molly's corpse, he steps back in horror, looks first at the revolver then at the pay-off money from Casimir, puts the revolver down behind him grinning and declares: 'Das Leben ist eine Rutschbahn . . . ' (Life is a slide . . .). The actor must convey what the three dots show, that this is not The End.

The visual metaphors of the rocket followed by the breathless slide downwards deny the rising dialectic of Keith's and Scholz's dreams of synthesizing contradictions. Life is aimless, without final purpose, absurd. To adapt the close of Goethe's *Faust*: 'Wer immer strebend sich bemüht . . . ' (Who constantly strives . . .) will have a bumpy ride to nowhere in particular. The corrosion of absurdity spreads to the women too. Who can believe that Anna will live happily ever after with Casimir, or that the children will flourish? Molly's deed changes nothing: the closing image is of a grinning man holding a bundle of money. At the end of Molière's *Don Juan* (1971: 85) only the valet Sganarelle is left unsatisfied by the triumph of virtue: 'Il n'y a que moi seul de malheureux. Mes gages, mes gages, mes gages!' (I alone am unhappy. My wages, my wages, my wages!). Keith fares better. Like his predecessors, Melchoir and Lulu, Keith has until now played the hubristic part of lawless defiance, a Faust, a Mephistopheles or a Don Juan. Clutching his wages, he has now become a lackey in a world ruled by Casimir.

What do Keith's grin and the intimations of absurdity mean as a response to the social evils the play explores? Like an animal snarl in its inconclusiveness, the human grin is nonetheless different in its self-consciousness; it is also different from the mad laughter of the insane. A grin is a demonstrative actorly gesture directed at an implied audience who can read irony. Keith's grin is ambiguous. What it conveys will depend on production of the play as a whole. Inside the world of the play he grins to himself as his own audience; but the grin will carry across the footlights, inviting the audience to share the joke, perhaps to reach a judgement. The grin could convey Keith's final corruption as he succumbs to a handful of money and turns his back on dead humanity; this would be the ending in keeping with black morality: a villain's grin which could touch only an audience of monsters. Such a grin would make us inclined to endorse the butcher boy's judgement on Keith, and would align Keith with Jack the Ripper, another character with red butcher's hands. Keith does indeed have affinities with Jack's earlier manifestation, Schön. More subtly, the grin has the Jacques-like cynicism of a romantic idealist who finally recognizes that all is vanity. Cynicism is a complex psychological balancing trick, a darker version of the humour of *Spring Awakening*. As Allan Rodway (1975: 36) puts it, it is a way of seeing and still surviving by pretending to be bad, much as the hypocrite pretends to be good: 'such comedy is based on despair and its purpose is not so much to defend values as to defend defeat.'

This comes close to Keith's mood, but it need not be the mood of the play as a whole. The audience may see beyond the cynic's defence to the absurity of despair when there was never any reason to hope. Where there is nothing to win, defeat is a meaningless term. Rodway later describes Beckett's *Waiting for Godot* as existing 'at the common vanishing point of tragedy, farce and nihilistic comedy' (p. 221). Perhaps this is where Wedekind's play stands. It exhibits the hypocrisies, the ridiculous roles, in such grotesque distortion that their function in bolstering power may be lost in inconsequential absurdity. Is Raspe, the theologian–criminal–policeman, a satiric distillation of a critical literature stretching back at least to that masked monster, Tartuffe? Or do the three terms simply cancel out, as I have suggested earlier, destroying all basis of judgement? The same question arises from the threatrical modes which meet and clash within the play. The male absurdist vision undermines but need not obliterate the comic and tragic stances of the women. Anna's practical concerns, the need for the weak to adapt if they are to survive and feed the children, the bitter outrage of Molly, whose love is a dead weight in a world where women cannot aspire to soar except by clinging to the heels of a man – these may remain powerfully felt if the play is so produced. We should also take into account the concrete analysis of specific power-relations that are not a timeless evil. The world in flux may mean that nothing means anything and nobody is anybody; but it may mean that human beings can change, even if Keith and his creator admit with a grin that they do not know how. The rocket and the slide may suggest that we are on a bumpy road to nowhere – they certainly deny metaphysical salvation or historicist utopias. But the play also resists this kind of absurdist closure by inviting the audience to wonder what will happen next. The ups and downs of life are at least movement, and, as such, are better than being dead.

7
Wedekind and the 'Woman Question'

German culture bears out Michel Foucault's (1976) view that, far from being a repressive age of enforced silence, the nineteenth century produced a cacophony of discourse on sex. By the end of the century, the so-called 'woman question' had become a topic of heated debate. The political issue of votes for women, pursued by the organized women's movement, touched on fundamental questions concerning women's biological role and their proper social function, as well as on sexual morality and the supposed natural differences of instinct, intellect, and temperament between the sexes. In the first two sections of this chapter I shall outline some German traditions of thought on family roles and sexuality with a view to determining where Wedekind stands in this cacaphony. I shall then look at two less well-known texts where Wedekind's entanglement in some more virulent sexist ideas is especially clear, before drawing conclusions about the four plays which in varying degrees subvert the very ideology with which they are imbued.

Marriage and the Family

First, a few comments on terms and method. As Foucault argues, sex is not an unchanging and unruly drive which threatens power and must be repressed. Sexuality is socially constructed as a complex transmission-point of power-relations between men and women, old and young, teachers and pupils, administration and population. Foucault warns against thinking of power in modern society in monolithic terms as a prerogative exercised from above producing a clear-cut opposition of dominators and dominated. Men and women do not confront one another in opposing armies, and relations between the sexes change along with social change. Nonetheless, I wish to ask precisely the questions Foucault cautions against: 'who has power in the order of sexuality?' and 'who has the right to know and who is forcibly kept ignorant? (1976: 131). Indeed, they follow from the questions he does advocate: 'what were the most immediate and local power-relations at work?' and 'how did they make possible those sorts of discourse, and conversely, how did these discourses serve to support those power-relations?' (pp. 128–9).

In medical discourse, for example, one local power-relation was the enforced ignorance of women through their exclusion from medical schools, while physiological arguments were used to support the division of society into a public male realm and a private realm of women and the family, an ideology effective far beyond the medical schools. Foucault's stress on the local threatens to fragment the social world; yet he allows that large-scale cleavages link the local struggles to produce what he calls 'major dominations'. The questions he warns against throw into relief otherwise hidden connections. They show, as the feminist tag has it, that the personal is the political, that apparently disparate phenomena do interact to produce a major domination, a cleavage between the sexes across a whole range of domains. That cleavage means that Foucault's comments on repression need modification. The weight of opinion concerning what was proper for women to think or know affected what women did think and know, even if it did not produce an absolute opposition of feminine repression and ignorance versus monolithic masculine power and knowledge. At the time Wedekind was writing, the women's movement was beginning to make an impression even on the medical schools. But constant emphasis on sexual difference backed up by formal inequalities had complex effects across a whole range of social relations: the sexual knowledge of the prostitute is connected with the ignorance of the middle-class virgin.

I shall be concerned less with actual powers and practices than with patriarchal ideology. The term patriarchy is sometimes used ahistorically to suggest a universal male power over women. It may elide distinctions between paternal power and male domination of women; between formal law and varying social practices; between economic structures and individual attitudes in personal transactions. Michèle Barrett (1980: 19) argues forcefully that the term presents insuperable difficulties in analysing women's oppression and its relation to capitalism. It remains useful, however, not as a blanket term for the whole social structure but as a noun to designate formal powers and as an adjective for modes of thought which divide the sexes and attribute powers to men over women. In examining patriarchal ideology, I shall consider both the typical structure of binary oppositions which thinkers constantly posit between the sexes, as well as the way in which arguments change over time.

Hedwig Dohm (1833–1919) was a noted novelist, essayist and feminist. She was the wife of the editor of the satirical journal *Kladderdadatsch*, and grandmother of Thomas Mann's wife, Katja Pringsheim. In an essay of 1876 (1978), she documents women's supposed qualities according to what 'on dit'. Overwhelmingly of the male sex, 'on' has, through the ages, produced an immense volume of opinion which also weighed on those women who ventured to add their voice to the cacophony. Before the nebulous chaos of the female soul, man the creator utters his 'Let there be woman' to conjure forth whatever image suits his mood. Given men's greater powers at any level of society, compared with women of the same class, it is often only sensible that women struggle to assume the desired shape. Woman appears mysterious because masculine discourse is astonishingly contradictory. Faced with this pot-pourri, Dohm suggests four principles to guide critical reading. First, qualities arising from particular social circumstances are taken to be sexually specific to all women. Secondly, claims so often and for so long asserted authoritatively harden into powerful stereotypes. Thirdly, the stereotypes conflict because desirable qualities in a housekeeper, proclaimed to be essentially womanly, conflict with equally essential requirements in a bedmate. This is why men declare the female of the species dangerous (an attitude brilliantly captured in the figure of Schön). Fourthly, men deny women the qualities they claim for themselves. Logic is a prime example: logical women are either honorary men or else plagiarists out of touch with their deep intuition. Conversely, feminine attributes turn out to be a lack or negation of the valuable qualities men possess: women are practical, that is they lack depth. Dohm concludes that woman's psyche is the site of a battle between 'Natur und Dressur', nature and training, but refrains from definitions of nature which would turn into limiting prescriptions. Dohm's essay reads like a premonitory analysis of Wedekind's work, while her principles anticipate later feminist thinking: women's attributes, defined relative to men's needs so that woman remains an object, are deficiencies relative to the universal human attributes of men. This captures the essence of Simone de Beauvoir's presentation of woman as the Other.

Mary Ellmann (1979: 131) has proposed a rule which amounts to a gloss on Dohm's second and third principles:

> The Mother is particulary useful as an illustration of *the explosive tendency*: each stereotype has a limit; swelled to it the stereotype explodes. Its ruin takes two forms: (1) total vulgarization and (2) a reorganization of the advantage, now in fragments, about a new centre of disadvantage. In this second form, the same elements which had constituted the previous ideal make up the present anathema. (p. 131)

To that can be added the see-saw effect: the antithetical stereotype, previously an anathema, rises to become an ideal. In *Spring Awakening*, Frau Bergmann is a satire on the vulgarized image of the mother, and Frau Gabor the anathema which sinks as the antithetical Ilse and her successor Lulu rise. The see-saw effect is particularly clear in an early play by Wedekind of 1887, *Elins Erweckung* (*Elin's Awakening*: *GW* 9), which anticipates both *Spring Awakening* and the Lulu plays and throws light on the stereotype of the mother, so salient in *Spring Awakening*, so notable in its absence thereafter. The hero of *Elin's Awakening* is a theology student committed to monogamy, who finds that the image of his sister keeps coming between him and his fiancée. He feels that his sister has been forced into marriage, and is jealous of her husband. This hothouse of feelings where sex is tabooed is highly reminiscent of the Freudian family, and behind the sister surely lies the mother: the more the fiancée cooks and serves, the services of a mother rather than a sister, the more impossible she becomes as sexual partner. Besides the Freudian problem of transference of desire, there are other ways in which the devoted and chaste mother interferes with sexual feeling in the son. As an ill-used victim, servant of her husband and children, her abuse arouses anger towards the father, and, in the son she served, both guilt and fear that he will also be imprisoned, as a husband, by his own wife's services. Wedekind's anger at his mother's life is evident in Notebook 5 (p. 16; 44r) where he refers, under the heading of *The Spouses*, to the servant without a wage at Schloß Lenzburg; and Tilly Wedekind (1969: 16) comments on his horror of domesticity in women. Elin's fiancée anticipates Molly Griesinger, who arouses in Keith an agonizing mixture of love, resentment and guilt. There is pity, too, for the frustrated middle-class girl forced by her theologian fiancé into such a role. The anathematized mother is a product of the combined effects of patriarchy and family love. By means of the see-saw effect, this anathema calls up its antithesis, a former anathema. Female sexuality divorced from motherhood and affective ties is embodied in Ella, who travels the world with a tramp called Schigolch. The hero saves her from Graf Schweinitz, a swinish marquis who was about to have his gruesome way with her. To the Marquis she is detestable, her body a vessel of iniquity and filth; but to the hero she is a saviour come to banish the fiancée-mother, who promptly turns into a witch. Her transformation anticipates the witchlike Mutter Schmidtin of *Spring Awakening*, who preserves the ideal of the chaste mother by killing the pregnant child. One could hardly wish for a clearer instance of Hedwig Dohm's scenario; Creator man utters his 'Let there be woman', while dispatching a fallen idol back into the chaos.

The mother brought advantages to the husband and children she served; but the stereotype swelled to such proportions that, as Ellmann puts it, the advantages became disadvantages and it exploded, the fragments reassembling to become an anathema. The kind of mother anathematized in Wedekind's work belongs in what Lawrence Stone (1979) calls the nuclear family of affective individualism, a bourgeois ideal which began to emerge by at least the seventeenth century and has gradually spread through all social levels in our culture, though how far practice conformed to the ideal is a matter of controversy. The ideal modern family is a small household of two generations bound by ties of affection. Choice of marriage partner is determined not by the father, but by personal compatibility and later increasingly by sexual passion or 'falling in love'. Both partners are faithful and both care for their children's growth and welfare. Ideally, the child develops as a free individual, emotionally valuable in loving and being loved rather than economically valuable as a pawn in a marriage market or as a wage earner. The nuclear family lives in a private household separated off from economic activity, in contrast to the older extended household – in *Buddenbrooks* Thomas Mann portrays a shift from one to the other among the Lübeck patriciate. Husband and wife are spiritual equals, but economic activity outside the household is the man's sphere. The woman finds fulfilment as mother and guardian of the household. The bond between mother and child starts with breast-feeding, which is preferable to sending the child out to a wet-nurse. Of course, neither ideal nor practice grew in a simple linear way; and both were highly variable within and between social classes. Stone argues that from around 1770 onwards, there was a strong revival within the middle class of moral reform, paternal authority and sexual repression, later intensified by reaction to the French Revolution and the stresses of industrialization. Stone is writing about England where, by the eighteenth century, there was an established bourgeoisie linked with an independent gentry. In Germany, feudal relations survived longer, the bourgeoisie was less established, the Napoleonic wars fought across German soil brought greater political convulsions, while industrialization occurred later, along with great political changes. In view of this, it is not surprising that there was an extreme tension between affective individualism and patriarchal authority.

The points of stress in the ideal of the modern family are evident: first, it demands a noble indifference to economic advantage and social status; secondly temperamental compatibility and sexual passion cannot be neatly aligned; and thirdly, given modern longevity, fifty years or so of happy, sexually fulfilling monogamy is a tall order. The shift from paternal power in law to bonds of affection transfers the power struggle into the psyche of the individual: think of Toni Buddenbrook's contortions in marrying Grünlich, or of Wotan's agonizing in *Die Walküre* (Wedekind's favourite Wagner opera) as he longs to father a free individual but punishes his daughter Brünnhilde's defiance. There are also economic stresses. The lengthy education of middle-class sons left them dependent well into sexual maturity, and girls remained dependent until they could be married for love to a man who could keep them. Depending on the family's prosperity, wives might work as household servants, like Molly Griesinger, or be idle, like Lulu Schwarz. The good husband must respect, love and desire his servant or idle wife. The privacy within the middle-class household meant that to her children the mother appeared as a sexual being when pregnant, but otherwise presented an aspect of asexual purity, creating an ideal of chaste yet motherly womanhood and strong bonds of love laid down from infancy. She had to forgo all other interests and find fulfilment through husband and children. Such an ideal of womanhood could easily become oppressive to the whole family and anathema to the young male, in limiting his freedom and arousing sexual guilt.

The modern family freed young people from the absolute power of the father, but this freedom was unequally distributed. The affections were allocated in greater quantity to women, and individualism to men, a distribution backed up by the prevailing double morality. The enlightened ideal of marital companionship but separate roles was made the more lopsided by the emergence of a middle-class patriarchal ideology, even as the cult of romantic love was strengthening. In *La Nouvelle Héloise* (1761) Rousseau, high priest of affective individualism, contrives to glorify love and sustain patriarchal order simultaneously. In *Emile* (1762), he propounds the ideal of the child's free growth. But the child is a boy; his sister's education is entirely subordinated to male needs for affection and service, which will begin with breast-feeding. *Les Confessions* (1770) documents both the search for selfhood and a ruthless refusal to be bound by affective ties. German educationists ignored the cult of love, but enthusiastically endorsed female education for domesticity (Blochmann, 1966).

Patriarchal ideology gained strength in step with the rhetoric of freedom. In 1793, Fichte demanded that the princes of Europe restore that freedom of thought which they had suppressed, but in his *Naturrecht* (1796) he propounded a reactionary conception of marriage. On her marriage, a woman surrenders her personality and her property as well as her person. She becomes part of her husband's life, just as she assumes his name: 'The conception of marriage involves the most unlimited subjection of the woman to the will of the husband; not from legal, but from moral reasons. She must subject herself for the sake of her own honour.' The legal consequences are then deduced from this moral base: 'her marriage utterly annuls her as far as the state is concerned . . .' (1970: 417–18). It is as if the newly reclaimed rights of man had to be redefined as the rights of men, lest women claimed them too. Where there is no risk of conflict, however, Fichte does grant some rights to widows and fatherless spinsters.

Hegel seems more even-handed; both sexes freely surrender their personality in marriage. But the male as head of the household conducts transactions with civil society and the state, while the individual achieves universality only as a citizen of the state, which is a male realm:

The difference between men and women is like that between animals and plants. Men correspond to animals, while women correspond to plants because their development is more placid and the principle that underlies it is the rather vague unity of feeling. When women hold the helm of government, the state is at once in jeopardy, because women regulate their actions not by the demands of universality but by arbitrary inclinations and opinions. Women are educated – who knows how? – as it were by breathing in ideas, by living rather than acquiring knowledge. (Hegel 1958: 263–4)

These are only two of the more famous voices among many. The sociologists continued the argument. Ute Gerhard (1978: 148–52) cites especially W. H. Riehl's *Die Familie* (1855), which reached a seventeenth edition in 1935. For Riehl, the family is the basic cell of the authoritarian state. Natural sexual inequality proves the impossibility of social equality between classes and sexes alike – a backlash against the liberal values earlier thinkers had upheld at least for men. Such views had concrete effects in family and industrial law, education and civil rights, so that women in the propertied classes were reduced by the mid-century to a condition of extreme marital dependence in grotesque contradiction of both the political and affective ideals of bourgeois individualism. Lower down the social scale, their exclusion from many fields of employment gave rise to an army of domestic servants and urban prostitutes. Since not all men were able to rise to the sublime indifference of a Rousseau, the restrictions on women necessarily limited the freedom of men too, resulting in, among other symptoms, the anathematized mother and the search for a model of freedom among proletarian prostitutes, a search doomed to fail unless accompanied by wilful blindness to the economics of prostitution. Early on in his diaries, Wedekind comments on the economics of prostitution in Berlin, though such clear-sightedness did not inhibit him in the pursuit of bought pleasures (Hay: 42–3).

At the time Wedekind was writing, the middle-class women's movement supported the family and attacked the double morality, prostitution, and women's exclusion from higher education and the professions – there were a million more women than men in Germany, and the rights of widows and fatherless spinsters meant little if they could not earn a living. Many men supported the movement, but there was also bitter opposition from men with vested interests. Socialist feminism, by contrast, attacked the family and private property: equal rights could not alter class inequalities or the sexual division of labour if childcare remained a family duty of women. Wedekind was scornful of demands for education and equal rights, sharing the socialists' view that they left untouched the root problem of the family. In a fragment of 1908, *Die Jungfrau* (*The Virgin*) he writes:

Die 'Frau' und die 'Jungfrau' sind Produkte der Zivilisation und nur durch den Bestiz des Hauses möglich. Ohne Haus keine Frau und keine Jungfrau.

Die Hure als Beschützerin der Frauen und Jungfrauen.

The 'wife' and the 'virgin' are products of civilization, only possible through ownership of the house. Without the house, no wife and no virgin.

The whore as protector of wives and virgins. (*GW* 9: 187)

The types are recognized as social constructs, and Wedekind is not wilfully blind to the economics or the social function of prostitution.

Up to a point, Wedekind's comments are quite close to Marxist argument; but since private property is equated with civilization, the liberation of women seems impossible. While such an equation is naive, so was Marxist faith in proletarian humanity. Marx had argued in 1848 in the *Communist Manifesto* that industrialization had destroyed the proletarian family; while Engels claimed in 1887, in *The Origins of the Family*, that proletarian relations were already cooperative and that the revolution would sweep away class exploitation and women's subjection in the bourgeois family. But the labour movement was far from united. The concept of the family wage for men and protective legislation excluding women from some kinds of employment found much support, backed up by restrictive practices among male workers fearful of cheap female labour. Among the proletariat, paternal power over property and marriage scarcely existed, but to infer that relations must therefore be cooperative was wishful thinking. Middle-class family ideals were spreading and childcare fell to women at all social levels. That is not say that the nuclear family cannot be cooperative; but precisely because of its emotional values the stresses caused by sexual divisions are the more painful. For all the rhetoric, patriarchy in the sense of paternal control of children was a lost cause in an ever more mobile society. Its death throes are reflected in the father–son conflicts of Expressionism: in Kafka's work, the patriarch without real powers becomes a monster of the mind. But as the father lost his powers and women were increasingly freed from formal constraints, the so-called battle between the sexes intensified.

Sexuality

Wedekind's attack on middle-class patriarchy, the cult of virginity, and the scapegoating of prostitutes, is progressive and historically interesting. But his contempt for equal rights and his inability to see beyond current economic relations mean that he cannot be accounted an honorary feminist in either the liberal or the socialist camp. Of more than historical interest, however, is his portrayal of sexuality, especially male sexual attitudes. Largely ignored by the political movements of the time, sexuality is crucial in personal relations and may be little affected by changes in law or the ownership of the means of production. This is where Wedekind's work is interesting, both as a response to the stresses of his own time and because of the light it sheds on still recognizable modes of feeling.

In a play of 1905, *Tod und Teufel* (*Death and Devil*: GW 5) Casti-Piani, still in the brothel trade, does battle with the feminist Elfriede. Prostitution, he claims, allows women to earn an independent living, play a useful social role and have a richer sex life than middle-class virgins. But his robust view is not borne out. He commits suicide on discovering that his virgin enemy loves him, and that for the whore Lisiska sensual desire is a raging, never-stilled agony: female love and female sexuality are equally deadly. If prostitution is necessary in bourgeois society – this is Casti-Piani's defence – two questions arise: why is the whore necessary, and if the whore is not a model of free female sexuality what is?

The first perceived threat to wives and virgins is predatory male desire, a force which seemingly cannot be denied; hence the necessity for the whore to protect patriarchal prerogatives. The second threat is the liberation of female sexuality, which would instantly destroy marriage. As Krafft-Ebing (1893: 13) puts it: 'If she (woman) is normally developed mentally, and well bred, her sexual desire is small. If this were not so the whole world would become a brothel and marriage and the family impossible.' Casti-Piani would deny that women naturally feel little desire; it is good breeding which contains women in marriage; women not so contained become endlessly receptive whores. Thus women may appear as the passive objects of male control, whose sexuality, unlike the active male force, can be held down by breeding: there is no male equivalent of the whore. (In the literature of adultery, a less passive image of women is presented, but the conflict between desire and control remains.) On the other hand, they may be seen as the passive vessels of a force which opens them to the active male. More horrifically still, they may become active, the ultimate threat explored in the *Lulu* plays but not in *Tod und Teufel*.

Prostitutes are wage-labourers employed by a male pimp, their sex a commodity bought by male customers, their sexual labour no more an image of freedom than proletarian wage-labour. The human essence in Marx's early writing, from which human beings are alienated under capitalism, is a universal potential. Female sexuality, by contrast, is the alienated essence of one sex, whereas the desires of the other are shown to be active within society. Lisiska is a gloomy urban variation on Ella of *Elin's Awakening*, who belongs in a Rococo pastoral. Both are beyond the margins: Ella is woman as the Other emerging from nature – she actually bursts forth from the bushes with Schweinitz in hot pursuit; behind the commerical facade of Casti-Piani's brothel is the temple of a divine agony. This extrasocial essence may be either bestial and subhuman, or else a lofty ideal. Either way, untamed woman stands on the margin not as a complement to man and the other half of humanity, but tinged with bestial or angelic alienation. Pleasure and love become antithetical: chaste mothers, wives and virgins do not experience pleasure at all, whereas the essential female experiences sex mindlessly as undifferentiated pleasure, often in the form of masochistic pain-as-pleasure. The sexually voracious woman has an ancestress in the prostitute Marianne in Büchner's *Dantons Tod*, a woman whose life is an endless flow of sexual desire.

As Josephine Schröder-Zebrella (1985: 159ff) argues, Wedekind's later interest in spiritual and intellectual questions produced more integrated female figures, though the attempted syntheses never succeed; while in a late work of 1911, *Franziska* (GW 6) the heroine, a female Faust, ends up back in the family as a mother – the former anathema is reinstated in a resigned accommodation to bourgeois society. Geschwitz, a woman with intellect, is an interesting intermediate case, one of Hedwig Dohm's unnatural plagiarists in the shape of a lesbian. But in the main women come in two types. The sexual woman as sub-social nature or suprasocial mystery is a mindless object, but her passivity could give way to activity. In social woman, imprisoning love threatens the free male individual: the love of tamed woman and the *vagina dentata* of liberated woman are equally castrating. Wedekind generally allocates the two sets of qualities separately to a whore and middle-class virgin who would like to be a whore but is prevented by a propensity to fall in love.

These are stereotypes of the sort Dohm pinpoints: men are agents, women are objects; women are close to nature, that is, they are mindless; women are emotional and deeply if passively sensuous, that is, they have no identity except in relation to the other sex; if they show signs of non-sexual attributes such as interest in the law, they are botched men. All this bears out Mary Ellmann's (1979: 2–26) principle of sexual analogy. Sexual psychology, personality and social role are set in analogy to the mechanics of sex in the missionary position: a thrusting agent and a passive receptacle; more fatefully still, an energetic spermatozoon emerges from the ruck to penetrate the round blank surface of an egg. The roles are rooted in biology. The ultimate unnatural horror is the reversal of these functions, the active castrating female who destroys society and procreation.

The Post-Enlightenment and German Idealism

Different ages give these oppositions different content. I have already discussed the evolving tradition which allocates affections to women and individualism to men. The attributes of female sexuality in Wedekind's work can be related most immediately to the post-Enlightenment and to German idealist philosophy. I shall offer a sketch of this changing tradition – an in-depth approach would require another book.

Enlightened humanism extended to women, who were held to be gifted with reason like men; and there were calls for female education, based on recognition of women's autonomy and their role in educating children. But from the 1760s onwards, the tone changes in line with the pre-Romantic cult of nature and of feeling rather than intellect. Certain basic assumptions underlie the arguments. Women are granted three roles: the first two, mother and sexual partner, are rooted in biology; the third, woman as the bearer of virtue, is religious in origin. The ideals of Platonic friendship and the virtuous companionate marriage were part of a middle-class attack on the immoral aristocracy, and encouraged respect for women, but at the cost of denying sexuality. The tensions emerge in the antithesis of pleasure and virtue which pervades much eighteenth-century litera-ture. The heroine of Lessing's play *Emilia Galotti* of 1772 is robbed of her freedom by *force majeure* and chooses to die rather than lose her autonomy, which she sees as threatened less by rape than by her own desires. Her death is the result of a clash between an older patriarchy of princely power and the new bourgeois combination of individual-ism with a moralism which fell primarily on women: she is killed by her father, who thus preserves virtue threatened by pleasure.

Mozart/de Ponte's *Cos! fan tutte* is a belated comic satire of this kind of bourgeois moralism. In Goethe's *Werther* of 1774, Lotte's peace of mind as companion-wife to Albert and Werther's spiritual friend is destroyed when she responds to Werther's kisses. She gives Werther Albert's gun with which he shoots himself; the gift preserves the virtuous wife, while the suicide asserts the clashing masculine values of freedom and control, for Werther can neither accept Albert's rights as a limit to his own freedom nor rape or abduct Lotte without destroying her automony, which exists only within a supervening male control in marriage. *Werther* is here more radical than *La nouvelle Héloise*, for the hero at least avoids the fate of becoming a tutor/lackey in Albert's household, and the countryside idyll, which Rousseau leaves intact, is here punctured. But the radicalism extends only to Werther. In the subtext, Lotte refuses her own sexual desires. Her motherliness is also quite divorced from sex in the famous scene where she cuts bread for a bevy of brothers and sisters. In Goethe's *Iphigenie auf Tauris* of 1779 and 1787, the virgin Iphigenie retains her autonomy in refusing marriage. In these texts, women must choose between autonomy and sexuality; spirit and body are divided. Iphigenie's asexual spirituality found its absolute antithesis a hundred years later in Wedekind's cult of the purely sensual woman devoid of spirit. The spiritual woman escapes patriarchy by means of a negative refusal of desire; the active sensual woman is a more positive threat to the fundamental assumption of man as subject and woman as object in sexual commerce.

The cult of Platonic spirituality is at once the climax and the end of enlightened assertion of women's autonomy. Such denial of sexuality could hardly be sustained, and tended to alienate woman as the eternal feminine, raised to a spiritual realm beyond social existence, just as Wedekind's antithetical ideal remains asocial. The antithetical image of the purely sexual woman gained strength in keeping with Rousseau's tag 'Le mâle n'est mâle qu'en certains instants, la femelle est femelle toute sa vie, ou du moins toute sa jeunesse' (1964: 450); or as Byron puts it in *Don Juan*, 'Man's love is of man's life a thing apart, tis women's whole existence'. Kant (1960: 852) allows wives a little reading under their husband's guidance only when they are ageing, lest intellect interfere with the sexual charm they passively emit, remarking of the French bluestocking, Madame Dacier, that she might as well have had a beard. Kant's vision is ponderously Rococo, but Rousseau heralds the sexual ideology of German idealism which, as turned upside down by Schopenhauer and mediated through Edward von Hartmann, is the immediate ancestor of the stereotypes in Wedekind's work.

Fichte, the founding father of idealism, deduces his concept of marriage from nature. Nature uses sex as a means to an end, the propagation of species with permanent form. Two sexes are necessary, one passive, the other active:

> The system of all the conditions for the generation of a body of the same species had to be completely united somewhere, and, when put in motion, to develop itself after its own laws. The sex which contains these complete conditions is called throughout all nature the *female* sex. Only the first moving principle could be separated from it. The sex in which this principle generates itself apart from the substance to be vitalized by it, is called throughout all nature the *male* sex.

Man acts, woman is acted upon. Human beings, bearers of the active principle of reason, are not purely natural. The male is sexually an agent, hence it does not conflict with reason as an active principle for a man to desire sexual satisfaction as an end in itself, but it would for a woman, since her natural part is pure passivity, a sub-human condition. Thus woman can never consciously desire sexual gratification without loss of humanity, nor may she desire children as an end in themselves, since she could satisfy this desire with any possible man and this must be degrading. Fichte sums up the dilemma thus:

> The female sex stands one step lower in the arrangement of nature than the male sex; the female sex is the object of a power of the male sex, and no other arrangement was possible if both sexes were to be connected. But at the same time both sexes, as moral beings, ought to be equal. To make this possible, a new faculty utterly wanting in the male sex, had to be given to the female sex. This faculty is the form in which the sexual impulse appears to woman, whereas to man it appears in its true form. (pp. 396–7)

This faculty is love, which man learns only at second hand. An uncorrupted woman must remain innocent, unlike a man, who may become conscious of all that is within him. In contrast to the 'true form' of the sexual impulse, love 'had to be given'; the question is, who or what gave it? 'The sexual impulse received this moral form of love in woman, because in its original form it would have cancelled all

morality in woman' (p. 399). The source, then, is nature in obedience
to the moral law – a very odd proceeding. Woman does not love in
direct response to moral law; her love is an innate feeling.
Nonetheless, she is corrupt as well as unnatural if she consciously feels
sexual urges and acts on them. Fichte then deduces his law of
marriage from these facts of nature and moral necessities. Wedekind
simply turns Fichte upside down. The moral law is in reality
patriarchal law. Marriage is a corruption of nature. Woman is false to
her innate sensuality in giving herself to one man.

Fichte's argument is full of binary oppositions: male human reason
and female natural feeling; male active subject and female passive
object; male self-consciousness and female innocence; the true male
sexual drive and the female illusion of love; male Becoming and female
Being; the male creator who vitalizes and the female substance of
unchanging nature; moral man who chooses magnanimity and natural
woman who feels love. Woman is a paradox, more rooted in nature
than man, yet bound to deny nature. In order to preserve her
humanity she must deny her body, the passive receptacle of the
conditions for generation. Weighed down by such a body, she stands
below man and can never be a free spirit, a 'vitalizing' agent. The
virulent binary oppositions of German idealism have haunted discourse on sex through at least to Sartre and de Beauvoir's *The Second
Sex*, and by that route have also come to influence some feminist
argument of our time. Hegel's system is all about overcoming subject
–object opposition, but he too places woman lower than man,
and sets nature against culture. In the extract quoted above, woman is
placid and endowed with a vague unity of feeling. She is less alienated
than man, but only because she is closer to nature. She is more *an sich*,
less *für sich*, that is to say less blessed and cursed with self-
consciousness than men, and so less divided but also less capable of
rational reflection. Carol McMillan (1982; 6) sums up the antithesis:
'only those activities for which there is no counterpart in the animal
world and which are not contaminated by feelings can be truly human
and therefore based on reason.' For Hegel as for Rousseau 'la femelle
est femelle toute sa vie'. Woman's plantlike harmony of being is just
the sort of attribute Dohm notes. Man may transcend alienation and
recognize his oneness with spirit through the cultural projects of
politics, science, the higher arts and philosophy; woman is pre-
cultural.

Wedekind does not fundamentally alter judgements like Hegel's; he simply reverses the evaluations. Neither Fichte nor Hegel was a misogynist. For Hegel, the family is at least a staging post in the movement of absolute spirit. Unlike Rousseau, Fichte attacks rape, and is less ambiguous than Rousseau on the power of the father: an imposed loveless union is a denial of woman's humanity. He allows for divorce, should love fail. But in theory it should not fail, for woman's eternal love of the one man protects male powers, and she does well to accept the prevailing double morality. In such a marriage, the partners combine to create a full image of humanity. As Schön puts it, divorce would be like losing half of himself. Schön's fantasies show what happens to Fichte's love match if the double morality breaks down and woman ceases to be purely passive.

Though the idealist philosophers deny female sexuality in the interests of maternity and the patriarchal family, their literary contempories, the early Romantics, were more radical in their lives and their writings. Friedrich Schlegel's *Lucinde* of 1799 celebrates sexual pleasure in men and women alike, and attacks the double morality which makes the fallen woman an outcast. Lucinde seems to be an integrated figure and the equal of her lover Julius. She is sensuous, intelligent, independent, creative, loving and supremely lovable, above all when she becomes a mother. Their child will grow free of the fetters of punitive morality. But the illusion of integration is created by means of a technical sleight of hand – the dialectical structure of the novel. The hero moves upwards from his fallen woman to Lucinde and marriage as the higher ideal. Lucinde moves on from sensual passion to become the madonna-mother who must henceforth subordinate everything to motherhood. In a fantasy section she is alienated beyond the grave into a spiritual ideal. And the binary oppositions of female nature and male spirit remain. In Goethe's *Elective Affinities* of 1809 the clash between sex and motherhood re-emerges, while in Romantic literature generally the female images Schlegel tried to integrate fall apart. The sexual woman is alienated as the inaccessible object of desire, forbidden, dead, or threateningly asocial.

The Anti-Idealists

Turning from the idealists to the anti-idealist Schopenhauer, we come to a notorious misogynist. Schopenhauer thought Hegel 'a flat-headed, insipid, nauseating, illiterate charlatan', and pronounced the idealist project mistaken from the outset (Popper, 1962: 33). He restores the Kantian dualism of things in themselves and things as they appear, but devalues the phenomenal world as mere illusion. The originating principle is not the logos, but the will-to-existence made manifest in all the forms of nature. In organic nature, the will acts through the sexual drive. Fichte contrasts love in woman with the 'true form' of the sexual impulse in man. Schopenhauer makes explicit what Fichte leaves implicit: since desire is nothing more than the means which ensures the end of propagation, desire for a particular individual is an illusion driving humanity senselessly on from one object to the next. Schopenhauer (1977: 667–81) reserves his most vituperative venom for women and their bodies, as objects of illusory male desire. Wisdom begins when will wills its own denial. Subjectivity and individuation are illusions, but they must be experienced in order to reach wisdom, a state closed to woman since she is not even a deluded subject, but merely a vehicle for propagation.

Nietzsche also sees existence as meaningless, but he converts the terrible truth into the basis of freedom. Since no rational purpose is given, man is free to make his own meanings. The will-to-existence is transformed into the will-to-power and is sublimated in the *Übermensch*: will wills not its denial but its own more subtle expansion. The *Übermensch* is male. In woman, the will is directed towards pregnancy and the birth of a potential *Übermensch*. Love is an illusion; the male *Übermensch* is an end, the woman a means. The anti-idealists, then, are not so different from the idealists when it comes to women. As a subject, man is either alienated or else deluded; but he can follow Hegel and recognize his oneness with spirit, or Schopenhauer and attain contemplative wisdom, or Nietzsche and assert his existential freedom. Woman, by contrast, remains locked in biology, blindly loving the one man, or blindly bearing the baby.

A similar view of women emerges in the philosophy of Eduard von Hartmann (1842–1906), a pessimistic philosopher whose work was very much in vogue in the late nineteenth century. Hartmann mixes ideas drawn from Schelling and Schopenhauer with evolutionary theory. The originating principle is the Unconscious, or will, which sets in motion a dynamic evolution. The proximate end of the process is the emergence of consciousness, which from the start inhered in will as an idea. As long as consciousness remains subordinate to will it brings only conflict and illusion. But the essence of consciousness is the emancipation of intellect from the will; when the process is complete, intellect will finally deny will in an act of cosmic suicide bringing the universe to an end. In the meantime, Hartmann deplores individual pessimism and especially suicide. Man must carry forward the cultural process in the optimistic faith that cosmic suicide will eventually become possible. With woman, however, it is different:

> One ought to be quite particularly on one's guard against making the female sex too rational, for where the Unconscious must first be reduced to silence, success is only attained at the cost of repulsive caricatures; but where the unconscious tendency harmonises with the demands of consciousness, it is a useless and in general injurious task. Woman namely is related to man, as instinctive or unconscious to rational or conscious action; therefore the genuine woman is a piece of Nature, on whose bosom the man estranged from the Unconscious may refresh or recruit himself, and can again acquire respect for the deepest and purest spring of all life. And to preserve this treasure of the eternal womanly, the woman also should be as far as possible shielded by the man from all contact with the rough struggle of life, where it is needful to display conscious force, and should be restrained in the sweet natural bonds of the family. (1983, vol. 2: 43)

This, of course, is long before the cosmic suicide when intellectual man, become God the destroyer, will annihilate Nature, the family and all those unconscious women.

In Wedekind's work, the sweet bonds of the family are burst asunder; though the male characters do still recruit themselves, if less on the bosom than in the vagina. Yet with the exception of the hero of *Elin's Awakening* and of Melchior Gabor, they remain estranged from woman and the family, and fail to acquire respect for the deepest and purest spring of all life. And then there is Geschwitz, a repulsive caricature of the sort Hartmann warns against.

The Scientists

The anti-idealist appeal to biology overlaps with the scientific materialism which became prominent by the middle of the century among the anthropologists, biologists and doctors who added their voices to the general cacophony. Wedekind owned copies of H. Ploss's

Das Weib (The Female) of 1855, and Krafft-Ebing's *Psychopathia Sexualis* of 1887, which from the second edition onwards included a section on Jack the Ripper. The case studies Krafft-Ebing (1893) documents are mainly male, though there are a few female monsters. The author accounts for this by emphasizing men's natural sexual aggression, which makes them more likely than women, who are naturally passive, to overstep the limits of acceptable expression of desire. Otherwise, his comments on women are a farrago of banalities (pp. 13–16). He vigorously endorses the double morality, demanding virginity in brides and heavier legal penalties for female adultery. He argues that modesty is woman's most beautiful attribute, and that woman loves more than man but has a low sexual drive which disappears with motherhood. Here the stereotype has indeed swelled to its limits. Ploss's book is a typical example of academic writing, and its title is an index of the pervasive bias in scientific discourse. *Weib* is the technical term for the human female. There is no male equivalent, nor could one imagine a book called *Der Mann*; it would be called *Der Mensch (Man* or *The Human Being)*, for man is the human norm from which woman is a deviation. Ploss offers a cross-section of medical and anthropological opinion, quoting from male peers and occasionally sneering at anonymous feminists. He accepts that women have a smaller cranium and therefore less intelligence than men, in contrast to Georg Büchner's pro-feminist brother Ludwig who, alas, compares white American women favourably with idiotic male negroes (Sayers, 1982: 95). Ploss approvingly cites a Rousseau-like argument: for some thirty years woman's body is a reproductive apparatus. Man can grow as old as Methuselah without being ill; but woman must periodically fall ill. He cites Paul Möbius's *Die Nervosität* (1882) on women's tendency to hysteria. Möbius went on to produce his *magnum opus* in 1900, *Über den physiologischen Schwachsinn des Weibes (The Physiological Idiocy of Woman)*, which reached a ninth edition in 1908. Ploss is not a misogynist: woman may do anything that does not interfere with her vocation of marriage. But she already has that freedom, and to claim greater freedom would be to deny her womanhood: a woman standing all day long at the lectern, the judge's table or on the political platform would not be a woman (though whether she would still menstruate is left obscure). This apparatus who spends much of life as a hysterical invalid is nonetheless described a page or so later as a 'schönes, geschlossenes Ganzes, nur aus sich selbst verständlich' (a beautiful, perfect whole, intelligible only in her own terms: p. 18).

The academics were not all like Ploss: Runge (1896: 51) suggests that women students would waste less time through illness than men do through drunkeness, while Kirchhoff (1897: 3–4) conducted an enquiry showing only a minority of academics still opposed to higher education for women. Science was less uniformly anti-feminist than metaphysics, and the scientists who were anti-feminist manipulated their results to suit prejudices drawn from family ideology and the metaphysicians. Wedekind comes close to Ploss's views in a story of 1879, *Die Fürstin Russalka* (*The Princess Russalka: GW* 8): the aristocratic heroine breaks with her background only to find fulfilment in marriage and motherhood, while her socialist husband turns out to be a conventional patriarch. This is reminiscent of Ploss's attack on Mill and the English suffragette movement (p. 585): whatever the political system, woman remains woman. In a play of 1903 *Karl Hetmann, der Zwergriese* (*Karl Hetmann, the Dwarf-Giant: GW* 4), with the alternative title *Hidalla oder Sein und Haben* (*Hidalla or Being and Having*), Wedekind takes even more direct issue with Mill, Engels and some contemporary feminists as well as with the eugenics movement. The play is typically ambivalent in flirting with eugenics as a path to a utopia which fails; in voicing outrage at the double morality and male oppression of women; in half accepting then undermining female intellectuality, but decisively rejecting political feminism. Wedekind's notebooks are full of Ploss-like taxonomic lists of female types and speculations on physiology and nervous conditions. Yet reduction of the female body to an apparatus seems also to have been abhorrent to Wedekind. When, in the *Monstretragödie*, Jack carries off Lulu's genitals which he means to leave to science, Wedekind seems to be suggesting by means of this gruesome detail that materialist science is a mode of manipulative control which destroys eros.

Sexual Ideology at the Turn of the Century: the Hetaera

Wedekind differs from the metaphysicians and scientists alike in divorcing sex from propagation. The will becomes the imperious power of masculine desire whose object, no longer restrained within the sweet bonds of family, threatens to turn into a subject. The mixture of hope and fear invested in the sexual woman has affinities with apocalyptic ideas of sexual revolution current in anarchist and bohemian circles in Schwabing, Munich's artistic quarter. Men like Otto Gross, whose ideas passed to D. H. Lawrence via Frieda Weekley, and the so-called Cosmic Circle of irrationalist prophets of primitivism attacked patriarchy and advocated what they conceived to be a female mode of being centred on instinct and orgiastic sexuality, though as Martin Green (1974: 74) notes, most of them were actually more interested in men than women. A key figure was the hetaera, the sexually free woman. Franziska von Reventlow, a leading personality in Munich café society, might seem to embody the ideal. She practised the theory of free love, had a child by an unnamed lover, and even experimented in selling sex, although rather than being a Lulu from the lower depths she was a countess and an author. The concept of the hetaera was borrowed from the anthropologist J. J. Bachofen (1948) whose work *Das Mutterrecht* (*Mother-Right*) of 1861 enjoyed a vogue at the turn of the century, with a second edition in 1897. Several critics, notably Alfons Höger (1981), have related Wedekind's work to Bachofen. As Rosalind Coward (1983: 71) notes, the debate on patriarchy versus matriarchy was more than just academic. At stake was which elements of human society were unchanging and which variables. If patriarchy was both original and universal, there were contemporary implications for the possibility of social change.

Bachofen was interesting in making sexual relations central to social analysis. He claimed that patriarchy was preceded by societies based on matrilinearity or matriarchy. As Engels (1962: 175) comments, Bachofen's theory is a piece of mystical idealist historicism. Pre-patriarchal society, Bachofen argued, was a material culture based on the bodily link between mother and child before spirit emerged in the abstract principle of fatherhood. He posits three prehistorical stages. Before the advent of agriculture was the *ius aprhoditus*, emblematically associated with plants and animals of the rich swamplands. This was the age of original hetaerism, in the sense of promiscuity, when women were the random prey of men. Such a condition became insupportable to women, who in an intermediate Amazonian phase forcibly asserted their rights. A second stage of ordered naturalism supervened: matriarchy proper under the aegis of Demeter, and associated with ears and sheaves of grain. Both stages are tellurian: the female principle of the earth predominated over the Uranian male principle of the sea, in that generation was a female prerogative. Hetaerism survived in this second stage as religious ritual. Marriage and the matriarchal family were established and women held social power in a high culture: brave youths honoured noble and chaste women. Amazonian tendencies re-emerged, however, as women rebelled against their nature and flexed the muscles of power. But Dionysus, a new god from the East, reconverted women to pleasure, ushering in a new hetaerism under the twin aegis of Aphrodite and Dionysus. In this third stage, all bonds were loosed, all differences disappeared. A democracy of the undifferentiated mass brought an apotheosis of fleshy emancipation and universal brotherhood. (Stages two and three sound suspiciously like Romantic medievalism versus Fourier and the French Revolution. It was stage three which appealed to the Schwabing anarchists.) But the apotheosis had a worm at its heart. Whereas matriarchy proper encouraged masculine bravery, the Dionysian phase weakened men until they became disgusting to women. The Roman imperial idea restored order after the chaos into which stage-three hetaerism necessarily degenerated; and patriarchy, with its mental bond between father and child, brought individualism, hierarchical order and higher cultural activities.

Bachofen's image of women differs little from the commonplaces of the time: they are close to nature, more body and less spirit, low on individual personality but high on love beyond the self starting with the attachment to the embryo. The text is self-contradictory throughout. The utopias of stages two and three contradict one another, but both seem preferable to patriarchal egoism and imperial militarism. Equally contradictory is the evaluation of Amazonianism and hetaerism. The Amazons represent a positive step towards matriarchy, but they stand in opposition to nature when women under matriarchy assume real power backed up by physical force. The assertion of power by violent means remains the prerogative of male warriors and is necessary for the establishing of an empire. Hetaerism degrades women in stage one and men in stage three. The need for patriarchy to save masculinity highlights the fundamental assumption of the active male and the passive female which underlies all the stages, though this assumption is shaken a little in stage three. The hetaera, then, is ambiguous. In the first stage she is passive prey, in the third stage an equal sparring partner, but her activity threatens the masculinity which women themselves desire.

Bachofen's analysis has imperialist and racist undertones. Leafy swamps and orgiastic unity are associated with Africa and Asia, images and ideas which reappear in the work of Mann, Conrad and

Lawrence. The gooey mud of the swamps is perhaps an ancestor of 'le visqueux' in Sartre. Interesting too is the reliance on myth and the alignment of social forms with religious rites and enblems. Here too Bachofen is ambiguous: on the one hand the sexual utopias are set within social forms, on the other hand they are distanced in an abyss of prehistory before humanity was emancipated from nature. The original hetaera is clearly beyond the margins of society, but the second stage suggests that women's power is not incompatible with culture, though it clearly is with bourgeois society. The question whether the third stage of sexual liberation and equality is compatible either with civil society or with masculinity is more problematic. Wedekind is not interested in mother-right; the image of woman in stage two is dangerously close to his anathematized ideal mother. But the hetaera is attractive as a sexual woman who will not bind men – in many respects a prostitute, but without the demeaning commerce of actual prostitution. In Bachofen's tellurian culture descent is through the female line and fathers are either unknown or subordinate. To the tellurian division of fathers from children, Wedekind also adds the separation of mothers in the interests of sexual pleasure. The appeal to myth is present in *Spring Awakening* and the Lulu plays, though less so in *The Marquis of Keith*. Religious ritual, absent in the major plays, is a feature of some of his less well-known works, two of which I shall consider in the following sections.

Mine-Haha: The Fragmented Female Body

In the works we have considered, Wedekind reacts against the power of the father, the hypocrisy of the double morality, and above all against the bonds of love. His cult of sex divorced from affective bonds, otherwise close to anti-idealist thought, centres on desire rather than procreation. The ideal sexual woman, the hetaera, cannot live in bourgeois society but must bow to patriarchy as wife, mistress or common prostitute. I shall now consider two utopian speculations on the creation of a new sexual culture. Over a period of twenty years Wedekind toyed with plans for a *magnum opus* on sex, which Kutscher refers to as *Die große Liebe*. Much of his published work as well as unpublished material belongs in this complex. In an excellent study, Thomas Medicus (1982) pieces together the evidence for this project and follows the fluctuations in conception. My interest is limited to two texts which highlight the abolition of the family and the separation of sex from procreation. These features create an odd affinity between Wedekind's sexual woman and Goethe's spiritual ideal; in both cases babies are either never produced or are disposed of, though older children remain attractive as siblings rather than offspring. Wedekind's texts also reveal sadism and sado-masochism as key forms of desire. The first deals with childhood, the second with adolescence. I shall follow this fictional order rather than the order of composition.

Mine-Haha oder Über die körperliche Erziehung der jungen Mädchen (*Mine-Haha, or On the Corporal Education of Young Girls GW* 1) appeared in its final form in 1903. The material dates back to 1895, with the first published version in 1901. It focuses on childhood as the origin of sexual conditioning. The narrator is a woman recalling her strange childhood and the story is focused through the eyes of her earlier self. We follow the experience of a child brought up without adults in a hierarchy of children grouped by age, headed by eighteen-year-old girls. The patriarchal family has apparently been abolished, though there are occasional visits from male inspectors. The children's education is aimed at developing physical beauty and control. At first boys and girls work together, but from the start the girls are more graceful: they come to think with their hips. When they are about seven years old, the sexes are separated. The narrator is taken off in a coffinlike box with airholes to a new building in a park where she finds older companions who had mysteriously disappeared earlier. The girls return intermittently to take charge of the young children. They receive no intellectual education and do not know the facts of life. It is forbidden to enter the bed of another girl and there are no lasting relationships, only intermittent companionship.

It transpires that the institution is financed by theatre productions for adults, performed by the girls when they reach the nymphet stage. As the girls walk to the theatre their white socks are splashed with mud. Once there they perform a pantomime they do not understand, but which is greeted with coarse delight by a faceless audience. The first adult male voices heard by the narrator are those of two men criticizing her calves. The pantomime, a description of Wedekind's pantomime *The Gnat Prince*, begins with two gnats dancing. The prince arrives and kills the female gnat by piercing her with a pin. He then marries a magician's daughter, but at once excludes her from their bed into a cage, taking mistresses who become pregnant by a bite inflicted by the gnat in revenge for the murder of his mate. Eventually the gnat bites the prince whose stomach swells up. Enraged, the prince humiliates the wife before the court and peasants. The old magician returns, kills the prince and turns the gnat into a man who is united with the princess; all ends happily with no more swollen stomachs. At night, however, after the performance, the narrator dreams of the prince cutting off his wife's head. The girls experience the onset of menstruation and the growth of flesh in puberty as hateful. Shortly afterwards they travel to the adult world by underground railway where they see posters they cannot read. They emerge to meet youths of their own age. As the young people walk to the arena for the initiation rites, their white knee socks get splashed with mud and the flowers the adults throw down from their balconies hit them in the face with painful force.

The story can be read in three ways. In the first reading, the world the children inhabit is a utopia, an alternative childhood comparable to Moritz's ideas in *Spring Awakening*. A bodily culture of the senses is set against the mind as the source of illusion. The taboo on close contact inhibits illusory individual love which leads only to possessiveness. (Mother–child bonding is ignored, the narrator being past infancy at the time of her earliest memory.) Bodily culture does not mean a cult of raw instinct; the training is as austere as a ballet dancer's. Because of the focus and the abrupt close, we do not know whether the male body becomes a beautiful instrument and whether the boys are also illiterate. The greater grace of the little girls, however, suggests that the boys will not so exclusively think with their hips. The thought experiment is not followed through to a resulting adult utopia. The signs suggest that the children will enter the society which finances the institution and is portrayed in the pantomime, a world where men judge women by the shape of their calves and lock their wives in cages. The passage by underground into the adult world conveys the gulf between utopia and reality. It is the birth passage from a utopian womb which, like Keith's magic palace, is attached to bourgeois society by the umbilical cord of economic dependence. The womb of history is a common metaphor for the locus of change. But, like Frau Bergmann who acts by Wendla as her mother had acted by her, mother society will mould the children in her image as soon as they emerge, and will crush the few who resist. Apart from shadowy male inspectors, the initiators and educators with the power to set up the system in the first place remain unseen. Who is to educate the adult educators who stand behind the childhood utopia? The framework identifying the narrator as an elderly woman, with the allegorical name of Helene Engel (Helen Angel), is a later addition. It makes clear that the girls sink into an untransformed society, a fate suggested by mud splashing white socks on the way to the arena, echoing the mud that splashed the girls earlier on their way to the first contact with adults in the theatre. Only the narrator retains the memory of childhood and, as the title *Mine-Haha* suggests, for a while finds another utopia among Indians. But her experience there only intensifies the conflicts she suffers in Europe. The gulf between reality and utopia, whether in childhood or among noble savages, remains unbridged. Threatened with being confined in a madhouse to prevent her publishing her memoirs, the narrator committed suicide, fortunately having just handed over her manuscript to the author of *Spring Awakening*. The utopia founders, then, on the problem of the chicken and the egg; social engineering by way of education alone cannot succeed, since education cannot be divorced from the surrounding social conditions.

The story is difficult to read in utopian terms though some critics have done so by setting it an anti-idealist context (Gittleman, 1969; Höger, 1981). Even Trotsky (1975), who regrets the attack on intellect in women and fears the system would have resulted in overproduction of ballet dancers, concludes: 'The cult of the body and the struggle to perfect it lead the artist to call for socialist conditions of education. This fact says as much about Wedekind's artistic sensitivity as it does about the irresistible nature of socialist forms of existence' (p. 44). Be that as it may, to this female reader the story's dystopian features are more evident. It evokes a nightmare world of rigid control enforced not by an identifiable enemy-class of teachers or patriarchs who can be opposed or laughed at, but by the children themselves. The horror lies in the closure of a self-perpetuating cycle. The park where the girls live is surrounded by a gold-painted iron grille, and the gate is heavily barred. Corporal training is reinforced by corporal punishment when the children are whipped across the legs with willow-wands if they walk clumsily. As Medicus (1982: 135–47) shows, the bodily types correspond to pornographic commonplaces such as the booted woman with whip or the 'Luxusfrau', the image of silken-clad availability, all the more piquant because the children are innocent of the image they offer.

The motif of voyeurism becomes overt in the theatre episodes. In one of the plays, one girl beats another until she has bleeding stripes across her legs. The victim is always played by the youngest girl. Here, sado-masochism is not an instinct but is learned, and is performed for the same audience which so enjoys the princess's humiliation and the female gnat's death by impaling. The author of the text is unknown. The children do not understand what they perform, but the bodily foundation is set for a culture of sado-masochism: the girls come to take whipping and being whipped for granted. Such an outcome is utopian if utopia is a world where every desire can be satisfied, including the desire to inflict and feel pain; but it is dystopian as an image of the subject obliterated through internalized subjection to impersonal power. Self-awareness is reduced to bodily awareness. When anyone said 'I', the narrator comments, she meant herself from the crown of her head to the soles of her feet. She cannot remember how any of the girls spoke, only how each of them walked. Imprisoned in the body, they feel themselves in legs and feet more than in fingers and eyes, the organs through which we most come to know and interact with the world. The children develop grotesque physical powers. One girl could cross her feet behind her head and walk on her hands, like a walking star. (This may go back to an erotic fantasy, which plagued Wedekind for several days in 1889, of an imaginary daughter trained to walk on her hands and collect money on her genitals (Hay: 107–13). The father as trainer, an idea which troubled Wedekind in its commercial aspect, is replaced here by an impersonal institution in which females train one another.) The body fragments into separate parts judged like features of a pedigree horse. It is alienated from its human shape and turned into an instrument. The cult of beauty condemns some to exclusion. The narrator dislikes her ugly though gifted music teacher, but later suffers herself when the men disparage her calves. Paradoxically, to be a pure instrument of pleasure entails total repression of desire. The prime transgression is to enter another girl's bed: attachment to an individual body would limit desire and the body's disposability as an instrument to satisfy all conceivable desire. There are two horribly ugly old maidservants, the only adults in the institution. As a result of an earlier transgression, they can now never enter the adult world, but remain slaves subject to the girls' whims; they may even be killed. Punished with ugliness, they cannot attract girls brought up to esteem beauty. The monstrous ugliness of lesbian and individual love reveals the secret locus of desire as adult, male and heterosexual. It shows the threat of woman as unique person rather than interchangeable body, who might arouse personal attachment rather than impersonal desire.

A bodily education might seem to stand in the Rabelaisian tradition of the *abbaye de thélème* with its rule *fay ce que vouldras* (do what you will): the taboos of a spiritual culture are banished and the body can fulfil any desire. It is also an aesthetic ideal: instead of beautiful images in stone or on canvas, the body itself is transformed into endless beautiful forms, like the walking star. But the motto *fay ce que vouldras* leaves open the question of who is doing the wanting: the forms and objects of desire are not timeless, but represent the historically changing needs of social beings. Who is to set the norms of beauty? The experts are exposed as men critical of girl's calves. Rather than *l'abbaye de thélème*, Wedekind's institution is reminiscent of the libertine monastery in de Sade's *Justine*, where women also discipline one another to serve male pleasure. But in *Mine-Haha* the girls are imprisoned from infancy and internalize what in *Justine* is imposed by force. The utopia cancels itself out as a dystopia, all the more horrific because the girls are happily unconscious of their servitude.

Just as *Justine* can be read as a monstrous exaggeration of real power relations, so there is a third way of reading *Mine-Haha*: as a grotesque satire of the way in which girls are actually brought up. At first the sexes mix, but in the latency period they separate, coming together again after puberty. Like Wendla in *Spring Awakening*, the girls are kept in ignorance of sexual matters, so that menstruation comes as a shock. Their childhood is reasonably happy, but lacks variety because their social intercourse is, as the narrator puts it, reduced to such simple elements. They have no intellectual stimulus; they do not speak much; all that matters is what they look like. The fear of ugliness is inculcated early. They have learned to play a few musical instruments and have finely tuned bodies; but they are without other skills and have no means of acquiring any, having been brought up to think with their hips, not their heads. The difference between this and the education of many a middle-class girl is the grotesque exaggeration and absence of moral conditioning. Lacan argues that patriarchal power begins with the entry of the infant into the symbolic system of language. These girls, who scarcely speak and cannot read, who remain enclosed in their bodies, who disparage their own fingers and eyes, might seem to have escaped that initial trauma of separation and differentiation. They do not move as women in the male world of language, but remain in their female bodily world, an imaginary world that seems to have no temporal extension, a world, as the narrator puts it, where seven years pass like a dream. But they have to survive in the world of language signalled by railway posters they cannot read. They do not even know they cannot read, but see only strange meaningless signs. Libertarian demands for equal rights to education may ignore the fact that the only education available is conducted in patriarchal language. But these beautiful girls in their pre-linguistic state reveal not the way out of patriarchy, but the way into adult life as trained animals, the horror Lulu complained of in her marriage with Schwarz. Wedekind's utopian fantasy is simply a monstrous outgrowth of the very culture it set out to oppose. The fact that it so ludicrously cancels itself out is a redeeming feature brought about by the addition of the narrative framework; this framework adds to the child's view that of an elderly literate woman who no longer thinks solely with her hips and can regret the starvation of the mind.

The narrator-heroine embodies the contradictions of the female image. Somewhere along the line this beneficiary of a corporal education has learned to express herself in speech and writing. The innocent unconsciousness of the child provides subtle delights for the voyeur-reader; the conscious adult is necessary as a stand-in for the narrator, concealing the author-voyeur and the truth that her childhood is just a masculine fantasy. For technical reasons, then, a completely contradictory narrator-heroine emerges, her two aspects divided by the gulf that separates utopia from reality. She became a teacher, a potential bridge, but that step is already in contradiction to her original mindless condition. She mothered children, now all dead, and presumably educated them – their father, a brilliant musician who played in nightclubs, would scarcely have had time to bring up the children. Teaching and writing bring her dangerously close to the blue-stocking. But the framework narrator, the author of *Spring Awakening*, anxiously dissociates her from the women's movement with which she had no sympathy. In utopia Helene Engel, beautiful and good, is a mindless, innocent instrument of pleasure who rides prairie horses bareback, at one with nature: she is Mine-Haha, running water. In reality she is a mother, a teacher, and a handmaiden to a musician, a genius of course. She is also an old, intelligent, asexual woman to whom the author of *Spring Awakening* enjoys talking, and from whom he even learns.

This bundle of contradictions still bears a faint resemblance to Kant's ideal woman emitting sexual charm when young, reading books after the menopause. Kant innocently pictures wives charming a patriarchal husband; Helene Engel has to emit sexual charms of a kind Kant had probably not thought of, and her mindlessness is all the more necessary since the receiver is to be not just a husband, but the unfettered masculine imagination. The narrator is indeed an angel in the sense of a non-existent, impossible being; while the utopia is a voyeuristic and sado-masochistic fantasy. The combination produces a text which contradicts itself and attacks the desires it asserts.

Eden: Castrated Patriarchy

Eden is an unpublished fragment, identified by its title as utopian. It purports to explore a new social order based on free love. The fantasy lacks any explicit critical dimension and is thoroughly pornographic as none of Wedekind's published work is. Its interest lies in elements which it has in common with the published works, where, however, raw fantasy is transformed. The text I refer to is a typescript apparently copied from a diary of 1890–1, but not included in Gerhard Hay's edition of the diaries. It should be distinguished from the later material in Notebooks 38–42 which Medicus uses (1982: 175ff), and the account given by Kutscher (1970, 2: 138ff). Höger (1981: 77ff) mentions the *Eden* typescript, but he bases his comments on Kutscher.

Eden has affinities with *Mine-Haha* in imagining an alternative childhood, but it partially connects the childhood realm with adult society and continues through to initiation rites. Economic matters are briskly disposed of. Everyone, male or female, is responsible for making his or her own living, and between the ages of twenty and fifty all pay a tax to support children. Birth takes place in public hospitals. Mothers interchange their babies in order to prevent bonding, and after weaning children are brought up in self-governing institutions. From the age of ten onwards education is segregated. Boys have sexual experience with older women; girls remain virgin until the initiation rites. The young children wear unisex clothes similar to those imagined by Moritz: white wool tunics and big straw hats. For the rites both sexes wear a kinky variation of Alpine Lederhosen, a typically infantile detail. The rites take place amidst a general orgy during which the girls lose their virginity in a completely impersonal way. A special group of priestesses presides over the ceremony, virgins aged between thirteen and twenty who are chosen for their beauty. During the spring and autumn rites, the most beautiful boy and girl respectively are sacrificed. In spring a woman selects the male sacrifice who suffers alternate spells of beatings by the priestesses followed by intercourse with the woman until he dies. He can shorten the process by killing his partner, after which he must kill himself or be beaten to death; but if he keeps going to achieve death by intercourse the woman is spared. In autumn the girl is simply done to death by repeated intercourse with all and sundry.

The fantasy seems even-handed: sex culminates in suffering unto death for both sexes. However, the boy does have the opportunity to make his death a triumph of will and sexual potency, whereas the girl can only suffer her fate. The male acts upon one woman who becomes his victim in a personal relationship initiated by her. To desire a man brings mortal danger to the woman who so presumes, while male desire gives her identity of sorts during the ritual. If she survives she sinks back into the collectivity, no longer distinguished by her role in the male agony. The female victim, by contrast, bestows no identity on the faceless succession of men who have intercourse with her. She is pure receptacle without agency. The male victim has heroic status, the female has none. Medicus (1982: 191) notes a similar difference in the later version: in contrast to the maiden the boy victim makes a *conscious* sacrifice. On the other hand, women are apparently more highly esteemed. The priestesses bring the aesthetic refinement of humanity to a height which makes them genuinely superior to the rest of the people, we are told. They demonstrate their superiority by punishing the sexual male. The text is contradictory: human society finds its highest expression in sexual ritual, yet female sexuality must be denied in order to achieve pure humanity. (Actual deflowering is unimportant, and by the third day most of the girls have learned to see the humourous side of sex!) Although women priestesses appear to stand at the summit of the hierarchy, their power is symbolic; ultimate control, again signalled by inspectors as in *Mine-Haha*, is male. (Bachofen too makes no distinction between symbolism and reality; even under what he calls mother-right he regards the exercise of real power by women as unnatural.) Male administration appears to be inevitable, for among the fragmentary notes towards the end we find that the birth-house is directed by an impotent old man, a parody of the almighty father who apparently does not exist in *Eden*.

In this Eden, love is anything but free; rather, it is depersonalized as ritual. In a study of the female body in Western art, Edwin Mullins (1985: 138) comments on the remarkable lack of paintings showing satisfied love between the sexes: 'far from longing to be unrestrained in his love for woman, he (man) fears that he will be punished for it, even destroyed by it.' *Eden* shows man punished and destroyed. If the virgin is the highest form of humanity, sex is a falling away to be punished and pleasure becomes agony, a tragic rite with a male hero. The collective comic rites are not developed. The humorous side of sex the girls discover on the third day remains mysterious. This is Eden after the Fall. Guilt appears not as a subjective feeling but objectified in a ritual which integrates punishment and pleasure. The sexual urge wins a pyrrhic victory over guilt through sado-masochistic activity prolonged to the point of death. Wedekind later wrote that the value set on virginity is a sign of barbarity, a residue of human sacrifice (Notebook 5: 4; 5v). The core of the fantasy, however, is not virginity but sado-masochism. If sex is to give rise to heroic hubris a taboo is necessary, hence the absurdity of virginity as the supreme value in the Eden of free love. A utopia which banished sado-masochism would be without savour, for the whole point of utopia is to fulfil forbidden desires.

Eden does not portray an alternative sexual culture, but reveals a structure of desire embedded in the same culture Wedekind portrays critically in his plays. The logic of that structure divides women into three classes: punishing virgins; the initiating sexual woman who is punished in the male agony; and bodies disgusting in their endless capacity to receive, as the final humiliations of the girl victim reveal. Women are objects of fear, hatred or disgust. These emotions do not appear explicitly; instead there is veneration, lust and admiration of beauty. But the underlying feelings are revealed by the action. A painting of *Eden* would combine two traditions: the hellish *Garden of Earthly Delights* in the manner of Hieronymus Bosch and the cult of the Virgin. The difference is that Wedekind's text does not purport to show hell and the damned, but paradise and the liberation of sexual pleasure. In Christian tradition the cult of the Virgin justifies punishment of sexual evil; in *Eden* it makes possible sado-masochism as a sexual good.

The fantasy is not simply another manifestation of age-old sexual guilt rooted in Christianity. *Eden* conveys a vision of impersonal power no longer located in king or feudal lord and severed from procreation and fatherhood, bringing not an end of patriarchal attitudes but their transformation. It shows an apparently closed circle, a ritual in which all participants wield and are subject to power. After the age of twenty, even the priestesses may potentially become the woman who will choose a male victim, to become his victim in turn. The closure is conveyed in the round game where each child in a circle beats and is beaten in turn. There seems to be no way out, no final authority which might be overthrown to break the circle. But the circle is not as closed as it seems; the taboo sustaining the ritual, the value of female virginity, is one-sided and is in reality a male power. The god who might be overthrown is male; the male inspectors are his emissaries. But he remains an unseen god, and perhaps the only clue to his identity is the impotent old man who directs the birth-house.

The text does not suggest that control of births is important; the only interest is in separating sex from procreation. But the unseen, asexual impotent old man in charge of the collective production of children who keep one another under control in a cruel ritual of sexual antagonism is an oddly appropriate symbol of power in a society where economic interest in children has become impersonal. No power accrues to the individual who fathers lots of children; quite the reverse. Wedekind was writing before the age of the international corporation, when the family firm still had a patriarchal form. But the explosive growth of capitalism with its booms and crashes had already made clear the fragility of individual power. This was a society which promised power, not handed down from father to son, but to the emancipated unencumbered individual, yet which withheld power from the vast majority. It would be absurd to suggest that *Eden* is a representation of capitalist society, but it expresses an anxiety of powerlessness at a time when whole populations felt the effects of a power whose holders were difficult to identify, and when the traditional forms of patriarchy were coming under increasing stress as family structures changed. The stresses called forth a hysterical assertion of the rights of the *paterfamilias* just as economic changes were undermining the basis of father-power and feminists were attacking male powers over women.

Wedekind despised the tyranny of the father. Since in his view, the petty power of fatherhood offers no compensation for the chains of family duty, the family is destroyed to emancipate sex from all links with procreation. *Eden* abolishes the family. Parents are quite severed from children. For biological reasons it is easier to sever men; but practical arrangements such as interchanging infants are designed to detach women as well. In our day a comparable utopia would no doubt mechanize reproduction altogeter – Shaw's *After Methuselah* is an intermediate move. In *Eden* the phallus is severed from fertility, a castration of male power rooted in fatherhood. The ancient symbol of fertility has become empty and is replaced by the penis as an instrument of compensatory sexual power detached from procreation. The detachment purports to bring sexual liberation, presumably to increase the sum of human pleasure. There is no question of childcare being pleasurable: the female roles of sex object and mother are antagonistic. But *Eden* makes it equally clear that the sterotype of the virile male has more to do with the capacity to sustain a superhuman erection than with potency in fathering children.

Eden suggests that the power of the penis, which brings little socio-economic power, may yet act as a real force in sustaining oppressive power under which both sexes suffer; it shows people turned into instruments of power as each participant punishes and is punished. The symbols of power are whips and the penis. At the summit stands the virgin with whip, apparently an agent who wields but is not subject to power, but who will lose her aura with her virginity; at the bottom of the scale stands the sexual woman, wholly subject to power without wielding it. The value of virginity divides male power against itself. It sustains the patriarch, here ostensibly abolished, but limits the penis, a contradiction explored in the Lulu plays. The purely symbolic power of virginity is difficult to depict and has to be supplemented inconographically by the whip. The power of the penis, however, is also symbolic. The characters in *Eden* are trapped in a ritual of mutual subjection in which powerlessness is sexualized to become masochistic pleasure or sadistic compensation. Both sexes suffer, but the focus is male: the female characters play the necessary parts to produce a male drama.

Eden conveys a culture of aggressive masculinity in a society where traditional male powers were under threat. It shows the displacement of reaction to oppressive power into the sexual sphere. Sadism and sado-masochism are here a signal of castrated patriarchy. Later, in Pabst's film, a comparable but fully conscious sign is the implied impotence of Jack the Ripper who wreaks on the woman vengeance for his own powerlessness. In our time, the patriarchal value of virginity has almost disappeared. Fathers are more distant from their children, though mothers are not; and the impotent old person whose power has nothing to do with maleness is still a collectivity of men, aided and abetted by relatively powerless virile males who seek compensation for their state, a compensation expressed in *Eden* in a sado-masochistic rite of sexual antagonism.

In *Spring Awakening*, sado-masochism is divided into masochistic Moritz and sadistic Melchior. The virgin Wendla has the necessary female masochism to elicit Melchior's sad sadism, for he suffers as he punishes. She functions briefly as destroyed virgin come to inflict punishment when Melchior contemplates suicide; but Moritz then takes on her masochistic role, his pain transmuted into pleasure in his closing words. In contrast to *Eden*, however, the male gods celebrated by the tragic ritual are clearly visible, though they remain the lesser deities, the male inspectors, as it were, who keep patriarchal power functioning at a petty personal level. Female masochism and male sadism or sado-masochism are linked to the educational methods of teachers and fathers such as Martha's. But that hallmark of so much of Wedekind's work, the love of children alongside the rigid separation of sexual pleasure from procreation, is strikingly evident as Wendla is brushed aside by the Masked Man. The Life he promises is unlikely to centre on fatherhood.

The last scene of *Spring Awakening* seems to overthrow the male gods. But it ominously preserves the twin response of sado-masochism in Melchior and Moritz, a mode of desire which seeks and finds an object in the Lulu plays. Melchior and the Masked Man presage Schön and Jack, Moritz presages Schwarz and Escerny. In the *Monstretragödie* the focus is on the male agony, and Lulu is both more sadistic and more masochistic than in the later plays, according to the immediate requirements of male sado-masochism. The toning down of these features may initially have been intended to appease the censors, but it produces a marked shift in meaning. Lulu is no longer a demon who torments men and thirsts for the knife. She becomes at once more and less of a cypher: more of a cypher as a mirror reflecting masculine fantasies; less of a cypher in *Earth Spirit* as an emergent individual whose dehumanization in *Pandora's Box* is a response to the abuses of male power. The Lulu plays, more than their *Urtext* and certainly more than *Eden*, destroy the aura of sado-masochism. Jack the Ripper is no hero of a spring ritual; he stands at the blackest extreme of that mysterious humorous side of sex which remains unexplored in *Eden*. He is the sadistic pole of the complex whose masochistic counterparts are the ridiculous Schwarz and Escerny.

Sadism and sado-masochism are here unmasked as the ludicrous contortions of the masculine ego under bourgeois capitalism which promises power to the unfettered individual yet constantly witholds it.

8
Wedekind and the Critics

The Early Critics

The major work on Wedekind until the 1960s, and one which is still a valuable source, was Artur Kutscher's three-volume biography. Kutscher and other early critics wrote about Lulu in terms of a tragic clash of antinomies: life or instinct versus mind; matter versus form; nature versus spirit; nothingness versus life or being, and so the circle closes. According to Mary Ellmann's (1979: 2–26) rule of sexual analogy, the binary oppositions collapse into a fundamental sexual antagonism. For Kutscher (1922, 1: 362), Lulu personifies the female sexual drive at the centre of life; for Diebold (1921: 49), she is substance on which the men impose form; for Fechter (1920: 24), she is pure instinct with nothingness in her heart; for Jacobsohn (1965: 172, orginally 1918), she is a blind natural force whose victims we pity and who is justly punished. In Friedenthal's view (1914: 77), she is woman as the elemental principle of destruction; in Hamann's (1907: 77), she is the eternal feminine in modern form; in Dülberg's (Friedenthal, 1914: 160), she is instinctual woman, foam-born Venus Anadyomene become marble against which life is broken. A timeless battle between male order and female chaos overshadows social criticism, and the close is affirmed as a restoration of order.

Karl Kraus (1982) stands apart from the majority of critics. In his introduction to the 1905 production of *Pandora's Box* in Vienna, Kraus fears that the public will see Jack as freeing the world from ruinous disorder and will fail to recognize in Lulu the victim of destructive male possessiveness. But he too operates with binary oppositions. As Hugh Salveson (1981) documents, Kraus was heavily influenced at this time by Otto Weininger's *Geschlecht und Charakter* which came out in 1903. Weininger posits antagonistic male and female principles and draws on much pseudo-biology, making no distinction between biological sex and social gender. The female is always the negation of the positive male qualities which constitute personal identity. While actual men and women are a mixture of male and female characteristics, any man is superior to all women. Womankind comes in two types: the mother and the prostitute. Kraus has nothing of Weininger's misogyny, but he shares his preference for prostitutes. Kraus writes of Lulu as 'die Begehrende, nicht Gebärende', she who desires, not she who bears (p. 14). (According to Weininger most prostitutes are sterile!) She is the 'Vollweib' – in Weininger's terms fully female – without mind, memory or the dangers of spiritual continuity: 'Jedem eine andere', different for every man, she is more truly virginal than the domestic doll (p. 14). Kraus does not notice that such a creature is nothing more than a doll with changing costumes.

Franz Blei (1915) by contrast, is scornful of the high priests of hedonism, and sees Lulu as a typical fantasy of bourgeois man. His attack on the cult of woman as mindless vessel of pleasure can only be applauded. But Blei dismisses Wedekind's critique of economic inequalities and leaves the division of women into mothers or prostitutes untouched while Kraus, who did see in Wedekind's work a critique of male powers, conceived of women as saturated with sexuality, hardly a recipe for emancipation. These were perhaps only the views of bourgeois intellectuals: Kurt Martens (1921: 217) reports that at the 1898 Leipzig *première* of *Earth Spirit* the working-class sector of the audience saw Lulu as a proletarian scourge of the bourgeoisie. But most middle-class commentators identified in the play an unsettling vision of sexual anarchy followed by restoration of order, unsettling in making hypocrisies and hidden desires uncomfortably overt.

The early history of Wedekind and the theatre reflects this mixed effect. In Wilhelmine Germany, Wedekind offended against official morality and until 1918 suffered more than any other writer from censorship. Michael Meyer (1982) documents the work of the Munich Advisory Commission on Censorship, set up in 1908 to mediate between artists and the police and Peter Jelavich (1985) too gives an account of its operations. The judgements are reminiscent of present-day voices claiming to speak for the 'moral majority', with two notable exceptions. In 1908 Max Halbe defended *Spring Awakening* and *Pandora's Box*; he eventually resigned, though over a naked dancer, not in defence of Wedekind (p. 255). Thomas Mann resigned in 1913 over *Lulu*, a version of the two plays in combination. Despite the bowdlerizations, Mann recognized a work destined to be a classic and praised its grimly moral power (p. 280). Unfortunately, the master of ambiguity does not explain what the moral is. *Pandora's Box* was scarcely performed during Wedekind's lifetime, apart from occasional private productions. But despite official morality, his work was in tune with the changing tastes of an audience tired of Naturalist images of social misery. The director most successful in capturing that mood was Max Reinhardt, and *Spring Awakening* became the most frequently performed play in his theatre. Sally McMullen (1985) suggests that most of Reinhardt's early productions of 1902–3 – Strindberg's *There are Crimes and Crimes*, Wilde's *Salome*, Wedekind's *Earth Spririt*, Gorki's *The Lower Depths* (played with rhythmic subtlety), Maeterlinck's *Pelléas and Mélisande*, Hofmannsthal's *Elektra* – had two things in common: figurative language translatable into sensuous theatrical effects, and the theme of woman's sexuality and freedom. She concludes that on balance the productions stressed the dangers rather than the value of emancipation. After these early successes Wedekind's work became increasingly popular, and by the 1920s was among the most performed in Germany (Seehaus, 1964).

In the domain of theatre, then, sexuality was a transmission point of power-relations. Wedekind's work was the focus of a battle waged in the name of a public to be protected from corruption or liberated from tutelage; a battle fought out between a paternalist state and intellectuals concerned primarily with their own freedoms. In the Weimar Republic those freedoms were largely secured, until the National Socialists took over and immensely strengthened the state apparatus. Despite a flicker of sympathy from Goering, a lover of spectacle, Wedekind's work disappeared from the stage. An offer from Ufa, the largest German film company, to film *The Marquis of Keith* provided that Keith could be portrayed as a Jew was turned down by Wedekind's widow (Tilly Wedekind, 1969: 257–8; 284). The middle-class public to be protected or liberated held contradictory attitudes. In Wilhelmine Germany the family ideal, a central tenet of state ideology, scarcely corresponded to the way people actually lived, still less so in the 1920s; but it remained potent among the very public that flocked to the theatre to be shocked by Lulu's freedom and downfall. A measure of its strength is the appeal of

National Socialist propaganda concerning the role of woman. Filtered through the attitudes of producers, critics and public, Wedekind's plays were assimilable as exciting spectacle which reinforced rather than undermined the division of women into two types, however little these correspond to real social practice. Dr Schön's illusions held sway and Lulu was often played more as he would have wished than as his more subtle son Alwa, and the author, intended. Notable too is the far greater critical agreement concerning *Spring Awakening* and the need to free young men from the power of the father, while Jacobsohn (1965: 11; 172), writing in 1901 and 1918, justifies Keith despite Molly's dripping corpse yet vigorously endorses Lulu's punishment. The family ideal was right for women but unendurable for men.

Recent Criticism: *Spring Awakening* and *The Marquis of Keith*

Critical argument turns on whether Wedekind is a scourge of bourgeois society, as Kraus or the Leipzig workers described by Martens would have it, or the arch-bourgeois of Blei's account. Apart from during the early years of cuts and censorship, *Spring Awakening* has not aroused as much controversy among professional critics as the Lulu plays, though audiences have sometimes been shocked. Bourgeois liberals, socialists and moderate conservatives alike can agree that young men should be freed from the rule of the father. Most also agree with the Masked Man in absolving Melchior of blame for Wendla's death, giving little thought to the problems of a live, pregnant fourteen-year-old. Disagreement arises over whether the play goes beyond a social Darwinist concept of the egoism of nature to propound a radical revision of values. Peter Michelsen (1965: 52) argues that it does not, though he is less critical of *Spring Awakening* than of the Lulu plays; likewise Trotsky (1975) who, given the attack on patriarchy, is disinclined to be too harsh on the Masked Man's bourgeois aestheticism. Sol Gittleman (1969: 51) and Leroy Shaw (1970: 61) identify in the play an optimistic anti-bourgeois radicalism; J. L. Hibberd (1977) sees radicalism mixed with sceptical humour; M. H. G. da Silva (1986: 7) recognizes a radical utopianism blocked by fatalistic pessimism. Rothe (1969: 39) and Keith Bullivant (1973) see the import of the main action as more radical than the Masked Man's final ruthless accommodation with bourgeois society. Hahn (I: 6) sees the Masked Man as a symbol of the reality of capitalist society when the moral illusions are stripped away; as an affirmation of Life he is an illusion of the author. Similarly, Hans-Jochen Irmer (1975) identifies in the play vitalist amoralism (p. 113) *and* the spirit of capitalism (p. 96). Edward Bond (1980) does not like either Melchior or his mentor, rightly recognizing that neither is a socialist. Critics of *Spring Awakening* offer much comment on sexual repression, some on the forms of sexuality (Shaw, 1970; Rank) and little on sexual difference except for Rothe (1969: 37), who comments on masculine sadism and feminine masochism under patriarchy.

The arguments over *The Marquis of Keith* are rather similar: is the hero a prophet of freedom and vitality (Hartwig: 106; Maclean, 1968: 186–7; Gittleman, 1969: 86; Firda: 1972), a failed capitalist entrepreneur (Best, 1975: 109), or an ambiguous mixture of both (Kaufmann, 1969)? Hahn (1967), Rothe (1968) and Burghard Dedner (1975) see Keith as a deluded idealist in the mask of a cynic. His delusion is his faith in vitalistic individualism, the ideology of free enterprise, where the reality is the power of capital. Most critical analysis focuses on the male characters, though Rothe notes a new scepticism about prostitutes and Dedner comments on the petit-bourgeois possessiveness of Molly. Wolfgang Kuttenkeuler (1977), in a study which ignores the social situation of women, takes Keith to be the very essence of the dehumanized relations of capitalism, yet attacks possessive Molly and calculating Anna for their failure to appreciate his idealism. Alfons Höger (1979), by contrast, interestingly relates the female types to Riehl's *Die Familie*: the conservatism of the two women and their rounded personalities (which are comparable with Hegel's vague unity of being or Ploss's *schönes, geschlossenes Ganzes*) contrast with the divided, complex men.

Recent Criticism: the Lulu Plays

With the Lulu plays judgements depend crucially on views concerning sex and gender. In recent criticism the two programmes most commonly attributed to Wedekind remain those outlined by Karl Kraus: affirmation of order or affirmation of pleasure even unto death. Depending on the individual critic's own beliefs, the first programme of order is either defended or else attacked as baleful (generally by left-wing critics). Similarly, the second programme of pleasure is either defended as radically liberating, as Kraus would have it, or else attacked as an outgrowth of the bourgeois imagination, as Franz Blei argues. In the pleasure programme Jack appears either as the instrument of bourgeois-patriarchal revenge or as the high priest of pleasure, while Lulu dies either as a martyr or in a masochistic transfiguration. Some critics identify both programmes but give one predominance over the other; others of a less polemical persuasion leave the issue open. Three factors play a part in most readings: political views on the social order; views on sexuality; and aesthetic judgements on the interplay of allegory and realist social criticism.

Among critics who identify a single programme in the Lulu plays are Wilhelm Emrich (1960) and Peter Michelsen (1965), whose views are sharply contrasting. Emrich elevates Lulu as the matyr of a misunderstood female nature; but since justice for woman contradicts all law, women are left to choose between living as victims or dying as martyrs, while the aesthetic virtues of genuine tragedy seen by Emrich do away with the subversive mixing of modes. Michelsen, like Blei, underplays realist social criticism to attack sexist allegory: Lulu is a bourgeois fantasy fed by social Darwinism, Schopenhauer and Hartmann; rapacious and masochistic, she is the reduction of woman to flesh and vulva. John Elsom (1973), writing with Marcusean optimism, is kinder: Lulu was a monster set against the Hausfrau, a battle now won. Her abandoned dancing signals a common mythological confusion shared by Wedekind between life-enhancing Eros and the bloody rites of Dionysus, a confusion no longer prevailing in our enlightened times; hence the outmoded dark undertones in Wedekind's otherwise liberating vision. Wolfdietrich Rasch (1967: 66) also takes Lulu's dancing as a sign of instinctual primitive vitality. Both ignore the fact that in Wedekind's work dancing is an exploitation of the female body, a controlled skill inculcated by the whip and performed for male eyes. In a later essay Rasch (1969) sees Lulu as a symbol of instinct deformed by society. Freud was no doubt suffering from a mythological confusion in identifying Eros and Thanatos, principles underlying Höger's (1981) treatment of the *Monstretragödie*. Höger too stresses allegory and defends a programme of erotic liberation, arguing acutely that Wedekind's early work reflects a struggle to escape the mother bond. But his critical method is questionable; he reads the *Monstretragödie* as an adaptation of the material in *Eden*, which in turn he relates to Bachofen. Lulu, the hetaera, belongs to a pre-patriarchal sexual utopia which becomes overt in the timeless idyll of the close: masochism and sadism are the polar extremes of pleasure and Lulu's death a natural necessity, an assumption into a transcendent utopia. Pleasurable existence is finally centred on genital sexuality (p. 34), and Jack's excision of Lulu's genitals is a ritual celebration. Sadism and masochism are more prominent in the *Monstretragödie*, but even so Höger's ultra-strong reading is due to an oversharp division between allegorical and social levels and to reduction to a master-text, *Eden*.

As David Midgley (1985) shows, the Lulu plays are equally resistant to reduction to the *Monstretragödie*. Irmer (1975: 140) takes a similar view to Höger, and in a less drastic reading Walter Sokel (1966) sees Lulu's end as a tragic, rather than an idyllic fulfilment of an unconscious death wish. In a reading based on Freud as revised by Marcuse, Gittleman (1967) remains this side of the pleasure principle. In the titanic battle between Eros and Civilization Jack is society's henchman rather than Eros become Thanatos, while Lulu represents 'humanistic eroticism' (p. 74) and 'the female's sexual drive' (p. 65). Gittleman is uncritical of Wedekind's anti-feminism because he takes Lulu as a mythical figure rather than a real woman. But the move from mythical Eros to the biologism of 'the female's sexual drive' shows blindness to the sexual stereotype behind the myth, and Gittleman describes *Mine-Haha* as 'wholesome' (p. 131). Like Höger, Dagmar Lorenz (1976) places Wedekind in the ambit of the Munich prophets of sexual revolution and the socialist appropriations of Bachofen. Lulu represents matriarchy while Geschwitz speaks for Wedekind in her vision of feminist jurisprudence. This radical feminist appropriation, like Gittleman's Marcusean defence, depends on taking Lulu as a positive image of female nature and on an unduly generous view of Wedekind's attitude to feminism.

Turning now to critics who see in the Lulu plays two conflicting programmes, Rothe (1968) sees the close as both an allegorical *Liebestod* and the final assault of destructive patriarchy. Rothe's accomplished study subtly takes account of the interaction of allegory, symbol and social critism. He does not elevate allegory and avoids a strongly closed reading. Similarly, Hibberd (1984) sees a tension between hedonism like that of Heine, one of Wedekind's favourite poets, and the pessimism of Hartmann. Trotsky (1975) had been critical, seeing *Pandora's Box* as 'the bankruptcy of esthetic eroticism' (p. 43); all that is left is 'the psychological need to institute a certain control, an extreme censorship over the elementary rhythms of life' (p. 46). Audrone Willecke (1980) follows him in attacking a viciously circular pattern in Wedekind's work. The freeing of instinct in sadistic Jack and masochistic Lulu only confirms the patriarchal status quo, showing how close the sexual stereotypes in Wedekind are to Weininger; although Wedekind sees through the underlying power structure, his characteristic reaction is one of helpless, painfully distorted laughter. For Willecke, then, the programme affirming necessary order cancels out the programme of erotic liberation.

While agreeing with much of Willecke's criticism, I think the major plays are recuperable as theatre if not as doctrine concerning female nature. Even Weininger occasionally seems dimly aware that patriarchy, not nature, contructs masculinity and femininity, as when he writes of woman as man's guilt. How much more subversive is Wedekind's exposure of a power structure underlying the constructs of femininity, both those he attacks as constructs and those he intends as utopias. In an illuminating commentary Sylvia Bovenschen (1979: 43–61) warns against closed interpretation. Critical uncertainty, she suggests, has its source in the appeal to nature in both positive and negative definitions of the female. Differences of opinion arise when critics try to determine to what tradition the author himself belongs and whether Lulu embodies a radical call for emancipation or traditional misogyny. Interestingly enough, a similar ambiguity in the reception of Freud points to his roots in German metaphysics, and remarkably similar conclusions are reached by the critics who look back through Freud to Wedekind. The clashing antimonies of the early critics Emrich, Elsom, Hibberd, Trotsky, and Willecke are all roughly translatable into the argument of Freud's *Civilization and its Discontents*, the critics then differing on how to evaluate that argument. Kraus and Gittleman roughly concur with Marcuse's revision in *Eros and Civilization*, to which Lorenz adds a radical feminist twist. The differing views on Jack, most clearly Gittleman versus Höger or Irmer, are translatable into the pleasure principle before and after its link with the death wish.

All these readings either themselves operate with, or attribute to Wedekind, a belief in a sexual essence, analogous to the theory of a human essence in alienation, which is repressed or deformed by bourgeois society. That is, they posit a form of sexual idealism and a repression theory of the sort Foucault attacks, leading either to biologistic celebration of the liberating potential of sex or to biologistic pessimism. The masculine bias, which Willecke and Michelsen see but Kraus and Gittleman do not, stems from the mythical embodiment of the final object of desire in Lulu, who like her antithesis, the Freudian Mother, remains an object defined relative to masculine desire. Wedekind sought to discover the sexual essence, but closed interpretations ignore the way in which conventionalized images are fragmented. As Bovenschen argues, Lulu demonstrates the interchangeability of the clichés. She plays roles which are projections of completion for masculine self-images, but she also plays *with* the roles. Yet all she can do is adapt to and then deny each role in turn, thus remaining trapped as the positive or negative image of masculine projections. On this account the plays strikingly demonstrate the problems of articulating opposition to sexual stereotypes without falling back into binary oppositions. Bovenschen's radically open reading takes further the line of argument initiated by Rothe. The diametrically opposed programmes do not so much stand in tension as mutually destroy, or deconstruct, one another. Willecke by contrast gives primacy to one programme over the other. Wedekind's laughter is perhaps helpless, as she suggests, but the laughter of the theatre audience need not be so, for the texts reduce oppressive ideologies to absurdity. A tragedy which is ludicrous may not, *pace* Emrich, be necessary. Interesting too are Lulu's games *with* the roles, which leave room for an actress to indicate an emergent autonomy behind the social and the allegorical roles so that their deconstruction need not leave us feeling helpless but enlightened and angry. The plays can be liberating today not for what they show of female nature or the sexual essence but by virtue of their essentially theatrical effect in exploring roles played *as* roles, and so subverting constructs of femininity which reduce women to objects, whether those which are overtly misogynist or the more well-meaning hypostatizations of women's sexuality as man's redemption.

9
Wedekind and Modern Theatre

The prologue of *Earth Spirit* offers theatre not as Schiller's moral institution but as an immoral circus full of eroticism, grotesquerie and violence. Such a promise looks forward to Marinetti's Futurist programme for theatre as variety or music hall, to the Dadaist attack on high art, to the shock effects of Surrealism or Artaud's programme for a theatre of cruelty, to the plays of Genet or Peter Weiss's *Marat/Sade* – theatre as lunatic asylum. The pervasive theatrical metaphor of masks and roles, the characters dissolving into fantasies, dreams or nightmares, and the fractured language all look forward to dramatists as disparate as Sternheim, Pirandello, Ionesco, Beckett, Pinter and Handke. Wedekind's characteristic manner anticipates that most pervasive aspect of modern theatre, tragi-comic travesty of the modes. Categorizing modern theatre is notoriously difficult; I shall concentrate on key aspects of Wedekind's theatrical language as points of comparison or contrast with a whole range of works that may be otherwise disparate, whether ideologically or formally.

Anti-illusionism and denaturalization

I shall use three sets of terms as working tools. The first pair, illusion and anti-illusionism, is often used to characterize modernism as self-reflective literature which underlines its own fictionality and is closely related to the second pair, naturalism and denaturalization. Metaphor and metonymy, Roman Jakobson's (1956) categories, are the third pair.

By naturalism I mean a mimetic mode of writing which purports to represent a relatively stable and accessible reality and to preserve the illusion of authenticity, claiming that the world it conveys is indeed the real world. (Note that the illusion is of authenticity, not identity – even in the most naturalistic work we are not intended to mistake theatre for life.) The historical form of naturalism Wedekind broke with was late-nineteenth-century Naturalism; this was a complex movement and I shall touch here only on one or two trends of Naturalist theory. Accurate representation meant photographic and phonographic accuracy in conveying appearances and sounds according to Arno Holz's dictum: 'Art tends towards nature again. It becomes nature in accord with the conditions for imitation and how they are handled' (Rupprecht, 1962: 210–11). The world to be imitated was governed by laws which could be demonstrated with scientific objectivity. The material elements of the world in which the laws were active could be reproduced with mechanical accuracy. In that sense the world was stable and accessible, however painful it might be to live in. As Furst and Skrine (1971: 38) note, Holz's demand for objectivity goes beyond Zola's definition of 'un coin de la nature vu à travers un tempérament' (a corner of nature seen through a temperament). Wedekind's perspectivism – schoolmasters *à travers* the child's eye, the mélange of styles, the temperamental refusal of inevitable doom, the mixed modes – are all anti-Naturalist. They are also denaturalizing in a broader sense. Both Holz and Zola use the term nature. The assimilation of supposed social and psychological regularities to laws of natural science can lead to fatalistic undermining of protest against social injustice: nature is notoriously unjust and what cannot be cured must be endured. To denaturalize is to rob social phenomena of the aura of natural necessity. A crucial step in that direction is to deny the 'second nature' of the art work its illusion of authenticity, to show forth that it is an artefact, not a reflection of immutable laws.

Denaturalization and anti-illusionism are not interchangeable terms: anti-illusionism is a technique which may aid denaturalization. If used to undermine the sense of the represented world as closed and law-governed, it can denaturalize features of the real world the fiction purports to represent which might otherwise seem to be natural necessities. This is the essence of Brechtian alienation as an aesthetic technique and a political position. Low-life milieu is not the only kind of representation which may be broken open to denaturalize the 'laws' of heredity and environment; any represented world can be so undermined and divine or moral law or the ineluctable power of the will subverted. Brecht's anti-illusionism was an attack on ideology which proclaimed a particular social order a necessity of nature. But he was a realist; he did not dispose of the scientific claim but redefined law less mechanistically. He claimed to represent the reality of class society and to distinguish between real necessity and ideology. Anti-illusionism can, however, express a radical scepticism which dissolves any distinction between true and false because faith in the possibility of representation has gone. The scepticism may be ontological or epistemological: reality may not be susceptible of rational understanding or we as subjects may be caught in a web of cultural fictions and linguistic structures which make reality for ever inaccessible. Wedekind's work is Janus-faced, pointing towards both Brechtian realism and sceptical relativism.

Roman Jakobson's categories of metaphor and metonymy are the third set of terms. Summarizing Jakobson, David Lodge (1976: 483–4) writes:

> Selection implies the possibility of substitution, and the perception of similarity, and is therefore the means by which metaphor is generated. Metonymy (the figure which names an attribute, adjunct, cause or effect of a thing instead of the thing itself) and the closely associated figure of synecdoche (part standing for whole, or whole for part) belong to the combinative axis of language, since they operate with terms that are contiguous in language and reality.

While most discourses mix metonymy and metaphor, Jakobson suggests that in literature one pole tends to be predominant: realist writing is metonymic, Romantic and Symbolist writing metaphoric; the realist novel is metonymic, the drama metaphoric, so that metonymic realism in nineteenth-century theatre was an experimental deviation. Whatever the force of such general claims, the terms can illuminate aesthetic tendencies in the genres at the turn of the century. Lodge suggests that the contrast between metonymic titles like *Kipps* or *The Forsyte Saga* and metaphoric titles like *Heart of Darkness* or *The Wings of the Dove* signals a move towards metaphor in the modernist novel; while the masterpiece of modernism, *Ulysses*, is a uniquely rich combination of metaphoric totality with metonymic fullness. The game works with German literature too: *Effi Briest* or *Buddenbrooks* as against *Steppenwolf* or *The Magic Mountain*, with Döblin's *Berlin Alexanderplatz* as the uniquely rich mix. The game is less easily played with drama, which has a stronger metaphoric tendency. *Hedda*

Gabler, Miss Julie or *The Weavers* are metonymic titles of realist or Naturalist plays. But Hauptmann's *Vor Sonnenaufgang (Before Sunrise)* is a Naturalist play with a title that sounds as Symbolist as Ibsen's *When We Dead Awaken.* Hauptmann's *Hanneles Himmelfahrt (Little Hanna's Assumption)* is a hybrid which does not so much blend Naturalism and Symbolism as forcibly chain them together.

The terms I have discussed apply at two levels of analysis: texture and structure. Literary texts, with a few experimental exceptions, are always a mixture. I am concerned with a structural distinction between plays which as a whole are metaphoric and those which are metonymic. The difference at the structural level signals a different relation of the represented world to a putative real world, and generally reflects ideological differences. The title *Spring Awakening* conveys an extended metaphor carried by local textural motifs such as nymphs or the image of the river. It is metaphoric in the straightforward sense that the nymphs and the river are not literally agents of a life-force, but create within the represented world the sense of a force at work. This metaphoric subtext relates to a putative real world as a revelation of hidden forces imperceptible to the senses. Since the forces are immaterial and metaphysical, they are not reproducible by cameras or tape recorders and cannot be discovered by scientific experiment. But the material vehicles of verbal image, scenery and gesture carry the metaphoric tenor which, depending on production, may be highlighted or played down. Modernist metaphor is often part of a backlash against scientific materialism. It signals the pursuit of the mythic, ahistorical vision and a return to a religious sensibility; at the turn of the century this often took the form of a religion of natural vitality. Metaphor is the condensed expression a of total vision.

Metonymy and synecdoche are also devices of condensation. As a structural principle they serve to convey a whole world, particulary metonyms signifying effects of the thing meant and synecdoches signifying parts of wholes. Thus the image of an intellectual wearing glasses shows the effect of too much mind, and a weaving machine represents the Industrial Revolution. This is different from metaphor in that the bad eyesight and the machine are literally an effect and a part of the thing meant, and the connection could in principle be analysed scientifically or sociologically. On the face of it, then, the relation of the metonymic represented world to the putative real world is not revelatory but analytical, showing material features of the historical world which can be checked by other means. The mimetic exactitude of the metonym or synecdoche as measured against its counterpart in reality guarantees the demonstration; the expressive force of metaphor carries conviction without recourse to proof. The ideology sustaining Naturalist metonymy is faith in scientific explanation and in the concept of social structure which allows for synecdochic representation of whole by part. Iron causality and social structure, however, are metaphysical in the sense that they cannot be demonstrated empirically any more than God or the *élan vital*; and Naturalist metonymy is arguably metaphor for ineluctable necessity masquerading as metonymy. I have already commented on the way in which a particular conception of scientific law could lead to fatalism; in a similar way, the concept of structure can become rigid. Brecht's techniques are designed to reveal dynamic, mutable structure. If modernist metaphor is often a sign of ahistoric myth, Naturalist metonymy can turn history into fate.

Finally, it should be noted that different types of literature have different textural mixes of metonymy and metaphor. Symbolist works may convey a whole alternative world fleshed out with internal metonyms and synecdoches which in turn bear an internal aura of exactitude: in Wagner's *Ring* the rippling flow of the Rhinemaiden's hair or the grimace accompanying Alberich's curse stand for a whole universe. Such internal metonyms become symbols in the relation of that universe to a putative real world. In realist writing the metaphoric stratum expands the meaning of metonymic mimesis, but without the doctrinal precision of some Symbolist works. At the opposite extreme, in French *symboliste* and later hermetic poetry the metaphoric vehicle is detached from any tenor and the referential quality of metonyms disappears, so that in imagist poetry or the work of Trakl the distinction can scarcely be made.

Hybrid Forms: Theatre Turning to Novel

Dramatic realism in the mid-nineteenth century and its outgrowth in Naturalism can be seen as theatre aspiring to the condition of the novel, the bourgeois form *par excellence*, just as earlier the novel and novella were influenced by dramatic form, especially in the development of plot. The history of the novel is in large measure the history of a form adapted to exploring bourgeois life and articulating the concerns of a bourgeois public. It is doubly private: in its themes, the places it portrays, and the psyches it explores, and in entering the household to be read by a person alone in a room. Yet it is widely distributable without the complexities of theatre finance. As theatre too sought to draw a bourgeois public it is not surprising that the aesthetic influence of the novel should become marked in dramatic form. Above all, there is the decisive shift, notably in Ibsen, from verse to prose. There is the striving towards comprehensiveness in evoking milieu. Stage directions increase in length, and a page of text in a Naturalist play can look more like the page of a novel. The language becomes anti-poetic, punctuated by silences and non-verbal noises and imitating the gestural effect of colloquial speech.

A similar development towards the end of the nineteenth century was the Impressionist demotion of plot in favour of a suite of atmospheric scenes with no sharp beginning or conclusive end. Locations are increasingly private: rooms in a middle-class household, a Berlin tenement or a Silesian weaver's cottage. Such tendencies are metonymic, building up strings of contiguous detail, suggesting through synecdoche a whole milieu by means of a part. In this sense, comedy has always been more metonymic, and it is in tragedy that the awkwardness of theatre turning to novel is most evident. But even in comedy the symmetries of dramatic plot lie uneasily alongside the proliferation of metonymic detail. In the larger form of the novel to be read over a long time, plot can more easily be submerged yet still be active under the leisurely deployment of detail, atmosphere and meandering story.

In Germany the novel was less prominent as the leading literary form than it was in Britain, France or Russia, and aesthetic debate tended to focus on drama, though in the 1880s the novel was for a while the leading Naturalist genre. The centrality of drama doubtless had something to do with the numerous centres in Germany with their long theatrical and musical tradition, as well as with the classical heritage of Goethe and Schiller. The strongest realist genre was the bourgeois tragedy initiated by Lessing and Schiller. A hybrid mode, it uneasily combines classical form with contemporary themes and realist detail, a manner Wedekind apes in the opening scene of *Spring Awakening* with its echoes of Hebbel's *Maria Magdalene*. The German intellectual tradition also favoured a striving towards the total vision, most readily conveyed through the compression of metaphor and the closure of the strong plot. Yet theatrical Naturalism found its strongest expression in Germany, where Strindberg's Naturalist plays were most widely produced. Here, the most representative Naturalist writer was Hauptmann, whereas in France, for example, Zola the novelist held that title. But the underlying classical structures remained active in even the most Naturalist of Hauptmann's plays and he soon turned to symbolism and a regressive neo-classicism. German prose fiction also was often a hybrid, combining overt metaphoric structures with intermittent realism, a tendency conveyed in the literary-historical term 'poetic realism'.

In other cultures the novel moved inwards into the psyche and outwards to convey an ever broadening social panorama, a striving towards totality which in combination with metonymic realism produces long novels or suites of novels. In Germany, the most fascinating experiments in articulating inner states were Wagner's operas with their extraordinary oscillation between the overarching metaphor and a mania for contingent detail, as in the proliferating retrospective narrations which combine mythic gigantism with modern neurosis. The uneasy mixture of metaphor and metonymy and of symbolism and realism was evident in the creaking literalism of productions which can seem comic to the modern eye. In the Wagernian leitmotif, however, the distinction between metaphor and metonymy is difficult to sustain. The dramatic motif – a sword or an expression in eyes – begins as metonymy or synecdoche. The musical motif is metaphoric, but 'resemblance' across media, between musical phrase and visual image, initially has to be established through simple juxtaposition. The dramatic motif is transformed by the musical phrase into metaphor, and the two elements together assume accretions of meaning in a metaphoric expansion through repetition in new contexts. In this German tradition of hybrid forms Wedekind stands out as an iconoclast. He broke with traditional classical forms and the metaphoric total vision, and rejected contemporary Naturalism. Wedekind is Wagner turned inside-out. Wagner strives to unite metaphoric totality with metonymic exhaustiveness: *The Ring* is the equivalent of a Zolaesque suite of novels. Wedekind travesties both poles, anticipating the sceptical and subversive strain in modern theatre and its formal self-reflection.

The Subversion of Signs

The 'hereness' and 'nowness' of the theatre has a paradoxical effect.

The whole *Gestalt* of a character is instantly present on stage; the set is filled with palpably contiguous details in the seemingly contingent juxtapositions of furnishings; the captive audience sits through the length of an act, admiring the precision with which a milieu is caught in the synecdoche of a living room. But the movement of dialogue and action invites the construction of metaphor as a bridge between static set and dynamic action: Nora's living room turns into a doll's house, a metaphor linking the external and material with the experiential. Material objects are transformed into utterance and tell Nora what to be. They reduce the person to a thing, a doll in a doll's house, though the play as a whole denies the necessity of that reduction. Whereas *A Doll's House* is metaphoric, *Nora*, the title used in Germany, and *Hedda Gabler* are metonymic, suggesting that the social fabric can be conveyed by following a single thread connecting with innumerable others which could in principle be shown until the whole weave is revealed. The title *A Doll's House*, by contrast, is a metaphoric short cut: the picture in the weave, an instant *Gestalt*. The audience can see the set simultaneously as metonymy and metaphor.

Spring Awakening, *Earth Spirit* and *Pandora's Box* are metaphoric titles, suggestive of Symbolist verse drama rather than Naturalism; but in fact Wedekind's plays are as much anti-Symbolist as they are anti-Naturalist. The link between the action and the mythical meaning borne by the titles does not hold because the metaphysical basis which would sustain the metaphoric connection is progressively undermined. The undermining characteristically takes the form of incongruous juxtapositions of metaphor and metonymic detail – Lulu's mythical names in the mouths of men sporting the garb of the late nineteenth century, or Wendla replying on being addressed as a nymph: 'No, I'm Wendla Bergman'. Comparable in effect is Manet's *Déjeuner sur l'herbe* which so disturbingly undermines the tradition of the pastoral nude by juxtaposing arcadian female nakedness with men clothed in the fashion of nineteenth-century Paris. In *Earth Spirit*, the metaphoric subtext of life and death, timeless nature and temporality is too overt. It becomes blatant by being incongruously highlighted in its realist context, like the tigerskin rug as a metaphor for animal vitality in the studio of the inadequate Schwarz. The effect is not organic unity but absurd incongruity.

The Marquis of Keith, by contrast, is on the face of it a metonymic title. The label 'Marquis' seems to locate Keith in a social hierarchy which could be built up further through contiguous detail. Or else the eponymous hero may be a significant part standing for the whole, as Hauptmann's weavers stand collectively for a stage in the growth of industrial Germany. In context, however, the name and title lose their quality of precise designation. Naturalist metonymy depends on reliable correspondence between word and thing, language and reality; but the social reality Keith inhabits does not correspond to the discourse which makes sense of the title 'the Marquis'. What is it to *be* a marquis? It is a title inherited through the male line, or bestowed by a monarch. Like a family name, a title identifies nothing essential to the individual independent of the social relations he inhabits. Of all kinds of labels, forenames seem most adapted to pinpoint the unique individual. But names are given socially and rely on public recognition if they are to do their job; they are highly conventional, good indicators of sex, nationality, region, religious culture, sometimes even age and class. A name does not so much specify a unique individual as place an individual in a set.

'When *I* use a word', Humpty Dumpty said, in a rather scornful tone, 'it means just what I choose it to mean – neither more or less.' This subversive notion which so disturbs sensible Alice is rather similar to the disturbingly arbitrary naming in Wedekind's plays. 'The question is, which is to be master – that's all', Humpty Dumpty continues grandly in reply to Alice's objections. Lulu's names are all given her by men claiming to be masters of naming who determine what Lulu, the woman, is to be. A woman generally assumes her husband's surname on marriage, but her forename is *her* name, offering some continuity of identification, a minimal autonomy Lulu's men seek to overthrow. In *The Marquis of Keith* the characters who choose their names claim to override the collective power of society and to have mastery over self-identification detached from social definition. Keith's name and title subvert the social quality of names and the power-structures of aristocracy and the patrilinear family which give meaning to the sentence 'I am the Marquis of Keith'. The play's title *The Marquis of Keith* is anti-metonymic; it points to a loosening of the connection between words, here names, and things, and it questions the social relations to which the words refer.

The names in *The Marquis of Keith* are details which in Naturalist text would be metonymy standing for a social system existing simply and objectively to be referred to. In Naturalist theatre props on stage serve the same kind of purpose; they refer to an objective social reality through the telling detail. In Wedekind's plays what the detail tells is that the social reality is not simply there but is itself a historical construct, a kind of language the meaning of whose words is up for grabs. We may consciously or unconsciously accept the conventional meanings which in the case of 'the Marquis of Keith' are determined by a set of power-relations. Or we may succumb to a sense of absurdity on recognizing the lack of necessary connections binding together the signs and discourses of the culture we inhabit. Or, like Humpty Dumpty, we may reject the mastery of a contingent social system which determines meaning. Rejection may take the form of a critical unmasking of the power-relations which inhere in the language of any society. Or it may go futher, as in their different ways Humpty Dumpty, French *symboliste* poets, and some of Wedekind's heroes try to do, in claiming absolute mastery over meaning, an attempt doomed to fail since individuals and language are social entities.

Paul de Man (1979: 67) argues that Proust often works a trick in which 'contingent figures of chance (metonymy) masquerade deceptively as figures of necessity (metaphor)'. Characteristic in Wedekind is the double undermining of metaphor and metonymy through jarring incongruity between them or a tendency for the one to turn disconcertingly into the other. Metaphors turn to metonymy in a language of mixed metaphors drawn from a variety of traditions. In the furnishings of Schön's house the metaphors of power of a Renaissance prince turn into eclectic bits and pieces standing for a bourgeois life-style. Gold, the king of metals enframing Lulu's portrait, is a metaphor from a obsolete system of beliefs which has become an anachronistic myth concealing the reality of the stockmarket. Unlike other symbolic works of the time such as *The Ring*, Wedekind's plays do not construct a coherent metaphoric unity bodied forth by an internal free play of appropriate metonymic detail. Instead, metaphor and metonymy collide: nymphs, diptheria and abortion. Conversely, the metonyms of Naturalism are consistently imbued with metaphorical meaning as the characters live through their self-created fictions, drawing on an endless cultural hoard to transform their material surroundings into metaphor – Wendla floating above the carpet of her garden, Lulu barefoot on the carpet of her elegant drawingroom, Hänschen's lavatory become Bluebeard's castle. The shifting meanings undermine both the metaphysical systems of belief and contemporary positivist faith in material causal explanations.

Absurdist Subversion and Brechtian Alienation

Seen in this light, it is easy to identify those dramatic modes which have least affinity with Wedekind. These are the two extremes in his own time of Symbolist verse drama and Naturalism; their latter-day descendants such as the plays of T. S. Eliot or Christopher Fry; and the various waves of realism, whether of the kitchen sink variety or the public forms of documentary theatre. But Wedekind's iconoclasm, which destroys traditional beliefs and values to confront the resulting void with a tragi-comic grimace, clearly looks in the direction of Beckett and the Theatre of the Absurd. The title *Waiting for Godot* lies ambiguously between synecdoche and metaphor. Godot, the person who never turns up, is a synecdoche, part of a society signifying the whole; he is the kingpin who would complete and make meaningful the relations between the characters. By way of a pun, Godot is also a metaphor for a non-existent god and a total cosmic vision which fail to materialize. The comedy stems from the kind of incongruous juxtaposition of fragmented Naturalist details which no longer cohere with numinous intimations of a lost transcendent order which marks Wedekind's plays. Wedekind's Earth Spirit is a Godot who fails to materialize. Winnie's handbag in Beckett's *Happy Days* is a quintessential Naturalist object, full of a jumble of contingently contiguous things. It is a synecdoche for a whole culture, but estranged in its desert surroundings it turns into a metaphor of extreme ambiguity. It is a metaphor for Winnie herself as a jumble of contigency in a physical container. It is a metonymic attribute as a blade is of a sword: a sword without a blade is not a sword; Winnie without her handbag is scarcely a person.

One type of metonym is the designation of something by its cause or its effect. In as far as Winnie, the named person, is anything she is something constructed by her name and the tool of her handbag with its cultural bricabrac like Lulu seeking to reconstruct herself with the clothes, furniture and curtains she missed in her prison cell. Winnie is an effect of cultural *bricolage* and her handbag is a metaphor for the powerful illusion of metonymy. Beckett subverts the illusion of a metonymically representable social order. The contingency even of physical identity is suggested by the disappearance of Winnie's body in a sandy grave, leaving only the talking head. She is fragmented into bits and pieces.

However, as long as Beckett uses speech his ear for rhythm and idiom, whether French or an Irish-flavoured English, and the precision of many observed details are an umbilical cord attaching his plays to history. Bright islands of touchingly palpable reality float in the void, never quite sinking until the final end of death. In his best work, Wedekind also preserves the link with history. Even more than with her handbag, Winnie holds herself together with words. Words are a social gesture of communication to which someone may be listening, whether Willie or the theatre audience. Though the sentences are increasingly fractured and the references obscure, Winnie's monologue is not quite lost in the void; the play closes with Willie's effort to reach her and their intense mutual look.

Winnie is another example of woman as man's redemption who asserts Life against Death. She is a stereotype at the opposite extreme from Lulu, however, a practical housewife who talks while the man reads, a more cheerful Molly Griesinger who has kept going and taken the man's revolver from him. *Happy Days*, first produced in 1961, dates from the height of one of those periodic assertions of female domesticity, before the upsurge in the feminism of the late sixties. Winnie's chatter is deadly in its monotony – some of Willie's looks suggest feelings other than uxorious fondness – but it is the sign of life. The play must end, however, and the chatter stop. The mutual look at the end is ambiguous. The womanly body is hidden, all that is left is a talking head. Her smile turned off, Winnie gazes at a man kneeling on all fours looking up at her, the posture of worship or of hate-filled humiliation – a familiar double response to the feminine image in its domestic and sexual forms. Whether Willie has come to shoot himself, to shoot Winnie or to say something remains obscure, but the look from eye to eye leaves hope and the beautifully crafted chatter is not monotonous to the theatre audience. Wedekind makes an icon of the body. Here we are invited to love the talking head and look into the eyes. *The Marquis of Keith* with its dripping female corpse is a grimmer close, but the isolated hero's ambiguous last grimace remains a social gesture and we are invited to pity the dead body. Perhaps sometime the whole woman may survive.

Dürrenmatt, another absurdist playwright, owes a direct debt to Wedekind. As Marianne Kesting (1970: 336) notes, some of the paradoxical aphorisms in *Die Ehe des Herrn Mississippi* (*The Marriage of Mr Mississippi*) are quotations from *The Marquis of Keith*. Dürrenmatt's theatrical technique was also greatly influenced by Brecht (1967, vol. 15: 3–4) who early in his career payed tribute to

Wedekind's acting and singing, on which his own harshly etched delivery was based. Comparisons between Brecht and Wedekind generally concentrate on this direct line of influence on the young Brecht in his Expressionist phase: the theatrical shock effects, the mockery of bourgeois values, the amoral sexual vitalism, the Wedekind circus and the Brecht boxing ring. Max Spalter (1967), for example, stresses the cynical anti-idealism of both writers. From the start, Brecht travesties Expressionism in an incongruous playing-off of Naturalist detail against Expressionist symbolism with a two-way subversive effect, just as Wedekind travestied both Naturalism and Symbolism. The last scene of *Spring Awakening* with Melchior and Moritz as two aspects of one temperament or as dialectical stages on the way towards life recalls Expressionist monodrama and its prototype, Strindberg's *The Road to Damascus*; but Expressionist pathos, religiose idealism and absence of subversive humour are remote from Wedekind. Nonetheless, the technical affinities between Wedekind and Brecht can also be related to Strindberg. I have commented on the tendency of Naturalist theatre to gravitate towards the metonymic realism of the novel. Paradoxically, there is simultaneously a converse shift in the aesthetics of the novel away from epic narrative towards dramatic showing forth and the disappearance of the authoritative narrator, the tendency Henry James promotes in his call to dramatize. This was in keeping with Naturalist aesthetics which aimed, in theory at least, at objective representation, at dramatic showing forth or mimesis rather than epic telling or diegesis.

But just as the novel was divesting itself of its epic qualities, Symbolist theatre was moving in the opposite direction. Wolfgang Kayser (1954) saw the disappearance of narrative authority as a threat to the survival of the novel. Conversely, Peter Szondi (1965) sees drama as under threat. I cannot endorse such apocalyptic claims about the essence of drama, and as Steve Giles (1981: 279–81) has argued, Szondi's concept of drama is in any case questionable. But Szondi's (1965: 48–9) comments on Strindberg are suggestive. He argues that in the Symbolist plays extreme subjectivity broke drama apart into reflection of the one ego and the demonstrative gesture which points to that reflection. The result was a distance between the shown and the act of showing, comparable to the distinction in prose fiction between the story and its telling. As Kesting (1970: 201) suggests, the Prologue to *Earth Spirit* creates a comparable disjunction between the shown and the showing, but without Strindberg's solipsistic egoism.

So too does the perspectivistic game with modes: the meaning of the shown shifts as the gesture of showing points now towards the comic, now to the tragic or absurd. Such modal changes are borne in the fragmented styles and the shifts of pace. Brecht (1967, vol. 16: 697) uses the term 'gesture' to designate the general gesture of showing which must accompany each individual segment of what is shown in the epic style of acting. Sometimes he uses the term to designate combined showing and shown. Thus the 'gest' is a Naturalist nugget of observed social behaviour, shown forth for the audience to see through with x-ray vision. What is represented remains recognizable as an element of the real world, but it is denaturalized and made strange (p. 680). It loses the fatalistic aura of necessity. In epic style the actor and role, Charles Laughton and Galileo, are simultaneously visible (p. 683).

The Prologue to *Earth Spirit* is a gesture pointing to all that follows. In *The Marquis of Keith* the pointing gesture towards the role is all-pervasive. Wedekind was not a 'good' actor; as Brecht remarks in his appreciation, he even forgot his lines sometimes. But 'bad' acting was essential; when he played an alter ego such as the Masked Man, Keith, Schön or Jack the Ripper, Naturalist identification of actor with role would have been, as Marianne Kesting (1970: 202) puts it, merely embarrassing. Wedekind therefore masked his face with white make-up and pushed actorly stylization to grotesque extremes, both in body language and in the overtly theatrical and melodramatic dialogue. The white mask of the clown and the body language recall the programme for theatre as circus and anticipate Artaud's call for an anti-literary and sensuous theatre. But the cool intellectuality, the continuing centrality of words, the pointing gesture which is verbal as well as physical anticipate Brechtian theatre, which is not without its own sensuousness: as good productions of Brecht or Wedekind testify, the pointing gesture may create moments of stunning verbal and visual beauty.

There are other affinities between the two playwrights. Brecht's view that the knots binding the individual segments of the 'fable' or story should be visible is reminiscent of the Lulu plays, where the episodes avoid riverlike fluidity, that hypnotic effect Brecht's knots are designed to interrupt. Similarly, the lyric flow of *Spring Awakening* is constantly interrupted by grotesque insertions which remind us that we are in the theatre.

The two playwrights' handling of character, especially female characters, is also comparable. In his early work Brecht focused on sexual women, but in his Marxist plays he turns mainly to the antithetical stereotype, the mother. Both Brecht and Wedekind depict incomplete human beings whose humanity is stunted or deformed. In Brecht's work the mother instinct as shaped or frustrated by current social relations exemplifies both potential social humanity and its deformation: Kattrin and Mutter Courage, Grusche and Natalli Abaschwilli in *The Caucasian Chalk Circle*, Shen Te and Shui Ta in *The Good Women of Sezuan*. The characters presented in a positive light are all excluded from biological motherhood which assumes the anti-social forms of current social relations. In the Lulu plays, particularly *Pandora's Box*, it is the sexual instinct which is deformed. Sexually active Lulu, like Brecht's biological mothers, is dehumanized, her sexuality is twisted in order to be compatible with the predominant patriarchal structure. Geschwitz, the most human of the characters, is excluded from sexual relations by her lesbianism, as Kattrin is excluded from motherhood by her disfiguration, and Grusche by having to care for a strange child; while Shen Te is a not-yet mother on whom motherhood forces the mask of Shui Ta. As E. S. Roberts (1985) argues, Brecht allows only those who either reject or are excluded from biological motherhood to reveal the human potential. But Geschwitz is not as liberated from love as poor Kattrin is from motherhood. Like Kattrin's mother who cares only for her own children, through most of the play Geschwitz cares only for her own lover. Like the mother who fights bitterly for her own children but is indifferent to all others, she has no sisterly commitment to other women and rejoices in the death of Sister Theophila. Her isolated commitment cannot withstand the muderous violence of Jack the Ripper; but it does suggest that human beings are capable of commitment rooted in erotic attachment, just as Brecht roots sociability in a motherliness extended beyond blood relations. Geschwitz's brief flash of political vision is like Mother Courage's fleeting insight beyond her deluded faith in individual enterprise. But Brecht requires of his good women that they give up actual motherhood. Confronted with the immediate threat to Lulu, Geschwitz cannot desert her to fight for women in general, a shift towards collective thinking which Brecht's audiences have likewise often failed to make.

As Martin Esslin has argued, there are thematic connections between Brecht and the Theatre of the Absurd, notably in the breaking down of character as fixed and immutable. Esslin (1980: 377) cites *Mann ist Mann* with 'its thesis that human nature is not constant, and that it is possible to transform one character into another in the course of a play'. Brecht's play is more schematic than *The Marquis of Keith*, but the transmogrification of good Galy Gay into his destructive double is reminiscent of the alter egos, Scholz and Keith. Indeed the whole motif of doubles and split personalities going back to the Romantics and continuing into Modernism pervades Brecht's work too, and is a sign of a culture marked by ever more rapid change. The motif continues in the Marxist works, in *Herr Puntila und sein Knecht Matti* or *The Good Woman of Sezuan*. Esslin compares Galy Gay's loss of personality with a kind of rape. Such theft of identity is a theme in the Theatre of the Absurd – Esslin cites Ionesco's *Jacques ou La Soumission*. Genet and more recently Fassbinder also spring to mind. Keith once stole aristocratic panache from his spiritual brother Scholz, who in turn tries to steal Keith's identity and his mistress. The breaking down of fixed identity may signal fluidity of personality in a rapidly changing culture or the more political vision of personality threatened by the bruality of power. In this sense Lulu suffers multiple rape before she is finally butchered.

Whatever the ideological positions, the connecting link between Wedekind, Brecht, Beckett, the Theatre of the Absurd and many other modern playwrights has to do with quintessentially theatrical matters. Wedekind is a technician who appeals to other writers and men of the theatre, as the list of his translators indicates: Stephen Spender, Eric Bentley, Tom Osborn, Ronald Eyre, Peter Barnes and Edward Bond. John McGrath has cited him in a letter to me as the other German playwright who along with Brecht has influenced his technique. Wedekind avoids that naive naturalism which presents the mediated image as if it were a necessary truth or a fact of nature, immutable and independent of interpretation. He exploits the language of the stage. In subverting dramatic convention, Wedekind turns everything into theatre which mixes clownish slapstick, heightened melodrama, jolting gear shifts in verbal style and a sensuous language of things and bodily movement. Theatre itself becomes a metaphor for culture as a language which we can interpret and manipulate to rewrite ourselves or to change our world.

Bibliography

German Editions of Wedekind

Frank Wedekind 1912–21: *Gesammelte Werke.* 9 vols. Georg Müller: Munich. Referred to as *GW*. Quotations follow this edition.

1969: *Werke in drei Bänden.* Edited and introduced by Manfred Hahn. Aufbau: Berlin. Referred to as Hahn. Volume 3 contains extensive extracts from Wedekind's Paris diaries.

1986: *Frühlings Erwachen. Der Marquis von Keith.* Goldmann: Munich. This new annotated edition appeared too late to be consulted.

1976: *Frühlings Erwachen: Eine Kindertragödie.* Edited by Hugh Rank. Heinemann: London. Referred to as Rank.

1980: *Erdgeist. Die Büchse der Pandora.* Edited and annotated by Peter Unger and Hartmut Vinçon. Goldmann: Munich.

1965: *Der Marquis von Keith: Text und Materialien.* Edited by Wolfgang Hartwig. De Gruyter: Berlin. Referred to as Hartwig.

1924: *Briefe.* 2 vols. Edited by Fritz Strich. Georg Müller: Munich.

1986: *Die Tagebücher. Ein erotisches Leben.* Edited by Gerhard Hay. Athenäum: Frankfurt am Main. Referred to as Hay.

1961: *Erzählungen.* Goldmann: Munich.

1979: *Gedichte und Chansons.* Goldmann: Munich.

1982: *Ich habe meine Tante geschlachtet. Lautenlieder und Simplicissimus-Gedichte.* Insel: Munich. This contains music for the *Lautenlieder.*

Manuscripts in the Wedekind Archive in the Stadbibliothek, Munich

Notebooks 1–8
Eden. Typescript copied from *Tagebuch 1890/91.*
Die Büchse der Pandora. Eine Monstretragödie.
Emilie Kammerer-Wedekind 1914: *Jugenderinnerungen.*

English Translations

English quotations from Wedekind's work and other foreign texts are my own translations unless otherwise indicated.

Edward Bond 1982, orig. 1980: *Spring Awakening*. Methuen: London.

Tom Osborn 1978, orig. 1969: *Spring Awakening*. John Calder: London.

Stephen Spender 1977, orig. 1952: *The Lulu Plays and Other Sex Tragedies: Earth Spirit, Pandora's Box, Death and Devil, Castle Wetterstein*. John Calder: London.

Peter Barnes 1971: *Lulu. A Sex Tragedy. Adapted from Wedekind's Earth Spirit and Pandora's Box*. Translated by Charlotte Beck. Heinemann: London.

Ronald Eyre and Alan Best 1974: *The Marquis of Keith*. For the Royal Shakespeare Company. Unpublished.

Peter Barnes 1977: *The Frontiers of Farce. Feydeau: The Purging. Wedekind: The Singer*. Heinemann: London.

Other Works

Bachofen, Johann Jakob 1948, orig. 1861: *Das Mutterrecht*. Basel.

Bakhtin, M. M. 1984, orig. 1965: *Rabelais and His World*. Translated by Caryl Emerson and Michael Holquist. Bloomington.

Barrett, Michèle 1980: *Women's Oppression Today. Problems in Marxist Feminist Analysis*. London.

Barthes, Roland 1980: *La Chambre Claire*. Paris.

  1984, orig. 1968: La mort de l'auteur. In *Essais Critiques IV. Le Bruissement de la langue*, Paris, 61–8.

Beckett, Samuel 1965, orig. 1956: *Waiting for Godot*. London.

  1963: *Happy Days*. London.

Benjamin, Walter 1972, orig. 1929: Wedekind und Kraus in der Volksbühne. In *Gesammelte Schriften* vol. 4 (1), Frankfurt am Main, 551–2.

  1974, orig. 1939: Zentralpark. In *Gesammelte Schriften* vol. 1 (2), Frankfurt am Main, 655–90.

Bergson, Henri 1975, orig. 1899: *Le rire. Essai sur la signification du comique*. Paris.

Best, Alan 1975: *Frank Wedekind*. London.

Blei, Franz 1915: *Über Wedekind, Sternheim und das Theater*. Leipzig.

Bloch, Ernst 1959: *Das Prinzip Hoffnung* vol. 1. Frankfurt am Main.

Blochmann, Elisabeth 1966: *Das 'Frauenzimmer' und die 'Gelehrsamkeit': Eine Studie über die Anfänge des Mädchenschulwesens in Deutschland*. Heidelberg.

Boa, Elizabeth 1984: Der gute Mensch von Barnhelm: The Female Essence and the Ensemble of Human Relations in Lessing's *Minna von Barnhelm*. *Publications of the English Goethe Society*, 54, 1–36.

Bohnen, K. 1978: Frank Wedekind and Georg Brandes. Unveröffenlichte Briefe. *Euphorion*, 72, 106–19.

Boone, C. C. 1972: Zur inneren Entstehungsgeschichte von Wedekinds Lulu. *Etudes Germaniques*, 27, 423–30.

Born, Erich Karl 1985: *Wirtschafts- und Sozialgeschichte des deutschen Kaiserreichs (1867/71–1914)*. Stuttgart.

Bovenschen, Sylvia 1979: *Die imaginierte Weiblichkeit: Exemplarische Untersuchungen zu kulturgeschichtlichen und literarischen Präsentationsformen des Weiblichen*. Frankfurt am Main.

Brecht, Bertolt 1967: *Gesammelte Werke in 20 Bänden*. Werkausgabe edition Suhrkamp. Frankfurt am Main.

Brooks, Peter 1985: *The Melodramatic Imagination: Balzac, Henry James, Melodrama, and the Mode of Excess*. New York.

Bullivant, Keith 1973: The notion of morality in Wedekind's *Frühlings Erwachen*. *New German Studies*, 1, pp. 40–7.

Burns, Robert A. 1975: Wedekind's concept of morality: an extension of the argument. *New German Studies*, 3, 155–64.

Carter, Angela 1979a: *The Bloody Chamber*. London.

1979b: *The Sadeian Woman. An Exercise in Cultural History*. London.

Cerha, Friedrich 1979: *Arbeitsbericht zur Herstellung des 3. Akts der Oper 'Lulu' von Alban Berg*. Vienna.

Coward, Rosalind 1983: *Patriarchal Precedents: Sexuality and Social Relations*. London.

Craig, Gordon A. 1978: *Germany 1866–1945*. Oxford.

Dedner, Burghard 1975: Intellektuelle Illusionen zu Wedekinds *Marquis von Keith*. *Zeitschrift für deutsche Philologie*, 94, 498–519.

Diebold, Bernhard 1921: *Anarchie im Drama*. Frankfurt am Main.

Dohm, Hedwig 1907: *Die Antifeministen*. Berlin.

1978, orig. 1876: Die Eigenschaften der Frau. In Gisela Brinker-Gabler (ed.), *Zur Psychologie der Frau*, Frankfurt am Main, 27–44.

Dumas, Alexandre 1983, orig. 1852: *La Dame aux camélias*. Paris.

Dworkin, Andrea 1981: *Pornography: Men Possessing Women*. London.

Ellmann, Mary 1979: *Thinking about Women*. London.

Elsaesser, Thomas 1983: Lulu and the Meter Man. *Screen*, 24, 4–36.

Elsom, John 1973: Lulu Dancing. In *Erotic Theatre*. London, 84–104.

Emrich, Wilhelm 1960: Frank Wedekind – Die Lulu Tragödie. In *Protest und Verheißung*, Frankfurt am Main, 206–22.

1968: Immanuel Kant und Frank Wedekind. In *Polemik*, Frankfurt am Main, 56–61.

Engels, Friederich 1962, orig. 1884: The Origin of the Family, Private Property and the State. In Karl Marx and Friederich Engels, *Selected*

Works vol. 2, Moscow, 185–327.

Esslin, Martin 1980: *The Theatre of the Absurd*. Harmondsworth.

Evans, Richard J. 1978: Liberalism and Society: The Feminist Movement and Social Change. In Richard J. Evans (ed.), *Society and Politics in Wilhelmine Germany*, London, 186–214.

Fechter, Paul 1920: *Frank Wedekind*. Jena.

Fichte, J. G. 1970, orig. 1796: *The Science of Rights*. Translated by A. E. Kroeger. London.

Firda, Richard Arthur 1972: Wedekind, Nietzsche and the Dionysian Experience. *Modern Language Notes*, 87, 720–31.

Fläschen, Werner 1981: *Magister und Scholaren. Professoren und Studenten. Geschichte deutscher Universitäten und Hochschulen im Überblick*. Leipzig.

Foucault, Michel 1976: *Histoire de la sexualité I. La volonté de savoir*. Paris.

Freud, Sigmund 1982: *Studienausgabe*. Frankfurt am Main.

Friedenthal, Joachim (ed.) 1914: *Das Wedekindbuch*. Munich.

Fritz, Horst 1977: Die Dämonisierung des Erotischen in der Literatur des Fin de siècle. In R. Bauer, E. Heftrich, H. Koopman, W. Rasch, W. Sauerländer and J.A. Schmoll alias Eisenwerth (eds), *Fin de siècle. Zu Literatur und Kunst der Jahrhundertwende*, Frankfurt am Main, 442–64.

Furst, Lilian and Skrine, Peter 1971: *Naturalism*. London.

Gasser, Manuel 1977: *München um 1900*. London.

Gerhard, Ute 1978: *Verhältnisse und Verhinderungen. Frauenarbeit, Familie und Rechte im 19. Jahrhundert*. Frankfurt am Main.

Giles, Steve 1981: *The Problem of Action in Modern Drama*. Stuttgart.

Gittleman, Sol 1967: Frank Wedekind and Bertolt Brecht: Notes on a Relationship. *Modern Drama*, 10, 401–9.

 1969: *Frank Wedekind*. New York.

 1976: Sternheim, Wedekind and 'Homo Economicus'. *German Quarterly*, 49, 25–30.

Glaser, Horst Albert 1974: Arthur Schnitzler und Frank Wedekind – der doppelköpfige Sexus. In *Wollüstige Phantasie. Sexualästhetik der Literatur*, Munich, 149–84.

Graves, Paul 1982: *Frank Wedekinds dramatisches Werk im Spiegel der Sekundärliteratur 1960 bis 1980: Ein Forschungsbericht*. Ph.D. Dissertation. Colorado at Boulder. University Microfilms International, Ann Arbor, Michigan.

Green, Martin 1974: *The von Richthoven Sisters: The Triumphant and Tragic Modes of Love*. London.

Günther, Herbert 1979: Frank Wedekind. In *Deutsche Dichter erleben Paris*, Pfüllingen, 1979, 57–72.

Guthke, Karl 1961: *Geschichte und Poetik der deutschen Tragikomödie*. Göttingen.

Hager, Werner 1968: Zur Villa Stuck. In Renate von Heydebrand and Klaus

232 Bibliography

Günther Just (eds), *Wissenschaft als Dialog. Studien zur Kunst und Literatur seit der Jahrhundertwende*, Stuttgart, 1–10.

Hamann, Richard 1907: *Der Impressionismus in Leben und Kunst.* Cologne.

Harris, Edward P. 1977: The Liberation of the Flesh from the Stone: Pygmalion in Frank Wedekind's *Erdgeist. Germanic Review*, 52, 44–56.

Hartmann, Eduard von 1931, orig. 1868: *Philosophy of the Unconscious.* Translated by William Chatterton Coupland. London.

Hegel, G. W. F. 1958, orig. 1821: *Philosophy of Right.* Translated by T. M. Knox. Oxford.

Hermand, Jost 1968: Undinen-Zauber: Zum Frauenbild des Jugenstils. In *Wissenschaft als Dialog*, 9–29.

Hibberd, J. L. 1977: Imaginary Numbers and 'Humor': on Wedekind's *Frühlings Erwachen. Modern Language Review*, 74, 633–47.

1984: The Spirit of the Flesh: Wedekind's Lulu. *Modern Language Review*, 79, 336–55.

Hirst, David L. 1984: *Tragicomedy* (The Critical Idiom 43). London.

Höger, Alfons 1979: *Frank Wedekind. Der Konstruktivismus als schöpferische Methode.* Königstein.

1981: *Hetärismus und bürgerliche Gesellschaft im Frühwerk Frank Wedekinds.* Kopenhagen, Munich.

Irmer, Hans-Jochen 1975: *Der Theaterdichter Frank Wedekind.* Berlin.

Jacobsohn, Siegfried 1965: *Jahre der Bühne: Theaterkritische Schriften.* Reinbek.

Jakobson, Roman 1956: Two Aspects of Language and Two Types of Aphasic Disturbances. In Roman Jakobson and Morris Halle, *Fundamentals of Language*, The Hague.

Jelavich, Peter 1982: München als Kulturzentrum: Politik und die Künste. In Armin Zweite (ed.), *Kandinsky und München: Begegnungen und Wandlungen 1896–1914*, Munich, 17–26.

1986: *Munich and Theatrical Modernism: Politics, playwriting and performance.* Cambridge, Mass.

Jerome, Jerome K. 1983, orig. 1900: *Three Men on the Bummel.* London.

Jesch, Jörg 1959: *Stilhaltungen im Drama Wedekinds.* Marburg.

Johnson, Barbara 1980: *The Critical Difference: Essays in the Comtemporary Rhetoric of Reading.* Baltimore.

Jost, Dominik 1969: *Literarischer Jugenstil.* Stuttgart.

Jouve, Pierre Jean 1962: Lulu et la censure. *Mercure de France*, 1190.

Kant, Immanuel 1960, orig. 1764: Beobachtungen über das Gefühl des Schönen und Erhabenen. In *Werke in sechs Bänden*, Wiesbaden, 825–84.

Kassner, Ilse and Lorenz, Susanne 1977: *Trauer muß Aspasia tragen: Die Geschichte der Vertreibung der Frau aus der Wissenschaft.* Munich.

Kaufmann, Hans 1969: Zwei Dramatiker: Gerhart Hauptmann und Frank Wedekind. In *Krisen und Wandlungen der deutschen Literatur von*

Wedekind bis Feuchtwanger, Berlin, 47–84.

Kayser, Wolfgang 1954: *Entstehung und Krise des modernen Romans*. Stuttgart.

Kesting, Marianne 1970: *Entdeckung und Destruktion. Zur Strukturumwandlung der Künste*. Munich.

Kirchhoff, Arthur 1897: *Die Akademische Frau*. Berlin.

Klotz, Volker 1972: *Offene und geschlossene Form im Drama*. Munich.

Krafft-Ebing, R. von 1893, orig. 1887: *Psychopathia Sexualis*. Translated by C. M. Chadwick from the seventh edition. Philadelphia, London.

Kraus, Karl 1962, orig. 1905: Die Büchse der Pandora. In *Literatur und Lüge*, Munich, 5–15.

Kuhn, Anna Katherina 1981: *Der Dialog bei Frank Wedekind: Untersuchungen zum Szenengespräch der Dramen*. Heidelberg.

Kutscher, Artur 1970, orig. 1922–1931: *Wedekind: Sein Leben und seine Werke*. Munich. Facsimile reprint AMS Press, New York.

Kuttenkeuler, Wolfgang 1977: Der Außenseiter als Prototyp der Gesellschaft – Frank Wedekind: *Der Marquis von Keith*. In *Fin de siècle*, 567–95.

Lenman, Robin 1978: Politics and Culture. The State and the Avant-Garde in Munich 1886–1914. In Richard J. Evans (ed.), *Society and Politics in Wilhelmine Germany*, London, 90–111.

   1982: A Community in Transition: Painters in Munich. *Central European Studies*, 15, 3–19.

Lessing, Hans-Erhard 1982: *Fahrradkutlur I: Der Höhepunkt um 1900*. Stuttgart.

Lodge, David 1976: The Language of Modernist Fiction: Metaphor and Metonymy. In Malcolm Bradbury and James McFarlane (eds), *Modernism 1890–1930*, London, 481–96.

Lorenz, D. C. G. 1976: Wedekind und die emanzipierte Frau: Eine Studie über Frau and Sozialismus im Werke Frank Wedekinds. *Seminar*, 12, 38–56.

Maclean, Hector 1968: Wedekind's *Marquis von Keith*: An Interpretation based on the Faust and Circus Motifs. *Germanic Review*, 43, 163–87.

McMillan, Carol 1982: *Women, Reason and Nature. Some Philosophical Problems with Feminism*. Oxford.

McMullen, Sally 1986: Sense and Sensuality: Max Reinhardt's Early Productions. In Margaret Jacobs and John Warren (eds), *Max Reinhardt. The Oxford Symposium*, Oxford, 16–33.

Man, Paul de 1979: *Allegories of Reading*. New Haven, London.

Mann, Heinrich 1960, orig. 1923: Erinnerungen an Frank Wedekind. In *Essays*, Hamburg, 243–62.

Mann, Thomas 1977, orig. 1914: Über eine Szene von Wedekind. In Michael Mann (ed.), *Thomas Mann*. Essays vol. 1, Frankfurt am Main, 69–74.

Marcuse, Herbert 1969, orig. 1955: *Eros and Civilization*. London.

Martens, Kurt 1921: *Schonungslose Lebenschronik* vol. 1. Vienna.

Medicus, Thomas 1982: *Die große Liebe und Konstruktion der Körper im Werk von Frank Wedekind*. Marburg.

Mennemeier, F. N. 1980: Frank Wedekind. In Walter Hinck (ed.), *Handbuch des Dramas* vol. 2, Düsseldorf, 360–73.

Mérimée, Prosper 1965, orig. 1841: *Carmen et treize autres nouvelles*. Paris.

Meyer, Michael 1982: *Theaterzensur in München 1900–1918*. Munich.

Michelsen, Peter 1965: Frank Wedekind. In Benno von Wiese (ed.), *Deutsche Dichter der Moderne*, Berlin, 51–69.

Midgley, David 1985: Wedekind's Lulu: from 'Schauertragödie' to Social Comedy. *German Life and Letters*, 38, 205–32.

Miller, Karl 1985: *Doubles: Studies in Literary History*. Oxford.

Molière 1971: *Oeuvres complètes* vol. 2. Paris.

Mullins, Edwin 1985: *The Painted Witch. Female Body: Male Art*. London.

Natan, Alex 1963: Frank Wedekind. In *German Men of Letters* vol. 2, London, 103–29.

Nietzsche, Friedrich 1980: *Sämtliche Werke. Kritische Studienausgabe in 15 Bänden*. Munich.

Panofsky, Dora and Erwin 1956: *Pandora's Box: The Changing Aspect of a Mythical Symbol*. London.

Peacock, Ronald 1978: The Ambiguity of Wedekind's Lulu. *Oxford German Studies*, 9, 105–18.

Perle, George 1985: *The Operas of Alban Berg* vol. 2: *Lulu*. Berkeley, Los Angeles, London.

Ploss, H. 1885: *Das Weib in der Natur- und Völkerkunde*. Leipzig.

Pickerodt, Gerhart 1984: *Frank Wedekind: Frühlingserwachen. Grundlagen und Gedanken zum Verständnis des Dramas*. Frankfurt am Main.

Popper, Karl 1962: *The Open Society and its Enemies* vol. 2. London.

Prévost, l'abbé 1967, orig. 1731: *Histoire du chevalier Des Grieux et de Manon Lescaut*. Paris.

Quiguer, Claude 1962: L'érotisme de Frank Wedekind. *Etudes germaniques*, 17, 14–33.

———— 1968: Actualité de Wedekind. *Etudes germaniques*, 23, 88–91.

Rasch, Wolfdietrich 1967: Tanz als Lebenssymbol im Drama um 1900. In *Zur deutschen Literatur seit der Jahrhundertwende*, Stuttgart, 59–78.

———— 1969: Sozialkritische Aspekte in Wedekinds dramatischer Dichtung: Sexualität, Kunst and Gesellschaft. In Helmut Kreutzer (ed.), *Gestaltungsgeschichte und Gesellschaftsgeschichte*, Stuttgart, 409–26.

Rauck, M.J.B., Volke, G., Paturi, R. (eds) 1979: *Das Fahrrad und seine Geschichte*. Stuttgart.

Reid, J. H. 1984: En route to Utopia: some Visions of the Future in East German Literature. *Renaissance and Modern Studies*, 27, 114–28.

Ritter, Naomi 1975: Kafka, Wedekind and the Circus. *Germanic Notes*, 6, 55–9.

Roberts, E. S. 1985: *A New Role for Women: the Revolutionary Implications of the Rahmenhandlung in Brecht's play Der kaukasische Kreiderkreis*. M.A. Dissertation, University of Warwick.

Rodway, Allan 1975: *English Comedy: Its Role and Nature from Chaucer to the present Day*. London.

Rothe, Friederich 1968: *Frank Wedekinds Dramen: Jugendstil und Lebensphilosophie*. Stuttgart.

1969: Frühlings Erwachen, zum Verhältnis von sexueller und sozialer Emanzipation bei Frank Wedekind. *Studi Germanici*, 7, 30–41.

Rousseau, Jean-Jacques 1964, orig. 1762: *Emile ou l'éducation*. Edited by François et Pierre Richard. Paris.

Runge, Max 1896: *Das Weib in seiner Geschlechtsindividualität*. Berlin.

Rupprecht, Erich (ed.) 1962: *Literarische Manifeste des deutschen Naturalismus 1880–1892*. Stuttgart.

Rutschky, K. 1983: Erziehungszeugen. Autobiographien als Quelle für eine Geschichte der Erziehung. *Zeitschrift für Pädagogik*, 29, 499–517.

Sade, Marquis de 1966–7: *Oeuvres complètes*, 16 vols. Paris.

Sagarra, Eda 1977: *A Social History of Germany 1648–1914*. London.

Salveson, H. 1981: A pinch of Snuff from Pandora's Box. *Oxford German Studies*, 12, 122–38.

Sattel, Ulrike 1976: *Studien zur Marktabhängigkeit der Literatur am Beispiel Frank Wedekinds*. Ph.D.Diss. University of Kassel.

Sayers, Janet 1982: *Biological Politics: Feminist and Anti-Feminist Perspectives*. London.

Schopenhauer, Arthur 1977, orig. 1851: *Parerga und Paralipomena* vol. 2 (1). Zurich.

Schröder-Zebrella, Josephine 1985: *Frank Wedekind's religiöser Sensualismus: 'Die Vereinigung von Kirche und Freudenhaus?'*. Frankfurt am Main.

Seehaus, Günter 1964: *Frank Wedekind und das Theater*. Munich.

1974: *Frank Wedekind in Selbstzeugnissen und Bilddokumenten*. Hamburg.

Shaw, Leroy L. 1970: The Strategy of Reformulation. Frank Wedekind's *Frühlings Erwachen*. In *The Playwright and Historical Change*, Madisom, Milwaukee and London, 49–65.

Silva, M. H. G. da 1985: *Character, Ideology and Symbolism in the Plays of Wedekind, Sternheim, Kaiser, Toller and Brecht*. London.

Sokel, Walter H. 1966: The Changing Role of Eros in Wedekind's Drama. *German Quarterly*, 39, 201–7.

Spalter, Max 1967: Brechts Tradition. Frank Wedekind. In *Zur deutschen Literatur seit der Jahrhundertwende*, Stuttgart.

Stein, Jack 1974: *Lulu*: Alban Berg's Adaptation of Wedekind. *Comparative Literature*, 26, 220–41.

Stopler, Gustav 1967: *The German Economy 1870 to the Present*. Completed and edited by Karl Häuser and Knut Borchardt. London.

Stone, Lawrence 1979: *The Family, Sex and Marriage in England 1500–1800*. Harmondsworth.

Szondi, Peter 1965: *Theorie des modernen Dramas 1880–1950*. Frankfurt am Main.

Tanner, Tony 1979: *Adultery in the Novel: Contract and Transgression*. Baltimore.

Theweleit, Klaus 1983: *Männerphantasien I: Frauen, Fluten, Körper, Geschichte*. Stuttgart.

Tirso de Molina 1982, orig. 1630: *El Burlador de Sevilla y convidado de piedra*. Madrid.

Trotsky, Leon 1975, orig. 1908: Frank Wedekind: Esthetics and Eroticism. Translated by David Thorstad. *Boston University Journal*, 23, 40–7.

Tymms, Ralph 1949: *Doubles in Literary Psychology*. Cambridge.

Ude, Karl 1966: *Frank Wedekind*. Mühlacker.

Vinçon, Hartmut 1986: *Frank Wedekind*. Stuttgart. This appeared too late to be consulted.

Völker, Klaus 1965: *Frank Wedekind*, Hanover.

Wagener, Hans 1979: *Frank Wedekind*, Colloquium, Berlin, 1979.

  1979: Frank Wedekind: Politische Entgleisungen eines Unpolitischen. *Seminar*, 15, 244–50.

  1980: *Frank Wedekind: 'Frühlings Erwachen'. Erläuterungen und Dokumente*. Stuttgart.

Weber-Kellermann, Ingeborg 1982: *Die deutsche Familie*. Frankfurt am Main.

Wedekind-Biel, Kadidja 1961: Introduction to 'A Scene from an Unpublished Version of Frank Wedekind's *Lulu-Tragedy*'. *Modern Drama*, 4, 97–100.

Wedekind, Tilly 1969: *Lulu, die Rolle meines Lebens*. Munich, Bern.

Weiniger, Otto 1980, orig. 1903: *Geschlecht und Charakter*. Munich.

Weis, Peg 1982: Kandinsky und München. Begegnungen und Wandlungen. In *Kandinsky und München*, 29–83.

White, Alfred D. 1973: The notion of morality in Wedekind's *Frühlings Erwachen*: a comment. *New German Studies*, 1, 116–18.

Willecke, Audrone B. 1980: Frank Wedekind and the 'Frauenfrage'. *Monatshefte*, 72, 26–38.

Wismatt, W. K., Beardsley, M. C. 1946: The Intentional Fallacy. *Sewanee Review*, 54, 468ff.

Zweite, Armin 1982: Kandinsky zwischen Moskau und München. In *Kandinsky und München*, 134–77.

Index